D0407060

Praise for *Fly a Little Higher*

Once in a blue moon, you meet someone who changes you. Though I never met Zach Sobiech, his grace in the face of a devastating prognosis was a beautiful thing to witness. The fact that his mother, Laura, and entire family were able to accompany him on his journey with such strength and courage (not to mention love and laughter) is a powerful lesson, not about dying, but about living.

—KATIE COURIC

Zach is an example of how one can *choose* to live one's life powerfully. His life and music will live on, sharing a beautiful message.

—JASON MRAZ, GRAMMY-
WINNING ARTIST

Through a few chords and a simple song Zach Sobiech inspired millions of voices to sing along to a message of courage, grace, and the acceptance of love. *Fly A Little Higher* is proof that one of God's great gifts is music. Sing loud and rejoice.

—SCOTT HEROLD, CEO AND
FOUNDER, ROCK THE CAUSE
RECORDS

Zach Sobiech's voice will live forever. He left the most powerful gift of all, a soundtrack of poignant melodies inspired by the boundless love of family and friends. This is the story of how a teenage boy—cursed with an evil disease—fought back and lifted his soul beyond the clouds. Zach's story will make you cry, make you feel life is unfair. But in the end Zach taught us how to live and how to cherish every single gift, every moment. I'm honored I got to share his story around the world. My time with Zach is a gift I'll cherish forever.

—ED LAVANDERA, CNN
CORRESPONDENT

Fly a Little Higher

HOW GOD ANSWERED *a* MOM'S SMALL
PRAYER *in a* BIG WAY

Laura Sobiech

NELSON
BOOKS

An Imprint of Thomas Nelson

For Zach

I am so grateful I got to be your mom

Published in Nashville, Tennessee, by Nelson Books, an imprint of Thomas Nelson. Nelson Books and Thomas Nelson are registered trademarks of HarperCollins Christian Publishing, Inc.

The author is represented by Joelle Delbourgo Associates, Inc., 101 Park Street, Montclair, NJ 07042.

Thomas Nelson, Inc., titles may be purchased in bulk for educational, business, fund-raising, or sales promotional use. For information, please e-mail SpecialMarkets@ThomasNelson.com.

Bible translations are from the THE ENGLISH STANDARD VERSION. © 2001 by Crossway Bibles, a division of Good News Publishers.

This work is the author's recollection of events, and the details are portrayed to the best of her memory.

ISBN: 978-0-529-10075-7

ISBN: 978-0-529-12179-0 (IE)

Library of Congress Control Number: 2013957741

Printed in the United States of America

14 15 16 17 18 19 RRD 6 5 4 3 2 1

Author's Note

. . . .

OVER THE YEARS WHILE WALKING WITH MY SON ZACH THROUGH HIS battle with cancer, there were moments I tucked away in my heart, knowing that eventually I would write them all down.

What resulted is not a story about how Zach died.

Rather, this story is about a boy who found himself tested by pain and loss. It's about a boy who learned to live while dying and in doing so brought hope to countless people who desperately needed it. But most of all, it is a story about a boy who showed his family, his friends, and eventually the world that everyone can choose to fly a little higher.

One

· ·

September 2012

ZACH DROVE UP THE DRIVEWAY, AND I HELD MY BREATH, WANTING—
and not wanting—to hear how the first day of his senior year of high
school had gone.

He got out of the car and pulled his backpack and crutches out of
the backseat. I stood in the kitchen, far enough from the living room
windows so he wouldn't see me watching. Even from here I could see
the heaviness in his gait and on his face.

As he walked in the door, I greeted him from the kitchen, keeping my distance, allowing him the space a seventeen-year-old boy
requires from his mom. My heart raced, but I remained steady and
focused. I'd seen this look before, though it was a rarity. He was the
kind of kid who could take a lot before he got down. Setting his
crutches aside, he glanced at me long enough to see the questions in
my face. He hobbled the few steps to the big chair with the ottoman
in the corner. The oversized pendulum clock that hung on the wall
above the chair was ticking, my heart surpassing its rhythm.

He wouldn't look at me, his face turned down and eyes averted. I remained grounded in the kitchen, not wanting to jump in too soon. I crossed my arms and leaned my head and shoulder against the wall, then asked, "How did it go?"

He took a deep breath, rested his forehead in his hand, and with huge tears spilling from his eyes, said, "I don't know how to do this."

And then he sobbed.

Though my heart was breaking, my mother's mind was bent on fixing his pain. I walked to the chair and sat on the armrest next to him. I leaned over and laid my cheek on his thinning hair, my hand on his shoulder. "Okay. Tell me what you mean."

Of course I knew what he meant. How do you do "this"? How do you pretend that life is normal when there is nothing normal about cancer slowly eating away at your bones and lungs? There is nothing normal about taking nineteen pills a day or finding out that the osteosarcoma has spread to your lungs for the third time in three years and has invaded your pelvis and the soft tissue surrounding it. And there is certainly nothing normal about learning, at seventeen, that you're terminal. How do you do this? How?

He took a moment to get control of the tears.

"The first assignment in English was to write a college essay," he said. "In every class the teacher was emphasizing how this is our last year of high school and that we should take it seriously and use it to prepare for college. What am I supposed to do with that? What's the point?" he whispered and finally raised his eyes to meet mine.

He went on to tell me that the toughest part of the day, and the past few months, was watching his friends making plans for the next phase of their lives. He felt like they were leaving him behind, and it was lonely. Zach, who had always been a social creature, was experiencing something he never had before. The friends whom he loved to be with were becoming sources of agony.

"We'll be hanging out downstairs just watching a movie or whatever, and everything is fine. Then one of them will bring up college, and all I can think about is how I'll be dead." He turned his face away and pinched the bridge of his nose to stop the tears.

I cupped his head in my hands and kissed the top of his head. I moved to the couch across from him, took a deep breath, and looked into this brave, weary, and heartbroken boy's soul.

And I prayed.

I prayed the desperate prayer of a mother who knows her child is beyond the reach of her wisdom. In my head, I screamed, *Give me the words! Please . . . just give me words.* With a clenched jaw, I took another breath, exhaled, and without any words ready, I spoke.

"How many kids are in your class?" I asked.

"I don't know, maybe around seven hundred," he replied.

"Zach, the likelihood of one of them dying within the next few years is pretty good. Think about that. There is a kid in your class who is going to die soon but just doesn't know it. You know you're going to die, and you have a pretty good idea of when. You have the advantage of preparing your soul. You get it. That other kid—he thinks he's just preparing for college. So what's really going on here isn't that your friends are moving on and leaving you behind; it's the opposite. You've moved on and have left them behind."

He lifted his head, intrigued yet still troubled.

"Yeah. But what am I going to do with my time? It just seems so pointless to be doing this stuff," he said, gesturing to his backpack.

I was relieved. The words he needed to hear had been given. I trusted there would be more.

"You'll have to decide; it's your choice. If graduating is important to you, maybe you can reduce your schedule and just take the classes you need to graduate. If it's not important, then decide how to fill your time. Do you really want to be at home while everyone else is at school? You could get a job or give guitar lessons. You have the freedom to make your life whatever you want it to be without the worries of planning for a big, long future like the rest of the kids." My heart rate quieted as I saw the sadness on his face ease into thoughtful consideration of the possibilities.

We kicked around some ideas. He decided graduating was a worthy goal (should a miracle happen, he wanted to be ready for college), and attending school would allow him to see his friends daily and keep up with their lives. But he didn't want to tie up more time at school than was absolutely necessary. He wasn't feeling great and didn't have the energy for a full class schedule.

We hammered out a plan that he felt good about: a later starting time and a pared-down schedule. I said a silent *Thank You!* to God for giving me the words Zach needed to hear. He wanted to be happy, and when he couldn't do it on his own, he was perfectly willing to let someone throw him a rope. I am grateful I got to be on the end of it every so often.

ZACH WENT INTO THAT SECOND DAY OF SCHOOL WITH A PLAN AND A renewed sense of what he was doing and how it was going to go. I wish I could say it was easy flying after that. It wasn't. He came home the second and third days much like the first, discouraged and broken. I continued to throw desperate prayers up to heaven, and heaven continued to respond.

"Zach, remember where you live. Remember this small space," I said as I used my thumb and forefinger to measure out an inch and then drew a vertical line up and down in front of me. "You are here. In the present. Yes, you have cancer and yes, you will likely die from it. But not today. Today is where you need to be. Not tomorrow and not six months from now. Just today."

That gesture, two fingers measuring a thin space in time, became a code for us over the next several months. We used it to encourage each other when things were tough and we needed to reset our thinking: keep it in the present and leave the future in the future.

ONE MONTH INTO HIS SENIOR YEAR, ZACH WAS IN A GOOD PLACE emotionally; he had figured out a routine that worked for him, and had gained some measure of peace in the belief that God had a plan that was bigger than him. Zach knew his suffering had purpose, even if he didn't see the reason. He was waking up cheerful and whistling in the shower again—one of my favorite sounds, second only to his strumming on the guitar.

We were driving home after a clinic visit at the University of Minnesota Amplatz Children's Hospital where Zach continued to receive a new treatment that his oncology doctors hoped would slow the growth of the cancer. I treasured those precious thirty-minute car rides. They were sacred times when we were alone and could have our deepest discussions about suffering and sickness, death and dying. Death was a topic we had learned to talk about openly; we touched on it sparingly, but with purpose.

Zach had been due for his port to be flushed, a procedure that involved a needle being stuck into his chest like a tack into a bulletin board, then flushed with saline. It was the only procedure he ever complained about. The pain, the pressure from the fluid pushing into his veins, and the taste of the saline grossed him out. But it never seemed to get him down; he just rolled with whatever came his way. I, on the other hand, hated needles to the point of having a phobia and wasn't sure if I would be as compliant and patient as he had been.

"Have you ever been angry that you got cancer and have to put up with all the junk you have to go through?" I asked, keeping my eyes on the road. We had left the city and were driving through what remained of the sparse farmland and sun-fried fields that held their ground in the midst of the Twin Cities' suburban sprawl.

I could see out of the corner of my eye that he had turned to look at me. After a moment of thought, he turned his gaze back to the road ahead. "No. Actually, I think I'm the lucky one. If somebody has to have cancer, I'd rather be the one to have it than to be the one who has to watch and then be left behind. I don't think I could handle watching someone I love die. You all have it worse, and I'm so sorry for putting you through this."

As we descended into the St. Croix Valley, I thought about what he'd said. The enormity of his compassion enthralled me, and I wondered if I would feel the same if it were me who was dying.

He had always been a compassionate soul; empathy was so natural for him. Even from a very young age, his heart would ache for people who were suffering. I recalled a memory I'd held in my heart from years earlier when he was four and his little sister, Grace, was nine months old. She was born with a ventricular septal defect, a hole in her heart, and had it repaired with open-heart surgery.

She was recovering in the ICU when Zach, who had insisted on visiting her rather than spending the hot summer day at Grandma and Grandpa's pool, walked into the room. He was too short to see over the edge of the metal crib so he stepped on the bottom rail, hoisted himself up, and peered in at his baby sister with all her bandages, tubes, and wires.

I will never forget that precious little boy with his sun-bleached hair and huge green eyes quietly gazing at his baby, at his Grace, his little heart breaking, tears welling up in his eyes. My own heart filled with an unnamed emotion that a mother feels when she sees her child rise to an occasion that is beyond his years—a mixture of pride, love, and heartache.

Now, ten years later, I thought about Grace and Zach and how they had become the best of friends. He was fiercely protective of her.

A few months earlier, the day we'd found out the cancer was in his pelvis and he didn't have long to live, Zach's concern turned to Grace. The thought of his little sister having to deal with his death destroyed him. He knew she would be devastated, and he wanted to soften the blow.

That evening as I was making dinner, he sat down at the counter. "Mom, I was thinking. Grace is going to be really bummed that the cancer is back, so I thought it would be nice if I bought her a pair of custom Converse. She and I could design them together, and I'll let her pick out whatever she wants. I think it will make her feel better."

I paused while chopping the onion and set the knife down. "I think she would love that," I said as I wiped a tear from my cheek. "Darn onions."

That was three months ago. As we turned onto our street, I wondered if a pair of custom-designed shoes was enough. Zach and Grace's mutual love for shoes made them the perfect gift, and designing them together would be a memory Grace would cherish. But did they convey the whole message? Did Grace really know how much Zach loved her? Had he ever just told her? If he had, surely they would be words that she would keep tucked in her heart forever, more than a well-worn and loved pair of tennis shoes.

We pulled into the driveway and stopped next to the abandoned basketball hoop. I turned to Zach. "You know, letters would be a good way for you to tell people how you feel about them. You might want to think about writing some." Several years earlier, I had seen a story on a local news station about a woman who was dying of breast cancer. She spent the last months of her life writing letters to her children to be opened on their birthdays and important events. The memory of the story surfaced when we found out Zach was terminal. Letters seemed the perfect way for him to be raw and honest without the fear of the awkwardness that can sometimes come when people aren't ready to hear what needs to be said. I'd been meaning to mention the idea to him, and hoped desperately he would write them, knowing what a comfort they would be for his loved ones when he was gone.

"Yeah. I should probably do that," he said as he flipped a guitar pick between his fingers. (He had one in his pocket wherever he went, and I was constantly picking them up around the house and especially in the laundry room.) "Who do you think should get one?"

"Your sisters, brother, and best friends would be a good place to start." I left it at that. I'd planted the seed, but wouldn't pester him. He'd do it if he felt up to it.

A COUPLE WEEKS LATER, IT WAS MID-OCTOBER. THE DAY WAS SUNNY and warm, the air was clean, and the leaves were a noisy riot of color.

Zach and Grace were at school. Zach's older sister, Alli, who was a senior at the University of Minnesota Twin Cities, was working at her magazine internship, and his older brother, Sam, was in his second year at the University of North Dakota in Grand Forks. Everyone was where they should be. They were safe, and they were happy. Life felt good again.

It was my day off from my job in a dental office where I worked in the claims department, and I'd spent the morning running errands. I couldn't wait to roll up my sleeves and get some work done around the house, and I was planning to start by purging the family room where Zach spent most of his time. I threw open the windows to let the fresh air fill the house. I took a deep breath and got to work.

I started with the couch. Daisy, our miniature dachshund, stood close by, knowing that Zach's couch was always a good place to visit if she was looking for a broken cookie. It was the first place she would go in the morning when she was let out of her crate.

To put it mildly, Zach was a slob. A huge slob. Wrappers, chip crumbs, bottles, and cans lay everywhere. It was easy to spot his roost because it was the only place on the couch that wasn't cluttered. It used to drive me crazy the way that kid could leave a mess; I didn't mind as much anymore. There's something about knowing your child is going to die that causes you to cherish stupid things, like cleaning up their unreasonable messes.

Mixed in with the monstrosity of a mess were folded pieces of paper, notebooks, and stacks of various assignment-looking papers. I didn't want to throw anything important away, so I opened each piece and looked it over carefully. After about a half hour, I'd made some pretty good headway—the couch was clean, the coffee table was cleared of debris, and the room smelled more of fresh air and less of goats-who-had-eaten-tacos. I had one last pile of crumpled notes to go through, so I lifted the pile onto my lap and began sorting.

About halfway through, I picked up a sheet of notebook paper that had been folded multiple times. These words were written in Zach's handwriting across the page:

> *I fell down down down into this dark and lonely hole,*
> *there was no one there to care about me anymore,*
> *I needed a way to climb and grab a hold of the edge*
> *you were sitting there holding a rope*

And that's how "Clouds" rolled into my life.

Two

. . . .

ON A SPRING EVENING SHORTLY AFTER ZACH'S FIRST BIRTHDAY, I was making dinner while he scooted around the kitchen on his bottom, his preferred method of travel. As I was popping a casserole into the oven, I suddenly realized I hadn't heard Zach in a while. I checked around the kitchen table, then the living room.

He was neither place, so I turned my attention downstairs to Sam and Alli who were playing "Lava," a game that entailed hopping between couch cushions they had spread out on the floor. One misstep meant landing on carpet-lava and being burned alive.

"Hey, guys," I called down. "Is Zach down there with you?"

"No," Alli called up breathlessly as she hopped cushions. "He's not down here!"

As I turned to check upstairs, I caught sight of the open sliding screen door that led from the dining area of the kitchen directly to a three-foot drop to our backyard. The glass door had been open to let the fresh spring air in, but the screen door had been shut. I ran to the door to check the backyard where I saw Zach, who had safely scooted about fifteen feet into the yard, kneeling at a T-ball tee. He had a brown plastic bat in one hand and a big white plastic ball in the other. I watched as he carefully balanced the ball on the tee and, while still kneeling, swung and hit the ball a good ten feet.

I learned to lock the door after that.

On his second birthday, Zach was given a three pack of toddler-sized balls: a soccer ball, a football, and a basketball. One of our favorite home videos is of him opening that gift and shaking with excitement when he saw what was in the package—he couldn't get the wrapping paper off fast enough.

Zach especially loved football, and like his dad, his favorite team was the Minnesota Vikings. From the time Zach was a toddler, he would sit on Rob's lap, and they would watch the games together. It was their thing, their way of spending time together. As he got older, Zach and his dad would connect by talking sports, but when he was little, Zach would act the plays out. While the game was on, he would have his little toy football ready and pretend to hike the ball, or he would tuck it into the crook of his arm and pretend he was going in for a touchdown. One of his first words was "bootball."

In our family, we had a one-sport-a-year policy, and Zach had chosen football from the fourth grade through the sixth grade. His fifth-grade team won the championship game played at the Vikings stadium, and his sixth-grade team came within a touchdown of winning the championship. It was a glorious time for Zach, and he proudly displayed the trophies until the day he died. The Catholic school where he went did not have a middle school football team, so in order to play, he had to walk to the public junior high school a few blocks away after school. He didn't enjoy it much; the tone of the coaching and the attitudes of some of the players were not his style—too much emphasis on individual success at any cost and not enough on team building. That was his last year playing football.

Zach spent nine years attending St. Croix Catholic School, kindergarten through eighth grade. While not every child who attends a faith-based school embraces the education, Zach did. He loved his Catholic faith and was comfortable with exploring it and growing in it. Part of this had to do with his class. They were a unique group of kids who had decided early on they would have no cliques. If there was a party, then everyone was invited—no exclusions. And they made a conscious effort not to gossip but rather to build each other up. By the end of the eighth grade, the group of fifty kids was very close and cared deeply for one another.

Zach, who was so naturally empathetic and willing to see the good in those around him, blossomed in this environment. Surrounded by people he knew cared for him, he was able not only to be open about his faith but also to try new things with confidence. He had taken an interest in music and, in particular, guitar; so when he was in the sixth grade, my husband, Rob, and I gave him his first electric guitar. It was a cheap guitar I'd picked up on sale; I wasn't sure it was something he would retain an interest in and didn't want to invest in a more expensive guitar until he'd proven he was going to stick with it. He surprised me with his enthusiasm and dedication. He was a natural and spent hours practicing new songs. He'd found a new passion.

In the seventh grade, after a year of taking guitar lessons, he and his friends Reed and Adam played for the first time in front of an audience at the school talent show. I was so proud of him, standing up there in front of the whole school and playing like a pro. I was amazed at his confidence and obvious love for the stage; every time he looked up at the crowd, a huge grin would break out on his face.

When Zach and his friends finished their song, the crowd went wild, clapping and cheering. The noise was deafening. Kindergarten children and even some of the older kids approached him after the show and asked for Zach's autograph. It was his first taste of performing on stage, and he fell in love with it.

Sports were still a big part of his life. Zach was asked to join the basketball team in the seventh grade. The team needed another player, and Zach's height was a definite advantage. He jumped at the opportunity.

The first year went well. He picked up on the game quickly, and the team ended the year with an equal number of wins and losses. By eighth grade, the team was solid, and they went undefeated, ending the year by winning the championship, despite half the players coming down with the flu. It was a glorious end to the year. Zach was elated! He couldn't wait to play more, and I looked forward to more too. I had dreams of watching Zach running down the court in the high school colors and me cheering from the stands.

But there was a problem.

Though we didn't know it yet, a little cell in Zach had changed and become ugly and unholy. It decided not to follow the rules cells should follow but decided to make up its own. It grew and divided into more and more rebels. They were sneaky and quiet for a long time, just long enough to make a nice little army.

Three

. . . .

ON NOVEMBER 13, 2009, CANCER SHOWED ITSELF LIKE A DEMON peeking out of a dark bedroom closet. It was the disease I thought would never haunt our family—we had no family history with that monster lurking in the background. As it turned out, sometimes the things we think are impossibilities are the things God uses to turn our world upside down. We learn to hang on tight that way. We learn to trust. Which is why, from the very beginning, I knew cancer would be as much of a spiritual journey as it was a physical battle.

August 2009

LATE THAT SUMMER, A FEW WEEKS BEFORE ZACH WOULD BEGIN HIS freshman year at the public high school, he and his older sister, Alli, went for a run. Alli had just graduated from high school and was headed to college in a few weeks. She was ready to take that next step into adulthood, to move away from home and start working toward a career in journalism. Knowing that she would be leaving soon, Alli wanted to spend some time with her younger brother. She'd been busy with work all summer, and Zach had spent a good portion of his vacation lounging on the couch in the family room in front of the television. They were both in serious need of some exercise.

"Hey, Zach," Alli called down to the family room where Zach was clicking through the channels, "it's a nice day. Let's go for a run."

He set the remote down and reluctantly got up from the couch. He knew there was no point in blowing Alli off. She wouldn't allow it. Alli stood at the top of the steps dressed in running shorts and a faded tank top she'd picked up at the Goodwill. Her blond hair was pulled back into a ponytail. Zach towered over her five-foot frame, but it was he who looked up to her. She was tenacious and driven. When she set her mind to something, there was no stopping her.

"Okay. I'll be up in a minute," he mumbled. He lumbered up the stairs, his bony body topped with an unruly mop of blond curls.

They left the house and, after a half-hour run, stumbled back in the front door.

"See! That wasn't so bad." Alli nudged him in the ribs. "We need to get in shape. I'm going to be walking around campus for the next nine months, and you've got to get ready for basketball if you want to have a chance at getting on the team. It's not like St. Croix Catholic, Zach. You're actually going to have to try out if you want a chance on the team." She walked to the kitchen sink and filled a glass with water.

"Yeah, I know," Zach replied, still catching his breath. "I'm not too worried about it. I'm probably taller than half the guys who'll be trying out." He loved the fact that he had inches on most of the kids his age and was a little prideful about it.

"It's not just height that's going to get you on the team, Zach. It's skill." Alli was good about making sure her brother didn't get too big of a head. "And you're not gaining any skill by hanging out on the couch all day. Ya gotta get out there and get some exercise," she teased as she walked down the steps to her bedroom.

"Come on, Al, it's not like you're out there running every day," he shot back.

Zach made a quick trip down to his bedroom and emerged with a two-liter bottle of some unnatural-looking bright blue drink. He always kept a hidden stash of various drinks he'd purchased on sale at the local gas station; he just couldn't pass up a deal. He planted himself at the kitchen counter next to Grace as I prepared dinner.

"So, Ma, I was thinking. There are, like, billions of earthworms in the ground and each of them poops. If you think about it, pretty much all the soil in the world is basically earthworm poop." He loved sharing unusual facts. He had a collection of dog-eared copies of sports and science fact books, and his favorite television channels focused on the same topics.

"Discovery Channel?" I asked.

"No. I was just thinking about it, all those worms."

"Not so sure that's true. I'm thinking there is more to the soil than just earthworm poo." I knew he was looking for a debate. "I think bacteria has a bigger part to play in the whole soil scheme."

"No way. Think about it. It's the worms that are little soil-making machines. They eat the rotting stuff, then poop it out, and voilà! Soil," he retorted.

"Nope. Not buyin' it, Zach. I'm sticking with bacteria."

He furrowed his brow in mock discouragement, a sparkle in his eye, and slapped his open hand on the countertop.

"Don't test me, woman," he scolded in a crotchety-old-man voice.

Grace and I busted out laughing. Zach didn't take himself too seriously, and most times would handle defeat with humor. If he couldn't win, he'd go down laughing.

Rob walked in the front door, set his keys and wallet on the shelf in the closet, and kicked his dress shoes off into the closet.

"Hey," I said as I tossed a hot pad on the table and set a pot of noodles on it. "How was your day?" I asked.

"It was okay." He loosened his tie and unbuttoned the top button of his shirt, then took a seat. I wondered if he would surprise me one day by declaring he'd had a wonderful day. But exaggerating wasn't something Rob was prone to; he was much too conservative for that.

"Hey, Dad," Sam said as he stepped into the kitchen.

"Hi, Sam. What have you been up to today?"

"Not much. Just reading up on an Airsoft gun I'm thinking about buying. All my friends' guns surpass my gun's speed and distance. If I'm going to be competitive, I need a better gun," Sam responded as he pulled out his usual chair at the table.

Zach greeted Rob as he walked to the table and sat down. He hadn't complained of anything, but I noticed he was favoring his left side and there was a slight hitch in his step. *Well, of course he's sore*, I thought. *He hasn't moved all summer!* I set the salad on the table and, once everyone settled, we said our mealtime prayer, then proceeded to fill our plates and continued talking about the events of the day.

"How was your run?" I asked as I got up to retrieve the Parmesan cheese from the refrigerator.

"Great! It felt so good to just get out and move," Alli answered. She piled salad on her plate, then took a bite. Grace sat quietly and consumed her pasta. She loved pasta.

"How about you, Zach? Did it feel good to get out there again and move a little? Basketball tryouts are coming up," I said in my best not-a-lecture voice.

"Yeah, Zach. You need to prepare," Rob chimed in a teasing tone. "E is for Effort!" It was a saying that didn't make much sense, but Rob used it often. "Don't expect things to be handed to you. You have to work for them."

I rolled my eyes and smirked at Alli. Rob had hounded her with that same phrase through high school. It drove her crazy, but she also found it endearing.

Zach shrugged his shoulders as he loaded noodles onto his plate. "I know. I'll start going for more runs. It felt pretty good, I guess, except at the end when my hip started to hurt."

"I saw you limping. Do you think you overdid it?" I asked.

"Yeah, I probably just went out longer than I should have. It's been awhile."

"Well, pop some ibuprofen, and go out again tomorrow," Rob said. "You don't want to be a quitter."

"Maybe rest a day, then go out again; loosen things up slowly," I interjected. "But let me know if it keeps hurting so we can get it looked at."

"Okay," he nodded and took a bite of his food.

A week later, two weeks before the school year started, Zach came to me after I got home from work. He was in his basketball shorts that barely hung on his narrow hips and his favorite Gibson T-shirt.

"Mom, my hip still hurts." There was concern in his big, round green eyes. "I thought it might be getting better, but it's not. It hurts more now than it did a week ago; it just keeps getting worse."

I wasn't about to blow this off like I'd done earlier in the year when Zach showed me his black-and-blue hand right as he was leaving to walk to the bus stop. He'd hurt it the night before while wrestling with Sam. "It's fine," I'd insisted as I shoved him out the door and waved good-bye. The school nurse called a few hours later and said she thought it looked broken. Turned out, it was.

Taking Zach's concern seriously this time, I called our clinic and made an appointment with a family practice physician who had an interest in sports medicine. Aside from the broken thumb incident, it had been ages since Zach had needed to go to the doctor. He hardly ever got sick.

"Whoa," the doctor exclaimed as he walked into the examination room. "What size shoes are those?" he asked as he took a seat at a little desk with a computer. He was a tall guy himself with some pretty big feet.

"Fourteen," Zach answered with a grin. "Same as my age." He loved his big feet. I wasn't a huge fan of them, especially when I was tripping over his haphazardly kicked-off shoes in front of the door. Zach and the doctor bantered back and forth about different style shoes and where the best places were to shop for the tough-to-find bigger sizes. Then the doctor got down to business.

"So what brings you in today, Zach?" the doctor asked.

"My hip feels sort of funny, sort of like there's something in there," he said as he pointed to his left hip. "Not on the outside, but on the inside, when I walk and run."

"What about when you're just taking it easy, when you're relaxing?"

"It just sort of aches sometimes, but not all the time."

"Does it keep you up at night?"

"No, not really. Sometimes it aches when I lay down in bed, but it doesn't keep me from sleeping."

"Okay. Well, let's get an X-ray and see if we can figure out what's going on," the doctor said as he wrote up an order, then pointed down the hall to where we needed to go. Once the X-ray was done, we met the doctor in an X-ray viewing room. He popped the film onto a lighted viewing board on the wall and began looking it over.

"Well," he said and paused as he concentrated on the hip, his nose inches from the film, "there's nothing obvious. I don't see any cracks, breaks, or deformities."

I looked at the X-ray too, and with my untrained eye didn't see anything obvious either. "So what should we do?" I asked.

"There might be a soft tissue injury, possibly the hip flexor." He scribbled out a referral and handed it to me. "I'm going to send you to physical therapy. They should be able to give you some exercises that will help with the pain and strengthen the muscles," he said to Zach.

Unfortunately, X-ray readings aren't foolproof.

The small lesion in Zach's left hip, the little spot a specialist with a trained eye would have noticed, went unseen and quietly grew and grew. Through two months of physical therapy, the lesion had time to get bigger and bigger, until it was so big that Zach could no longer walk without a severe limp or even bend over to tie his shoes.

His therapist sent him for an MRI.

Cancer never entered my mind.

Four

IT WAS FRIDAY, NOVEMBER 13, 2009. ROB HAD TAKEN THE DAY OFF work, and we'd spent a leisurely morning together at home before going out for lunch and heading into town to the MRI appointment. It was a rarity in the hustle and bustle of our busy lives. We didn't have much time to spend together.

For most of our marriage I was a stay-at-home mom, though I usually had some kind of side job that brought in a little money. I had worked as a day-care provider, screened phone calls for a local charity, and taught CPR classes at a hospital. By the time Grace, our fourth and youngest child, was in school full time, I had taken over as coordinator of the CPR education program at the hospital and had taken a part-time job at a dental office. An itch for adventure led me to join our local fire department where I served as an EMT and firefighter. I was busy, and I loved it.

Rob worked full time as a logistics manager at a medical diagnostic test company. His mother, who was eighty-one, widowed, and failing in health, lived on a farm two hours from us. Her only other child,

Rob's brother, lived out of state, so much of her care landed on Rob. He hadn't had a day alone in months, and I knew he was due for one.

"Why don't you just hang out at home today?" I said to him that morning. "It's just a routine MRI. I'm sure we'll be in and out. The doctor probably won't even look at it until next week, anyhow."

"No, I'm going," he insisted. "I want to be there." I was pleasantly surprised he wanted to go. I enjoyed our time together, when we could find it. We were getting to that point in our marriage where I sometimes wondered if we had anything in common apart from the kids. We got along just fine, but I felt like we were drifting apart.

It was early afternoon. The colors of fall had given way to the drab gray of winter, and the snow wouldn't come to brighten it up for another couple of weeks. Rob and I pulled into the school parking lot and waited a minute or two before Zach stepped out of the school entrance onto the sidewalk and hobbled toward the car. He looked nervous but managed to give us a grin and a wave as he approached, then hopped into the backseat of the car.

"Hey, hon. You ready for this?" I asked as he did his best to arrange his long legs into a comfortable position and buckled himself in. His hip and height made small spaces difficult to maneuver sometimes.

"Yeah. I asked around to see if anyone else in my class has had an MRI before. A girl from first hour had one last year. She said it took a long time and was noisy but that it wasn't a huge deal." I caught his eye in the rearview mirror as I backed the car out of the parking spot. "She said the trick is to get comfortable before you go into the tube."

"I'm sure it will be fine, Zach," Rob encouraged. "You can put up with anything for a half hour. You're tough. You can handle it. Heck!

You've been through a full day of school with a broken thumb," he teased while giving me a sideways glance.

"Not fair," I scolded while I slapped Rob's thigh. "Every mom gets at least one epic fail."

Zach laughed from the backseat. "Yeah, Mom. Major epic fail."

At the hospital, a nurse led us down a hall to a changing room.

"You'll need to take all your clothes off. Everything, even underwear," she said as she held out a plastic bag and a gown. Zach glanced at me. I raised my eyebrows as if to say, *Sorry*. The nurse continued, "You can put your clothes in here, then put the gown on; it ties in the back. When you're done, just step out and I'll take you down the hall to the procedure room."

Zach took the bag and gown and closed the door behind him.

The nurse turned to us to explain the procedure as she led us to a waiting area.

"We'll do an X-ray guided dye injection directly into Zach's hip, and then we'll take him to the MRI machine just down the hall," she explained. "The injection will take about twenty minutes, and the MRI should only take about a half hour."

"Will he be in a lot of pain?" I asked.

"He'll be a little sore, but it shouldn't last too long. A little ibuprofen should do the trick," she said.

Rob and I took a seat in the waiting area, and twenty minutes later Zach emerged from the procedure room. He looked pale and miserable.

"How'd it go?" I asked cautiously.

"Bad." He looked like he'd been punched in the gut.

"Oh, babe. I'm sorry," I said as I took the bag that held his clothing from his hands. "The worst should be over." I glanced at Rob. He frowned with a look of concern in his deep blue eyes as he peered through his glasses. Zach wasn't one to complain much, but when he did, we knew it was bad. Rob hated to see his son suffer.

The nurse led Zach down the hall to the MRI room, and Rob and I took a seat in the main waiting area. I pulled a book out of my over-sized purse, grateful for the distraction and rare opportunity to read, and Rob grabbed a *Business Weekly* from the magazine rack. A half hour passed, then forty minutes, then fifty, and I wondered what was taking so long. After an hour, the nurse came back out with a clipboard and a form and called us into the hallway just outside the MRI room.

"We spoke with your doctor on the phone; he would like us to do an IV dye injection. It will allow us to get a clearer picture," she said as she handed me the clipboard. "If you could just sign the consent." She was a middle-aged woman, a few years older than me, with short dark hair and pale blue eyes.

"What do you think?" I asked Rob. I was reluctant to put Zach through more pain, and he'd already been in the machine for an hour.

"Well, we're here, we might as well get it done," he replied. "The sooner we have this done, the sooner we'll know what's going on."

I signed the form and handed it back to her. She immediately turned and walked back into the MRI room, the door clicking shut behind her. I walked with Rob back into the waiting room, and we sat down.

"That's not good," Rob said, shaking his head.

"What do you mean?" I asked. "They just need a better view."

"Or they see something concerning and want to double-check it."

It annoyed me sometimes, how Rob tended to see the dark side of everything. I was sure this was just routine stuff and nothing to get worried about. If he wanted to worry, there was nothing that would stop him. I picked up my book and settled back into the story.

After another half hour, the nurse peeked around the door and into the waiting room to tell us Zach was done and would join us momentarily. I set my book down and stepped into the restroom. When I came out, Rob was standing in the corner of the room by the lobby phone. I walked across the room to where he stood.

"The nurse came back out and said the doctor wants to talk to us right away." He answered the question playing out on my face. The phone rang, and Rob picked it up.

"Hello," Rob answered.

And life changed . . . forever.

I STEPPED IN CLOSER TO ROB, THE PHONE HELD TO HIS EAR. *WHY IS the doctor so eager to catch us before we leave?* I wondered. We had been told earlier that the doctor would call with the results on Monday. I was impatient and wanted to listen in, so I pressed my ear to the back of the phone, hoping to catch a little of what the doctor was saying, as Rob listened to the doctor on the line. Zach was seated across the room, exhausted and miserable, looking like a cat who'd just been dunked in a pool of water, but he watched us intently.

The words were muffled. ". . . tumor . . . it's bad . . . hard year ahead," were all I could hear.

I stepped away as Rob continued to talk to the doctor. Tumor? I saw the X-ray two months ago; how could there be a tumor? My legs went weak as my brain worked to process what I'd just heard, and I could hear my heart pounding in my ears. I looked across the room at Zach where he sat patiently waiting. *What do I tell him?* I wondered.

Of course, the first thought that filled my mind was cancer. I assumed it would be the first to enter his mind as well. But there were so many unknowns, and I didn't want to burden him with so little information. I didn't have enough to put him at ease, but I certainly had enough to scare him.

Zach watched me as I walked toward him. He wore a look of expectation; he needed to know what was going on. Rob finished the conversation with the doctor. I had no idea what to tell Zach as I sat down next to him, my body numb and my brain scurrying to process the news.

By the time I turned to him and opened my mouth, I knew all I could do was tell him the simple truth. I couldn't make this easier, and I couldn't protect him from this enemy, whatever it was. The only loving thing I could do was give him as much information as I had.

"The MRI showed a tumor."

Zach held my gaze for a moment, then looked away from me and closed his eyes as he processed the news. My heart was breaking. In that moment he looked so small and vulnerable. Not like the tall, confident kid who just months earlier ran down a basketball court with ease, but like the three-year-old Zach who had pleaded with me through tears as he was strapped to a board in the doctor's office so he would stay still enough for his forehead to be stitched up. That little boy had quieted his crying, pinched his eyes shut, and turned away from me when he realized I couldn't save him.

"What is it?" he asked after a few moments.

"We don't know yet."

"Okay," he said as he rubbed his eyes to stop the tears from coming. A woman sat on the other side of him and noisily flipped through a magazine. "Can we go home now?"

As we drove home, I was in agony. I needed the details. I needed to know exactly what the doctor had said, and I needed the scary questions that banged around in my head to be answered: *Where is it? How big is it? What is it? What is our next step, and what does "it's bad" mean?* Rob kept his eyes on the road, and we kept the discussion in the car to a minimum.

"How are you feeling, babe?" I looked over my shoulder at Zach, his head resting against the car window and his eyes closed.

"That was the worst thing I've ever had to go through," he mumbled back. "The injection was really bad, but laying in the machine for over an hour was the worst. I never want to have to go through something that awful again."

We pulled into the driveway of our modest multilevel home. It was late afternoon and the sun was setting; its remaining light filtered through the tall trees in the front yard and danced across the pale yellow siding and windows. A hard freeze had turned the once-colorful perennial flower garden that lined the front sidewalk to a now-dead brown mass of leaves and sticks. Grace met us at the door.

"Mom, I need help with my math homework." She stood holding out her workbook.

"Why don't you have Dad sit down with you while I get dinner started?" I asked.

"What is for dinner, Mom?" Sam asked as he pulled open the refrigerator door. "I'm starving."

"I don't have any idea," I said as I set my purse down and hung my coat in the closet. I went to the kitchen and pulled a pot out of the cupboard, filled it with water, and set it on the stove. I felt like I was in a bubble and everything was in slow motion except my mind— it was racing. All sorts of thoughts ran through my head. There would probably be surgery, plus a fair amount of time for recovery.

Basketball was out for this year. What about next year? School would be tough, but Zach would be able to keep up.

Zach tossed his coat on the chair by the front door and retreated downstairs to the family room. Rob sat down at the kitchen table as Grace set her workbook in front of them. I started frying up hamburger meat to make spaghetti.

I looked at the clock on the stove. It was five forty-five; Zach's guitar lesson was scheduled for six.

"Zach, are you feeling well enough to go to your lesson?" I called down to him.

There was a brief pause, then: "Yeah. I'll go."

"Sam, would you please give Zach a ride?"

"Fine." He scraped the last little bit from a yogurt cup and tossed it into the garbage.

Zach came upstairs, his guitar slung over his shoulder, and the two of them walked out the door. They would be gone for at least forty-five minutes. The anxiety had boiled up in me like the pot of water I'd put on the stove. Rob and I were finally able to talk freely, so I motioned to him to join me in the living room just off the kitchen.

"What did the doctor say?" I asked in a hushed tone. "Tell me everything."

"He said the MRI clearly showed a large tumor in Zach's left hip, in the femoral neck," he told me.

"How big is it?" I cut in.

"He isn't sure. He won't know exactly until the radiologist looks at it and measures it. But he said it was significant."

"I don't get it! How can that be? I took him in two months ago, and the doctor didn't see anything," I asked out loud but mostly to myself. I knew Rob didn't have the answers.

"There are three possibilities the doctor said it could be," he continued as he pulled a piece of paper out of his pocket where he had written them down. "Lymphoma, fibrous dysplasia, or osteosarcoma. Osteosarcoma is the worst of the three," Rob said as he carefully folded the paper and tucked it back into his pocket. "We have to see an orthopedic surgeon; he said he'd have his nurse set up an appointment for us. He wants us to get in right away because whatever it is, it's bad and we'll have a long and hard year ahead of us."

As Rob talked, I lowered myself down into a chair in the corner of the room, and I broke down and sobbed. The gravity of the news and the reality that Zach's life—all our lives—had changed forever was finally penetrating my brain. Rob sat down on the ottoman next to me and held my hand for a moment until Grace called needing help with a homework problem.

My racing mind began to slow as I mentally saw pieces of Zach's life fall away. Sports. Carefree teen years. A future of boundless opportunity. How would he handle missing out on sports? They were such a huge part of his life. *Thank God he has the guitar*, I thought.

Then my mind landed on the stripped-down and naked realization: Zach could die. We could actually lose him. My mind stopped clamoring, and I felt like my next breath would never come as the thought penetrated my whole being.

Zach could die. Zach could die. Zach could die . . .

Finally, I took a deep breath. A quiet but powerful peace began to fill my soul. It settled in me and surrounded me like an embrace or a warm blanket. In that moment of stillness there were two clear thoughts that surfaced. The first was, *I am so grateful to know Zach*, and the second was, *God is asking us for something big*. I knew I was being presented with a choice. A choice between faith in a loving

God who knew all things and was in control, or a choice to fall into despair and anger that this horrible and terrifying thing was happening to us. And then I had a vivid image of God's face turned to me, His gaze resting on us as He waited for an answer. I knew without a doubt that God was present, and He was asking us to trust Him.

Okay, I thought, *we'll do this. We will trust in You.*

LATER THAT NIGHT, AFTER ZACH GOT HOME FROM HIS LESSON AND dished up a plate of spaghetti that he brought downstairs, I went down to the family room and sat next to him on the couch. Without looking at me, he laid his head full of thick blond curls on my shoulder.

"What are you thinking?" I asked, loving the fact that this big boy was still okay with being close to his mom. He raised his head and looked at me.

"I think it's about something big," he responded. "I think God has something planned."

I was relieved at his ability to find God in all things. Even when he was very small, just a toddler, he would look at a flower and declare, "God made it pretty." Now he was being challenged to see God in the not-so-pretty things, his open heart ready to receive the grace that God would pour into it.

I reached out and touched his smooth face. Too young to have stubble yet wise beyond his years. I stood from the couch and walked up the steps to the kitchen. The soothing sound of Zach gently strumming his guitar reached my ears and caused my heart to swell with love for that precious teenage boy. While I knew he was about to embark on a path that would not be easy, he would be okay. We would all be okay.

Five

. . . .

AFTER A WEEK OF DOING AGONIZING RESEARCH OF THE VARIOUS possibilities but still hoping for the best, we went in for the biopsy. It was the Monday before Thanksgiving, and the waiting room was full of people. The ones who were there for routine surgeries stood out; their companions were lighthearted and chatty. The ones who were there for more serious reasons were quiet. Rob, Zach, and I were quiet.

Zach was called in. He was nervous; the MRI experience had left him shaken, and he was unsure of what the biopsy would feel like. When he was told he would be under general anesthesia, he relaxed a little. While Rob and I stepped into the hall, Zach pulled the privacy curtain closed in a small, glass-enclosed room. Then he donned an awkward paper gown, placed his clothes in one bag and his huge shoes in another, and lay down in a hospital bed that was about two inches too short. Loved ones of other patients milled around in the hallway, and doctors and nurses hustled from room to room.

Before the biopsy, doctors and nurses came in and out of the room to introduce themselves and explain their various roles. Zach was cordial and talkative with them. Several doctors double-checked his age; his size and maturity made him seem older than his fourteen years.

Finally, it was Zach's turn to go in for the procedure. As they wheeled him to the operating room, we came to the "kissing corner" where parents say good-bye before entrusting their precious children into the care of people they'd just met. Zach turned to us with groggy eyes from the "happy juice" the nurse anesthetist had injected into his IV line.

"I love you," he said with slurred speech, "and can you make sure you watch my iPod so no one steals it?" I chuckled a little and kissed his forehead.

"I'll keep an eye on it," I assured him and watched as they wheeled him through the steel double doors.

Rob and I walked silently back to the waiting room, hand in hand, and found a couple of seats in the middle of the room. There was no private place to sit where we could hunker down together and agonize alone. So we ended up sitting next to a family who were joyfully planning their holiday dinner, the mother-in-law and wife sorting through a recipe box and discussing various options. I wondered what our Thanksgiving would be like.

The cheerful chatter felt like an assault. It was surreal as we waited in the middle of all the prattle of other people's lives, knowing no matter what news the surgeon would bring, our lives would be changed forever; it was simply a matter of how much. Rob and I sat silently and anxiously watched the screen that hung on the wall for updates as "SobZ" made his way from pre-op, to op, to recovery. I'd brought a book to read but just stared at the page before me, my mind unable to escape to another world.

Hours later, the surgeon, still in scrubs, called our name and led us to a private consultation room. We sat down on a hard couch; he pulled a chair up close and leaned forward, hands clasped on his knees. He reminded me of Mister Rogers. Mild. Gentle. "Well, the biopsy confirmed Zachary has osteosarcoma."

The words hit me with the percussion of a bomb; I couldn't breathe and my ears rang. As much as I had prepared myself to hear those words, I wasn't ready for their impact. I'd spent hours on the Internet researching the different possibilities. None of them were good, but osteosarcoma was definitely the most difficult to treat and the most deadly. I'd read a blog by a teenage girl who had battled osteosarcoma. The desperation and sadness in her words were palpable, and I remember thinking, *We aren't doing that. We aren't doing osteosarcoma.*

While I had chosen to trust God, to hope rather than despair, fear still reared up inside me. The practical part of trusting God is hard and takes practice.

My gut in knots and fighting tears, I asked the surgeon what the chance of survival was. "Around 70 percent, depending on how far it's spread," he replied. An audible gasp escaped as I felt the knots tighten. I already knew these numbers. I'd spent hours sorting through the medical journals and studies looking for answers, for hope. Seventy percent sounded good until I heard it in the context of my own son. Suddenly the odds sounded horrible. All I could hear was 30 percent chance of dying . . . Your fourteen-year-old son has a 30 percent chance of dying.

The surgeon left the room, closing the door behind him. Rob and I stood and held each other. I sobbed, and Rob remained stoic. A volunteer, an older gentleman with an atrocious toupee and a theatrical mustache, peeked into the room and with an apologetic look told us we must leave, the room was for consultation only. We left the solitude of the room and headed back to our seats by the happy family. They were on to planning dessert.

I knew people at home were waiting to hear the news, so I moved to a seat that was a little more private and less noisy. Rob stayed in his seat so he could keep an eye on the screen and know where Zach was. Holding my emotions in, and doing my best to be pragmatic, I dialed the phone. My first call was to my parents. Mom answered the phone.

"It's cancer. Osteosarcoma."

"Oh! Laur . . ." she choked.

A sob caught in my throat. "Don't. Don't do that. I can't go there right now. We still have to tell him. I still have to go in and tell my son he has cancer, and I don't want to be a mess. I don't want him to have to deal with that." She cleared her throat and took her marching orders to call the rest of the family: my six siblings, grandma, and aunts and uncles.

My next call was to Alli, who was waiting for news in her dorm just across the Mississippi River.

"Hi, Mom." She answered her phone after the first ring.

"Hi, hon. It's cancer," I said. She immediately broke down into sobs. "We have to meet with oncology in the next day or two. I'm not sure what things will look like until then."

"Mom? Is Zach going to die?"

"There's a 70 percent chance that he won't," I answered. "Just pray, Al. Pray hard."

"I will," she said through tears. "I'm going to talk to my professors and see if I can get some time off. I don't know if it will be possible, with finals coming up and all."

"We'll figure something out. Babe, I have to call a few more people. I'll call you when we get home tonight."

I continued making my way down my list of friends and coworkers, breaking down a little more with each call until the tears finally forced their way out.

When I finished the calls, I looked up to see a woman around my age with dark, long hair and olive skin, whom I had seen earlier in the morning, seated in a chair across from me. She had entered the waiting room with a man I assumed was her husband, and he had been taken into surgery around the same time as Zach. A doctor accompanied by an interpreter had just exited the waiting room after speaking with her, and silent tears were streaming down her face. Beaten down by having to say the words *it's cancer* over and over again, I found myself in a similar state. We sat there together and cried freely without the pressure of having to use words to comfort each other. As I walked past her, I reached out and squeezed her shoulder. She grabbed my hand and held it for a moment without looking at me. I was so grateful for her in that moment. I needed her and she needed me; we were silent witnesses to each other's pain. When I look back on that moment, I know it was no accident that the seat next to her was free.

Our name was called again, this time by a nurse who would lead us to Zach's room. As we walked past the boisterous, recipe-wrangling family who was obviously waiting for a loved one they expected would come out of surgery better than he or she went in, the lobby phone rang. One of their members looked up and jokingly teased me, "You're closest! It's your turn to answer it." In my head I replied sarcastically, *Sorry! I get to go tell my son he has cancer.* On the outside I just smiled.

As we walked down the sterile hallway toward the recovery room where Zach was coming out of the anesthesia, I prepared myself to say those words: *Zach, it's cancer.* I'd practiced while in the shower for a couple of days, saying the words out loud, over and over again, trying not to cry. It hadn't worked. Every time I said those three words out loud, it was like throwing a switch in my heart with a line to my tear ducts. Tears would come, and there was no stopping them.

We walked through the nurses' station and into the glass-enclosed room. I pulled the mauve-and-green checkered curtain back to see Zach lying in the bed, a blanket pulled up to his chin. He was in a drug-induced slumber.

Rob and I sat quietly by his bedside, looking at him and wondering how he would handle the news . . . *Cancer . . . cancer . . . cancer.*

As I sat there and prayed for the strength to say that horrible word, a powerful sense of peace washed over me. It was like being wrapped in a warm, wool blanket after being out in a freezing Minnesota blizzard. The knot in my gut loosened, and the fear suddenly lost its power, replaced instead by resolve and confidence that things would be okay.

Rob looked up at me for a moment from Zach's bedside, all his attention focused on Zach. I walked over to him, and he grabbed my hand. "You doing okay?"

I nodded and smiled. I was okay. I was peaceful.

Zach started to come around as the anesthesia wore off. He asked for a sip of water, then dozed off a little bit. The surgeon walked into the room and quietly asked if we'd had a chance to tell Zach the news. We hadn't, so the doctor pulled a chair up alongside Zach's bed, then reached over and gently laid his hand on Zach's leg to wake him. Zach turned his head and did his best to focus.

"Zachary, we did the biopsy and you have osteosarcoma," he said in his oddly peaceful and gentle way, cancer a more normal part of his life than it was ours.

Zach groggily nodded his head and closed his eyes as the life-altering news settled in, the pain medication providing a buffer. I offered up a silent prayer of thanksgiving. God knew what He was doing.

As he gradually became more clear-headed, Zach seemed focused on getting home and getting on with it. He asked some questions about his diagnosis and what was going to happen next, but what he was really wondering was whether he would be able to go to school and how it would affect his social life. We gave him as much information as we had without being too overwhelming. We told him the next appointment would be with the oncologist in a few days. Once he was feeling well enough to move around and get dressed, he just wanted to go home.

We drove home in silence, each of us pondering the news, the sky thick with dark clouds on a rainy November afternoon. As we descended into the St. Croix Valley, the valley of the Holy Cross, there was a tiny break in the cloud cover and a single beam of sunshine broke through. A rainbow formed directly in front of us over the road ahead. As I rested my head on the cool, damp window, a silent tear ran down my cheek and I smiled. *Okay. I get it. You've got this*, I thought. I nudged Rob, who was intently focused on the road ahead, and directed him to look up.

WE PULLED INTO THE DRIVEWAY AROUND FIVE O'CLOCK IN THE EVE-ning, exhausted. The abandoned basketball hoop was silhouetted against the darkening sky, the net dripping from the rain. Once inside, Rob pulled his wallet out of his jacket and placed it in its usual spot on the shelf in the closet, then hung up his coat. Zach kicked his shoes off into the closet, tossed his coat on the floor, and took a seat at the kitchen table. None of us had eaten all day; Zach because he wasn't allowed, Rob and I because of nerves.

I hung my purse on a hook in the kitchen and hung my coat over it, then turned to Rob and Zach.

"When do you want to tell Sam and Grace?" I asked them both. I was grateful the two of them were in their bedrooms. I hadn't thought this far ahead, and it gave us a minute to plan.

"It's up to you guys," Zach said as he looked at Rob and me and shrugged.

"We should probably call them down now," Rob said wearily.

I went up to their rooms and knocked on each door. "Hey, guys? Can you come down? We need to tell you how things went today."

They both emerged from their rooms with looks of concern on their faces. I indicated for them to take a seat at the kitchen table where Rob now sat next to Zach, in their usual spots. Once everyone was seated, I nodded to Rob.

"Well, we got some bad news today," he started. "We found out that Zach has a cancer called osteosarcoma. We have another appointment in a few days with an oncologist." He turned to Grace. "A cancer doctor. We know he will need chemotherapy and surgery, but we don't know much more than that right now."

Sam dropped his eyes to his hands and nodded his head. "Okay," he said, raising his eyes to Zach. "I guess you just do whatever you have to in order to get better."

Zach nodded his head in silent agreement.

Grace sat quietly. At age eleven, she didn't understand what it all meant—cancer, chemotherapy, surgery—but she knew it was serious and it involved her big brother.

Headlights shone through the window in the living room adjacent to the kitchen. I walked to the front door and opened it. It was the assistant chief of the fire department, whom I had worked with for five years, and his wife. With a quick hello, they whisked by me and, with the help of Rob and the kids, spread out a feast of hot rotisserie chicken, fresh mashed potatoes, buttered corn, warm rolls, salad, and pie on the kitchen table. The mouthwatering aroma triggered our neglected stomachs to instantly rumble and reminded us we were starving.

As fast as they came in, they were walking out the door, mindful of our need to be alone and together as a family.

They backed out of the driveway, the daylight having given way to darkness. I turned to the kitchen table where everyone was finding their seats, the light above the table casting a Norman Rockwell-like glow on the scene. I sat down at my place at the table, where I'd sat since the kids were babies, and watched as everyone loaded their plates with slices of chicken and mounds of potatoes and gravy.

I picked up my own plate and began dipping into the delightful and unexpected banquet, and listened to the chatter as the kids and Rob shared the more interesting parts of the day, the parts that were about more than just cancer. I sat quietly for a moment and absorbed the scene. *So this is how it is,* I thought. *At the end of the day, we are just a family who loves each other.* We'd just received devastating news and yet here we were, together and joyful. In that moment, we were okay, all of us just happy to be back together after a long and hard day.

I took a bite, savoring the flavors, and wondered at how life, even in the darkest moments, could be so good.

Six

. . . .

December 2009

A COUPLE DAYS HAD PASSED, AND THE NEWS THAT ZACH HAD CAN-
cer had begun to sink in. We were back at the U of M campus at the
Masonic Cancer Center for an appointment with the oncology doctor. As we walked up the sidewalk, we passed several people smoking
cigarettes, some with hospital gowns on and hooked up to IV poles.
The irony didn't escape Zach; he looked over his shoulder at me and
cocked an eyebrow.

We stepped into the crowded waiting room with its scuffed
walls, outdated décor, and a big basket of hand-knitted caps on a
shelf just inside the door. There was a children's play area in the
corner, the only part of the room where an attempt had been made
to bring any cheer into the space. It smelled of hand sanitizer and
stale coffee.

Zach, the only patient under the age of forty, looked around trying to find a set of three chairs in a corner somewhere. He and Rob

headed for some window seats while I went to the desk to check in. The place was busy—bald people coming and going; people in wheelchairs parked in aisles between chairs and caregivers alongside. The staff was frantically trying to keep up, handing out doctors' orders for this test or that scan, doing their best to give directions to places in the farthest reaches of the expansive U of M campus.

I stood there, insurance card in hand, and thought, *I hate this place. Who wants to hang out with a bunch of sick people?* An extremely thin woman behind the counter with overdone hair and heavy makeup hung up the phone and turned to me. "Name?"

"Zachary Sobiech," I replied.

She reached over into a file drawer and pulled out a chart. I took a few squirts of the foam hand sanitizer from a canister that hung on the wall. The place looked so old and worn-out it made me feel dirty.

She handed me some paperwork and took the insurance card to scan into the computer. I walked to the chair beside Rob, sat down, and looked around. People of all different ethnicities packed the room. I could pick out the seasoned patients. They were the ones dressed in sweats, tennis shoes, and hats or head scarves. The caregivers stood apart from the sick, more talkative and a bit more polished in appearance. It was hard to tell the economic statuses of the patients; cancer treatments have a way of making people look generic.

I wondered what Zach would look like with no hair and how long it would be before we would blend in. Maybe Zach wouldn't lose his hair, I silently hoped. If he lost his hair but kept his eyebrows, that wouldn't be so bad. Bald eyebrows seemed to be the thing that turned a person into just another cancer patient. I finished the paperwork and walked up to the desk to hand it in. The clerk pointed to a file rack hanging on the wall next to a huge white board with all the doctors' names and magnets that indicated who was on time and who was running late. "Put it in there," she said.

I nodded and placed Zach's chart in the front and sat back down. A nurse came out a moment later, grabbed the chart, and called our name. As we walked across the room, I noticed a few dirty looks from people who had been there before us. Then I saw the sign above the file rack: "Place your file in the back." Oops. Wouldn't make that mistake again.

She brought Zach into the lab for a blood draw, the first of hundreds he would have over the next three years, then we were taken to a clean, very beige room to wait for the doctor. Zach was calm and patient, just taking it all in as it came his way.

A young woman in a black-and-white floral patterned skirt with a black blouse and short hair that she managed to pull back into a little ponytail walked into the room. "Hello. My name is Nicole. I'm the heme-onc intern working with the oncologist."

The what? He-monk? What's a he-monk? I didn't ask; I was too busy trying to keep up as she proceeded to hand me a few packets of information and a little yellow sheet with a calendar printed on it and handwritten script in various colors on each day.

"Here is the chemotherapy schedule that Zach will be starting," she said. "We start with chemo first because studies have shown that survival rates are better if we begin with chemotherapy. After around three months of the chemo regimen, Zach will have surgery to remove the tumor from his hip. Once he has recovered from the surgery, he will continue for an additional five months of chemotherapy."

My mind was racing. I had talked to a family from our church about their son who had been battling leukemia. He'd had six rounds of chemotherapy. I looked down at the little yellow calendar. Zach would need eighteen! Would he be in the hospital or would it be out-patient? He'd probably be missing a lot of school. Maybe it wouldn't be so bad . . . a day for chemo, a day to recover, and then back to school. Surely the school would be accommodating.

"Zach, you'll need to be homeschooled while you're on chemo-therapy," the intern said to Zach.

My brain turned from bouncing around with questions to abrupt slow motion. Hoooomeeschooool. I saw my terrified expression reflected in a mirror that hung on the door across from me. A scene popped into my mind: Zach, ten years later, standing on a street corner in front of the hospital and holding a sloppily handwritten sign that reads "Please help! Unable to find work. Laura Sobiech home-schooled me."

"He won't be able to go to school?" I asked, interrupting her.

"No," she said gently, taking the little yellow calendar from my hands and placing it on the counter between us. "So, Zach," she said, looking at him as he sat on the examining table and then back at me, "each one of these infusions will be done in the hospital and will take at least two days, most will be longer." She traced the little yellow card with her finger. "Your white blood cell count will drop with each infusion, leaving you with little immunity to infection. You won't be able to go to school because it will be too risky."

I looked over at Zach, his long legs, clad in baggy jeans, gently swinging as they hung off the edge of the table. Giant basketball shoes tapped the floor as his feet swung back and forth, his hands clasped and resting in his lap.

"What do you think?" I asked.

He shrugged, grinned, and said, "Who needs school?"

I smirked at him, picking up on the glint in his eye. Yes, his life was changing fast and in a big way, but he was up for the challenge and missing a little school wasn't going to hurt him.

Nicole went on to give us the outline of what the next several months would look like. Chemo would start in a couple of days, after a gamut of tests and X-rays and scans had been done. At around the fourteen-week mark, Zach would have surgery to remove the tumor and replace his hip. Then chemo would start back up according to how necrotic (dead) the tumor was: over 90% necrotic = less chemo, less than 90% necrotic = more chemo. Either way, it was going to be a long year, but Zach was ready. He didn't complain or even show fear; he just wanted to get through it, then on with life.

Nicole gave us the information we needed to get started down this new road, patiently repeating things as she could see the confusion play out on our faces. We had been bombarded with the details of a whole new life that included a whole new vocabulary: *heme-onc*, a hematology/oncology doctor; *cisplatin*, a chemotherapy drug; *doxorubicin*, another chemotherapy; *methotrexate*, yet another chemotherapy. Our brains were swimming.

We gathered up our packets of information, our little yellow calendar, and a list of scheduled times and places for tests, X-rays, and surgeries. We stepped out of the room and walked down the hall to the door, on our new path to our new life—our Via Dolorosa, our Way of Suffering.

ZACH'S RIGHT UPPER CHEST WAS TENDER AND SORE FROM THE PORT that had been surgically placed just under the skin earlier in the morning. He had been moved from the OR to his new home in a cramped room on 5B at Amplatz Children's Hospital in the University of

Minnesota Hospital Medical Center where he lay quietly waiting for his first chemotherapy treatment.

The nurse walked into the room dressed in a protective disposable gown and a mask that hung around her neck. She held a bag of yellow liquid in her hand, the first bag of chemotherapy, the poison that they would pour into my son to save his life. *This is so primitive,* I thought. *Someday we'll look back on this and shake our heads at how barbaric it all was.*

My stomach turned as I watched the nurse, who was nervous and apologetic about having to access Zach's newly placed and very tender port. It was supposed to have been accessed, the tack-like needles pushed through his skin into the port and the IV lines ready to be hooked up to the fluids, during the surgery, but due to a miscommunication it had not been. She put her mask over her mouth and nose and pulled her gloves on, then unfolded the port access kit. As she scrubbed the tender area with antiseptic from a preloaded sponge and proceeded to push each needle into Zach's chest like a tack into a bulletin board, I watched helplessly as Zach turned his head to the side with his eyes closed and a look of quiet agony on his face. He was trying so hard not to let it get him down, but pain was a worthy adversary and challenged his resolve.

My heart was pierced as I watched a look of defeat settle on his face. Pain had won the first battle. I wanted nothing more than to jump from my seat and comfort him like I had when he was a young child, to stroke his hair, kiss his forehead, and tell him how much fun we would have when we were done with this nasty place. But I couldn't. He was too old for the simple comforts of childhood. Yet he was much too young to bear so much suffering alone.

The nurse hooked the lines from Zach's port to the bag of chemo on an IV pole, then pushed a button. *Swish . . . click . . . swish . . . click . . . swish . . . click . . .* The poison slowly marched through the tube and into Zach's chest. As he lay there, not wanting conversation, we sat quietly and listened to the sound of the pump. It was a sickening sound that had a lulling effect.

Our journey with chemo had begun.

The hospital was old, worn-out, and cramped. Big kids and little kids had to share rooms with just a thin curtain separating them. Some hospital stays were tolerable if a few conditions were met: a quiet roommate with quiet visitors, the window side of the room, and our favorite nurses. Other stays almost made us crazy: noisy kids (or worse, noisy parents), no window, and people walking through constantly.

There were a couple of hospital stays that first year that stood out.

Zach's first roommate had a brain tumor, and there was some question as to whether or not the tumor had caused blindness. He was around seven years old, and his whole head, with the exception of a dark tuft of hair on top, was wrapped in bandages. I walked in the room one morning and found the bed empty.

"Hi, hon," I greeted Zach. "Where did your roommie go?"

"He got to go home this morning," Zach answered cheerfully. "And, Mom, he can see!" Zach never laid eyes on that little boy on the other side of the curtain, but he cared deeply about him and gave me updates each morning when I would come into his room.

"I'm not suffering. That kid is suffering," he would say.

Another time we were assigned a room with a little boy who had a mental disability, among other problems, and very loud. He loved cartoons and gave a continual commentary about them as he watched. "Oh boy . . . oh boy . . . he's in trouble now," he would yell.

His poor mother spent most of her time shushing him. Zach would look at me and roll his eyes and shake his head.

"It's going to be a long stay," he whispered.

There was one little boy who had the voice of an angel. He had osteosarcoma like Zach, and had to have his femur amputated and a procedure called rotationplasty performed to reconfigure his leg. He diligently did his homework with his mother's help and never complained, even when physical therapy came to work with him. Though we only roomed with him once, this little boy had a big influence on Zach.

"Mom," he said one day when we were alone in the room, "if I had to die instead of that little boy in the bed next to me, I would. It's not fair. No kid should have to lose their childhood to this." He was angry.

No teenager should either, I thought to myself.

Seven

· ·

IT FELT GOOD TO CROSS THE WEEKS OFF AS WE COMPLETED EACH treatment. I had decided when Zach was done with treatment, we would throw a big party to celebrate kicking cancer's butt. There would be music, dancing, and lots of laughter. Zach had been playing his guitar more than usual lately, and I had an image of Zach standing on a stage playing for a room full of people who were just as excited about our victory as we were. Then, when the party was over, we would pick up where we left off: Zach would go back to school, graduate, and move on to college.

Good news kept coming our way. The chest CT scan showed a small spot that was likely just residue from a previous infection, and the bone scan came back clean. It appeared that the cancer had not spread. The doctors were ecstatic.

If the little yellow calendar was the game board, then blood counts were dice. We were always waiting to see what the counts would be. If counts are good, proceed to the next square, and roll the dice again. If counts are bad, stay put until they are good. Each infusion was a crap shoot—we simply had to wait and see.

Zach's third infusion was scheduled for a couple days before Christmas. The infusion would take at least two and a half days, and then he'd need fluids to flush his system. It seemed Christmas would be spent in the hospital, and it was heartbreaking to think about not being together as a family on this, our favorite holiday.

Every year on Christmas Eve, we would spend the day buzzing about the house in preparation of our favorite evening together as a family. We would make our traditional Christmas Eve meal of tortellini soup, shrimp cocktail, and a special dessert. The table would be draped in a gold jacquard tablecloth and set with candlesticks and our finest dinnerware. The Christmas tree would be lit with hundreds of multicolored lights and decorated with ornaments the kids had acquired throughout the years. We would go to Mass in the late afternoon, have our simple candlelit dinner, then the kids would exchange their gifts with one another. It was our favorite night because it was just us, no one else.

As heartbroken as I was that we were going to miss this special evening together, I went into fix-it mode and did my best to come up with a solution. We decided to move our Christmas Day celebration with extended family up a week and planned for our immediate family to be at the hospital on Christmas Eve with Zach, then return to the hospital early Christmas morning. It was going to suck, but it was the best I could come up with.

Zach was heartbroken that he would have to be at the hospital, but what else could he do? He didn't have a choice. The other kids couldn't quite get it. They ganged up on me and asked, "Why can't they just delay the chemo? Why can't he go in after Christmas?" I'd thought the same thing myself. Was it really that big of a deal to delay a few days?

I asked Rob what he thought.

"No," he said with firm resolution. "The docs know what they're doing. We aren't going to delay Zach's treatment for Christmas no matter how hard it's going to be."

Rob is a methodical person, and once something is decided, that is the end of it, there is no more discussion. It was one of the reasons I fell in love with him, and after we got married, it was one of the things that drove me crazy. Over the years he had softened a bit, but Zach's cancer had him back to working by the book. Rob found comfort in routine.

Two days after our early celebration at Grandma and Grandpa's house, we went to the clinic for Zach's appointment, packed and ready to check into the hospital for his next infusion.

"Maybe you'll get to meet one of the Vikings' players. I hear they visit the hospital over Christmas," I offered lamely as we waited for count numbers after his blood draw. He raised his eyebrows and nodded with a look of "not good enough" written on his face.

The nurse came out and sat down in a chair next to us. "Well, I'm afraid you won't be checking into the hospital today," she said apologetically. "You didn't make counts; you're about five hundred too low." Zach's immunity was too low for additional chemo. He would have to wait.

A look of elation beamed on Zach's face. You'd think he just won the lottery, he was so happy. Christmas had been saved! Back at home the girls and I hustled about the house. We dressed the table while Zach fried up the spicy Italian sausage for the tortellini soup. Rob ran to the grocery store to pick up a couple of bottles of bubbling apple juice and a tube of ready-to-bake biscuits. Once everything was prepared, we all dressed in our best clothes and headed to Christmas

Eve Mass where friends were waiting. When we got home, we had our traditional candlelight dinner together, and then we gathered by the fireplace and the kids exchanged their gifts.

It turned out to be one of our most memorable Christmas Eves followed by a blessed Christmas Day. We opened our home for an impromptu gathering of our extended family. The house was bustling with activity the whole day, the cousins running through the house and the adults playing Rock Band on the Xbox for hours on end. It was a perfect Christmas.

THERE WAS NO WAY I WAS GOING TO TRY HOMESCHOOLING ZACH IN the midst of dealing with cancer. There were only so many things my shrinking brain could focus on at once, and cancer had called "dibs." So I'd worked with the school to find out what our other options were. He was a smart kid who picked up on things quickly. If he got a poor grade, it wasn't because he didn't understand the material; it was because he either hadn't turned in the work or hadn't studied enough. We had the option of a tutor coming to the house who would help Zach work through the material his classmates would be doing, or he could go at his own pace with online classes. We soon realized it would be too difficult even with a tutor for Zach to keep the same pace as his classmates; as chemo built up in his body, he got increasingly sicker and simply wouldn't have the energy to keep up. Things were too unpredictable to take that route, so he chose online classes.

One month in, we had a system. If he was home, Zach would sleep in until around nine o'clock, get up and shower, then come upstairs and sit in the middle of the couch in the living room with his laptop and do schoolwork for three hours a day. If he was in the hospital, he would spend the morning hours in bed with his computer, working on schoolwork until I came from home to spend the afternoon and evening with him.

After he was done with his schoolwork and if he was home, he would head down to the family room and play Rock Band on the Xbox until Sam came home from school, and then the two of them would hang out for a little while. If he was in the hospital, Zach would spend a good portion of the afternoon researching guitars, drum sets, and other instruments. We had learned from another family at the hospital about Make-A-Wish and what they had to offer children battling life-threatening diseases. We filled out the application for a wish to be granted and were told by the hospital social worker to dream big. Much to Grace's chagrin, rather than choose a family trip to Disney, Zach chose music.

Most evenings at home, a friend or two would visit Zach. If Zach was in the hospital, Rob would come in with Grace and some fast food, we would have dinner together, I would go home, and Rob and Grace would stay until around ten o'clock. The next day we would do it all over again.

I took leave from my job at the dental office after Zach was diagnosed. His treatment demanded much of my time, and I didn't want to leave him alone for long periods of time. But I continued teaching CPR classes when Zach was feeling well enough and volunteering at the fire department, going on calls as they fit between hospital visits; it gave me a chance to keep my foot in my pre-cancer life. I spent my days at home and by Zach's bedside in the hospital researching osteosarcoma. Osteosarcoma is considered an orphan disease, which means it's rare and doesn't get the attention of some of the "sexier" cancers like breast cancer or prostate cancer. Approximately four hundred children in the United States are diagnosed each year, most in their teens. The last real breakthrough in treatments for the disease happened over twenty years ago, and those treatments work for only 70 percent of patients.

While Zach pored over the Guitar Center website researching the instruments, I spent hours reading through studies that were over my head, doing my best to learn the medical jargon and research our options. I read books and articles, looked at diet therapies, and called clinics around the country to learn all I could. I was open to any treatment, but I needed to see numbers to be persuaded. Traditional medicine had the research and results to back up their claims, and that was the course we felt the most comfortable and confident with.

As word got out about Zach's diagnosis through CaringBridge, a website that enables families to share medical updates about loved ones with the community, Facebook, and word of mouth, we began to receive suggestions for various alternative treatment options. People were passionate about cancer, some on a level that approached religious zeal. Most people were sensitive in their approaches; they understood the limits of what they had to offer but needed to share the information they had just in case it might help in some small way. Others, however, were thoughtless, offering pointless suggestions or questioning our treatment choices without any real regard for how it would make us feel. Everything from pat suggestions like, "You should feed him more broccoli," to "You're killing him with the chemotherapy" were hurled at us.

I began to see how uncomfortable people become at the thought of dying young and how little people think before they speak. People would say things to make themselves feel better even though they didn't serve us any purpose. I'd often fantasized about writing a tutorial entitled "What Not to Say." It would be very basic, just a couple of hard and fast rules:

1. If the sentence you are about to say starts with the phrase "have you" or "you should," don't say it.
2. Unless you have had a child with the same disease and you've been through the exact same thing, don't offer advice.
3. Don't tell me about everyone you have ever known who has either battled cancer or died from cancer.
4. Don't tell me to be grateful.

Zach went through the same kind of intrusive questioning. At different times during his treatment, depending on where he was in his treatment schedule, Zach was bald. When he was bald, it was easy; no one asked questions because they already knew the answer—he had cancer. It was when he had hair that things would get tricky. Because the tumor had eaten away a good portion of the bone at the neck of the femur, he needed to use crutches, which would prompt people to wonder what was wrong.

One Sunday morning we were walking into church when a sweet, older gentleman walked up to Zach.

"What's your injury?" he asked, giving Zach a hearty slap on the back.

Zach, not wanting to make the man feel awkward, which undoubtedly he would, gave me a quick look of *Oh boy. Here we go.*

"I have cancer," he said plainly.

"Oh . . . Yeah . . . Well, geez," the man stumbled as he tried to find words of comfort. "That's tough," he finally got out.

Zach, seeing the distress on this poor gentleman's face, just smiled and assured him he was fine. We often found ourselves in this situation where people who wanted to bring us comfort ended up needing to be comforted themselves.

Zach hated watching people squirm; he didn't like to be the source of their discomfort. So one day he decided to experiment a little. He was out with friends when a man came up to him.

"Hey, what happened to your leg?" the man asked.

"Car accident," Zach answered, thinking that would satisfy him.

Unfortunately, the man was a paramedic. "What kind of injury?" he asked. "Tib/fib fracture?"

"No, hip injury," Zach responded.

"Dislocation?"

"Um. Yeah," Zach answered.

"Did you roll the vehicle?"

"Yep."

"Oh man, that stinks. Were you buckled?"

"Yep."

Buried under lies, Zach's only option was to continue the ruse. When Zach got home he was feeling so guilty, he sat down on the couch next to me and confessed the whole thing, chuckling as he unfolded the multiple lies he'd told. By the time the man finally stopped questioning him, Zach had rolled his dad's Mercedes, had dislocated his hip, and would have to miss the rest of basketball season because he would be on crutches for six weeks! I have to admit, I was proud of him for having a little fun with it.

The words I found most comforting were from those people who said it like it was, something like: "Whoa, your son has cancer?

Well, that just totally sucks." No gushy stuff, no advice, just straight up naming it and acknowledging how awful it was.

One of the kindest and most thoughtful things anyone ever said was the question my best friend, Anne, asked.

"So, what do you want? Do you want me to call you every day and stop by to visit? Or do you want to be left alone until you get through it?" she asked. "If it were me, I'd want to tuck myself away for a year and come out when it's over."

"Don't you dare leave me alone," I answered. "There is no way I can do this thing without talking my way through it."

She called me almost every day.

Eight

. . . .

February 2010

THE RADICAL SURGERY TO REMOVE ZACH'S HIP JOINT AND SEVERAL inches of the femur and replace it with a metal prosthesis went well. The surgeon had to remove much of the surrounding tissue and muscle as well, which meant Zach would never have full mobility again. But Zach was determined to get back as much as he could, and by the second day he was walking up and down the hospital hallway. By the third day he was doing steps, and by the fourth we were going home.

For six weeks Zach had to wear a brace, the top strap wrapped around his waist and the bottom just above the knee, with a metal bar connecting the two straps. It held his leg at a thirty-degree angle; his knee turned outward continuously, a position that would aid in his hip healing properly. Zach was in pain, but didn't complain when I pulled out the checklist of exercises he was to do each day. He was determined to heal quickly so he could move on with the chemotherapy and then on with life.

We only had one close call, when Zach slipped in the bathroom. I had been standing outside just in case he needed help. (Of course, no fourteen-year-old wants help in the bathroom, from his mom of all people.) After a couple of minutes, I heard something crash.

"Are you okay?" I asked through the closed door.

He was silent. A few moments later, when he came out, his face was pale, and he was obviously shaken.

"What happened?" I asked, doing my best to keep panic at bay.

"The bench slipped when I sat down," he said with clenched teeth. "I heard something pop in my hip." He went into his bedroom across the hall and lay down on the bed without another complaint.

Since I am an emergency medical technician and had been with the fire department for six years, I have seen a lot of things and had to keep my cool while dealing with some very serious injuries. But never have I felt as unsteady as I did seeing the look on Zach's face as he came out of that bathroom and made his way across the hall to his bedroom; he looked panicked. I was terrified something had pulled apart and been displaced. I knew he was in extreme pain, but he just lay in the bed and kept quiet. It was one of those rare times when I wished he would complain. I called the doctor to see if I should bring him in, and he assured me that it would take a lot of force to pull the stitches or for anything to be displaced. Nonetheless, I brought Zach in to have an X-ray. Everything was fine.

Several days after Zach's hip surgery, we got a call from the oncologist. The tumor had been carefully dissected and examined to see if the chemotherapy was killing the cancer cells. We were thrilled to hear all margins were clear of cancer and the tumor came back 100 percent necrotic! The chemo was working—it was killing the cancer!

It was the best news we could have gotten. It was looking like Zach would be one of the 70 percent of kids who survive osteosarcoma. He didn't have any tumors in his lungs; they were completely clear, as was his bone scan. Everything pointed to him beating this horrible disease. Now it was just a matter of healing from the surgery and getting through the next five months of chemotherapy.

It was a tortuously boring several months, relieved only by Zach's progress in physical therapy in recovering from the hip surgery. He'd lost so much muscle tissue we weren't sure how much movement he would be able to recover. He amazed us all by his dedication to therapy. He would never have the same strength and range of motion he had before cancer, but he worked as hard as he could. He wanted to run again.

One of the chemotherapies he was receiving required several hours of fluids after the transfusion. This meant more hours in the hospital, sometimes an extra day or two. We arranged with the hospital to have Zach go home with a backpack of fluids that would continue to flush his system at home. They were able to train me to change the bags and remove the lines from his port when the flush was complete. A home-care nurse would come to the house once a day and draw blood for the lab and would call us when his numbers were low enough to discontinue fluids. It turned out to be a blessing and a curse. We were able to leave the hospital early, but we were bringing the misery of it home with us. Zach had to lug the pack around with him everywhere he went, and had to stay close to a bathroom because of all the fluid running through him. It also brought that sickening *swish . . . click . . . swish . . . click* of the pump, a constant reminder that life wasn't normal, into our house. But we were at home, together as a family. The intrusion was worth it.

May 2010

IT WAS LATE IN THE EVENING, THE NIGHT BEFORE ZACH WAS TO check back into the hospital for another infusion. It had been a long few months recovering from the surgery on top of being sick from the chemotherapy. His body was wearing down and so was his spirit. His bedroom door was cracked, so I gently opened it and walked over to his bedside. He was asleep, his favorite stocking cap topped his now bald head, and he held a rosary in one hand and a wooden cross in the other.

The past months had challenged Zach to examine his faith and its place in his life. His simple, childlike faith was maturing into something he could turn to for guidance and find comfort in during this time of suffering. He was ready to step into spiritual adulthood and be anointed in the sacrament of Confirmation.

Zach's Confirmation class was scheduled to be confirmed at the St. Paul Cathedral at the tail end of one of these infusions. It was going to be close, but home-care would be able to deliver the fluids in time for us to get the backpack hooked up and make it to the cathedral. The youth director and Confirmation leader, Annie, came to visit us in the hospital two days before Confirmation. She told Zach not to worry about making it to the cathedral with his class, that Zach would be confirmed one way or another.

He grinned at her and pointed at his suit that was hanging on the IV pole in his room. "I'll be there."

"Really, Zach, don't worry about it. It's not a problem to schedule something later," she responded.

"Nope. I'll be there. Count on it."

The next morning Rob and I arrived at the hospital dressed up and ready to head to the cathedral for Confirmation. Rob was in his suit and tie, and I clacked down the hallway in heels instead of my usual clogs. I'd informed the nurses the day before we would need clearance from the doc bright and early—no waiting around like a normal discharge. We were doing this. The nurses were on board with the plan and made sure the docs wrote up the orders right away after rounds that morning. The home-care pharmacy was there to deliver his backpack and fluids, so it was just a matter of Zach taking a shower, getting his port hooked up to the pack, and getting dressed. He was tired and feeling sick, but he was determined to go.

We taped him up with Saran Wrap to cover his accessed port, and he hopped in the shower. Moving as quickly as he could without making himself sick, he got dressed, and we got the fluids running and were out the door in record time. He'd done it—he was actually going to make it with the rest of his class!

We walked into the beautiful, cavernous cathedral with its stone arches and marble floors as fifteen hundred people were taking their seats. As Zach made his way to our reserved pew, one by one his classmates caught sight of him and hopped up to greet him; everyone was surprised at the small miracle of his presence. The next miracle would be getting through the entire Mass without having to use the restroom, as he was wearing a pack with two liters of fluid being pumped into his system. Still recovering from the hip replacement, bald, pale, and sick, the joy on his face was evident. Cancer would not win—it was just a minor setback.

While he waited in the long line to receive the anointing by the archbishop, one of the ushers asked if he really needed to bring the backpack up with him. I'm not sure what he thought was in the pack. Perhaps snacks? Alli was furious. She knew how hard he'd worked to get there, and he didn't need the interrogation. But before Alli had a chance to lay into the guy, Zach just nodded and said in a quiet voice, "Yep. I need it. It's keeping me alive."

We made it through the ceremony on that glorious spring day, and Zach was even well enough to go out for a celebratory lunch afterward, though he slept through the remainder of the day once we got home. As Zach rested peacefully, I sat on the patio in our backyard and soaked up the spring sunshine. It had been a good month so far. Just days earlier we had celebrated Zach's fifteenth birthday and now his Confirmation.

My heart sang with gratitude for this small miracle. It felt like we'd run a marathon with every ounce of energy we had left and crossed the line. But we were beating cancer and the end was in sight! Zach had shown extraordinary courage and enduring faith in the battle. Now I'd gotten to see Zach anointed into spiritual adulthood, and I looked forward to watching that faith grow and mature. It brought me peace.

Nine

. . . .

July 2010

I'VE NOTICED THERE ARE A LOT OF CANCER FAMILIES WHO END UP adopting puppies, as if cancer isn't enough of a powder keg. But having a puppy in the mix seems to serve as a needed distraction. Ours came seven months after Zach's initial diagnosis and four months after his hip replacement. Zach had done remarkably well with physical therapy and was nearing the end of his regimen of chemotherapy. He had gained significant function and range of motion in his hip and was able to bend over and tie his shoes again. Though not with the same flexibility he'd had before cancer, it was still a big deal. And he had started to walk without the assistance of crutches, as much of a relief as losing shackles. He was free. We all felt the eager hopefulness that comes after a long, monotonous journey; we could see the end, and we were restless and in need of some distraction.

Over the years, the kids had cared for various pets. We had owned three rabbits, a mouse, a spotted leopard gecko, several fish, and two hamsters. But what they really wanted was a dog. As every mother knows, dogs are like toddlers; they require a lot of work. And, as every mother knows, she will be doing all the work. So for years I resisted. But now my defenses were down after several months of hard battle, so when eleven-year-old Grace came to me and told me Dad was fine with getting a puppy and that it was all up to me, I said yes.

After weeks of research, we decided on a three-month-old miniature red dachshund we named Daisy. On the Fourth of July holiday weekend, Rob, the girls, and I drove two hours to a little town in southern Minnesota to meet this little bundle whose picture we'd fallen in love with.

The breeder had told us that she was the runt of the litter, and they had kept her longer than the rest to make sure she would thrive. Once she grew to a healthy size, they decided it was time to put her up for adoption. A family had come a week before us to see about taking her home, but she hid under a shed in the yard and refused to come out. We had been warned that she may not choose us to be her adopted family, so Grace, Alli, and I were thrilled when we stepped into the yard and the puppy immediately ran to us and jumped into Grace's lap.

Daisy promptly took on her role as major cancer distraction. When Zach would come home after a few days in the hospital, Daisy would happily greet him at the door, so excited she could hardly contain herself. Zach would lie on the floor, and she would jump on his chest and give a most thorough licking of his entire face and was especially fond of his nose and mouth. I'm not sure the doctors would have approved, low blood counts and all, but it was therapy for his soul that was worth the risk.

When Zach was sick, Daisy would dig her way under his arm

and nuzzle until she was comfy. Or if he was lying on his stomach on the floor, she would roost between his legs with her chin resting on his butt.

Her distractions weren't always welcome. One day Grace and I had been out shopping for a new middle school uniform. Upon returning home, we were met by a very guilty-looking puppy and a floor covered in stuffing torn from Grace's new teddy bear. Grace was furious!

"It's okay. See?" I held up the husk of what was left. "It tore on the seams. I can fix it, no problem," I said, trying to keep her from tears.

We began re-stuffing the bear when we came across a little recording device that had been inside the bear. Daisy's crime had been recorded. I pushed the play button, and we could hear her growling and tearing the bear to shreds. I couldn't help myself—I busted out laughing. After a few moments of stubborn protest, Grace joined me.

Daisy was good at making dark things lighter through humor, and this would become especially true in the days to come.

IT WAS THE END OF JULY, TIME FOR ZACH'S LAST INFUSION. AFTER eight months of chemotherapy and surgery, we were finally done. Done with hospital stays and boredom, done with blood draws and port accesses, done with backpacks of fluids and days of being sick just to feel better again and do it all over. We were leaving this hospital and not coming back.

It was during that last stay in the hospital that we met Lance and his mom, Laurie. Lance was a couple of years older than Zach and had been diagnosed with osteosarcoma just a couple of weeks before Zach had. It was odd that we had never seen him before, but that was kind of how it happened—you got in, you got out. The curtain between the beds often kept friendships from forming.

Lance didn't have the same prognosis as Zach. His tumor had not responded as well to the chemo; it was not "as dead" as Zach's was, so he would have to continue on for a few more months with a different therapy. Neither Zach nor Lance were really up for talking much since they had both been on chemo for a couple of days and chitchat took too much energy, so Laurie and I did the chatting for them. It was a comfort to talk with someone who knew what we were going through, who really understood the whole thing. I'd wished I had more time to get to know her and that Zach would get to know Lance, but we were leaving and would not likely see them again, unless it was at a follow-up clinic visit.

You would think that I would have been ecstatic, that I would have been doing cartwheels down the hallway. But I wasn't. There is this strange phenomena that happens with people who have battled cancer. As hard as it is to go through chemo and as much as you want so badly for it to be done, when it finally comes to an end and you are walking out that hospital door, it feels more like leaving a secure fortress than leaving a prison. You realize that you aren't leaving the battlefield behind but are actually taking it with you, and it will be a part of you forever.

Zach didn't feel all that upbeat about leaving either. He was a little sad to leave the nurses who had taken such great care of him all those months, some of whom he regarded as friends. They presented him with a card signed by all of them and an iTunes gift card because they knew he loved music from all the time he'd spent with his headphones on and the few times, when he'd had a private room, he'd brought his guitar in. We promised to stop by for a visit when we came for his CT scan and follow-up appointment the next week.

Then we walked out the door into the great, big world and wondered if life would ever really be normal again.

FIVE DAYS LATER I TOOK ZACH TO THE ONCOLOGY CLINIC FOR A routine CT scan. We had decided to take part in a study of osteosarcoma patients that was being conducted to see if this certain maintenance therapy would help keep the cancer at bay. It seemed like a good choice for Zach, and it gave us a little peace of mind to know that we were still actively doing something to combat the disease in others.

Zach had rebounded from the last chemo cycle and was feeling good. He had been home most of the previous year and was excited about starting back at the high school in just over a month. We were happily talking about my youngest sister, Maria's, wedding that was coming up in a few weeks when the doctor and nurse came into the room.

As the nurse pulled up some images on the computer screen, the doctor asked Zach how he was feeling, to which Zach replied that he was feeling great. After he brought me up to speed on Zach's current blood count numbers, he took a seat and turned the computer screen toward us.

"We have some disappointing news," he said with a sigh as he looked at Zach. "The CT scan we did this morning shows three new lesions on your lungs." He paused a moment to let the news sink in.

My mind was reeling. What were they? Where did they come from? And why was the doctor making it sound like a big deal? I knew that osteosarcoma liked to go to the lungs, but Zach had beaten it. His tumor was dead. The chemo had worked.

"What are they?" I asked, puzzled.

"We won't know until we take them out."

"What do you mean, 'take them out'?"

"We'll have to do a surgery called a thoracotomy on each lung and do a wedge resection to remove the spots. We won't know for certain what the lesions are until they are taken out by a surgeon," he explained. "At this point we shouldn't waste too much time worrying."

My mind was tumbling all over the place as the future I had just barely allowed myself to consider was being tossed like a chess board that's been flung off a table. We were supposed to be done with this thing; we'd done our time.

"Can't we just keep an eye on them for a while? Is the surgery absolutely necessary?" I pleaded. This poor kid had just started to feel somewhat normal again and he'd had a major surgery five months earlier.

Zach was calm and didn't betray any emotion, more thoughtful than stoic. He was the one who would be affected the most, yet he didn't seem rattled at all. Quite the opposite, he was serene.

"I'm afraid so. Given Zach's history of disease, it would be too risky to delay. We really need to know what we are dealing with and, like I said, the only way to do that is to go in after it and take it out. But there is a good chance it's just scar tissue from a previous infection," he said patiently. This wasn't the first time he'd had to explain this to a parent.

"Okay. When?" If cancer was going to crash into our world again, I needed to start picking up the pieces of life and arrange them back on the board. The wedding was weeks away and school wasn't far behind, and I wanted Zach to be able to do both.

"We've scheduled a consultation with the pediatric surgeon for next week." He handed me a card with the information written on it. "You can expect the surgery to be scheduled within the next week or two."

"What about the study?" I asked. "When do we start?"

"We'll have to wait and see what the lesions are. If they are in fact osteosarcoma, Zach would no longer qualify for the study. It's for non-recurrent patients," he said in an apologetic tone.

Later that afternoon, I called Rob to tell him the news.

"That's not good," Rob said more to himself than to me. Rob had always been a worst-case-scenario kind of guy. It was how he prepared himself for bad news. I was more of a stay-upbeat-and-positive kind of gal.

"It doesn't mean the cancer is back. It could be something else." I wasn't ready to go there.

"Have you told the kids yet?" he asked.

I hadn't. It was the part I really hated—watching their lives dumped again with no reassurance to offer them. It was so hard to leave that world where everything turns out fine for that other world where kids actually get sick and some of them die.

"Zach is going out with friends, so let's talk to Alli and Sam tonight after dinner. Maybe we should wait until we know for sure if it's cancer before we tell Grace," I replied. I wanted desperately to shelter Grace. She was a child, just eleven years old, and I wanted to protect her from the agony of waiting for bad news and the harsh reality of Zach's disease. And I was still hopeful that it could be something other than cancer.

After dinner Sam went out to cut the lawn, and Grace settled in to watch some television. We pulled Alli into our bedroom first to give her the news, and as we were talking, Grace walked by the partially open door on her way to her bedroom. She heard Alli start to cry as the news that the lesions could be cancer began to sink in. I looked out into the hall just in time to see Grace make a beeline for her bedroom, tears forcing their way from her eyes despite her obvious effort to stop them. I hadn't seen her cry about the cancer before this; she kept things tucked away pretty tight. I was shaken and heartbroken as I stepped out of the room to catch her and pull her into my arms.

"Did you hear what we were talking about?" I held her shoulders and pulled back a little to look at her. Sadness mingled with fear swam in her eyes.

"No. I just heard Alli start to cry, and I figured something bad was happening again."

"Come on. I think you need to hear what is going on." With my arm wrapped around her shoulder, I guided her into the room with Alli and Rob. Alli put her arm around Grace and pulled her into a hug as Rob and I proceeded to tell Grace everything we had already told Alli: there were new lesions on Zach's lungs, and he would need surgery to determine what the tumors were. It was difficult telling my little girl, but she needed to hear it all, just like the rest of us. I couldn't shelter her anymore. I could only be there to help pick up the pieces after they fell.

I watched Grace, this strong, confident girl, let the wall come down and the tears flow freely. I felt my own tears fight their way out. Like a good midwestern German, I'd hidden that part of myself from the children. A parent's tears seemed too much a burden to place on a child. But as the four of us stood there, huddled together in our little group, it became evident that by sparing them my tears I was asking them to spare me theirs. I finally let the tears go. Rob pulled the girls and me into a big group hug and for a few moments we all just sobbed.

Until Daisy bounded in and caught her reflection in the full-length mirror.

At four months old, she was still a little baffled by the other puppy in the house—the one who would show up periodically in the mirror and stare boldly back at her, even after she displayed her very best pouncing stance and her fiercest bark.

As Daisy's little tiff with the puppy in the mirror played out, we all turned and regarded her for a moment, then looked at one another and erupted into laughter as we wiped the tears from our faces. The tension and sadness shifted so easily into torrents of laughter. And I realized what a blessing this little beast was.

Ten

A FEW DAYS AFTER WE'D GOTTEN THE NEWS THERE WERE NEW lesions in Zach's lungs, we met with the pediatric surgeon. I was still a little annoyed Zach would have to go through another surgery. It seemed like such an extreme way to proceed.

"Do you have any questions, Zach?" he asked gently after examining Zach.

Zach shrugged and looked across the room at me. I could tell he didn't really know what to ask; he was just going with the flow.

"Do you want to know how the procedure is done?" I asked Zach.

"Yeah. Sure." He looked at the doctor.

"We make an incision about ten inches long between the ribs and then use a rib spreader to pull the ribs apart," he answered in a mild and matter-of-fact tone. "Once the ribs are spread apart, I will go in with my hands and feel the whole lung. Osteosarcoma feels like a piece of sand. It's very obvious. If we find anything suspicious, we will do a wedge resection and cut that part of the lung out."

I glanced at Zach as he listened intently from the exam table. He caught my glance and smirked at me, one eyebrow cocked. This guy sure wasn't pulling any punches! Initially I was shocked at his frank language. But once I got over the "rib spreader" part, I appreciated his candor. Zach deserved to know what he was in for; he needed to be prepared for it.

"Zach, do you have any questions?" the doctor asked as he pulled a business card out of a drawer and handed it to me.

"Nope. I'm good." Zach sat on the table and leaned back, his hand planted firmly behind him as he casually tapped his foot on the slide-out step.

"Okay. Well, we'll see you a week from today, next Friday." He indicated the date and time written on the back of the card he'd given me. "Do you have any big plans this weekend?"

"Yeah. We are going to a cabin up in Wisconsin with my mom's side of the family," Zach answered.

"Oh. What do you do up there? Hiking, swimming, boating?"

"We usually go kayaking, and we do a lot of swimming."

"Well, be sure to wear insect repellent. You don't want to get Lyme disease from wood ticks. And don't drown," he said with a sober face as he rose from his chair and showed us to the door.

"Okay," Zach chuckled.

As we walked down the hall, Zach laughed again and said, "He's like a sadistic Mister Rogers."

"Ya think?" I busted out laughing too. "He's an odd duck, but I kind of like him. He lays it on the line."

"Yeah. Me too. I don't know what it is about him, but I trust the guy," he said as we walked out the door of the mammoth concrete building that looked more like an oversized castle than a medical facility.

August 2010

BEFORE WE LEFT ON OUR CABIN TRIP, I CHECKED MY E-MAILS AND received a notice of a CaringBridge update for one of the children I'd been following for a couple of months. He was a little boy, around nine years old, who was tanned from the summer sun and had a head of dark, patchy hair that had struggled to grow back after chemo. He had been fighting osteosarcoma for a couple of years and was in his last days. The cancer had filled his lungs. A week earlier, Santa visited his home and delivered a surprise Christmas in July to accommodate his wish to have one more Christmas before he died.

He had died that morning.

I was heartbroken and devastated for his family. This was the first time it hit home how horrible this disease was. I'd allowed myself to believe that Zach would never have to go through what this little guy was going through because Zach was different—he was beating cancer. But now there were unexplained lesions on Zach's lungs that I knew in my heart weren't caused by an infection or a cold. The only explanation was the most obvious one. Cancer was back.

Denial is such a crazy thing. Sometimes it hinders people from seeing what is real and keeps them in a place they should not be, but sometimes it's the only thing that allows people to live freely in the midst of terrifying circumstances that would otherwise cripple them.

I was finally starting to understand the nature of this disease. It was sneaky and greedy, and it didn't follow any rules. It didn't care about statistics or formulas, and it certainly didn't care that Zach was a strong, healthy kid who'd never had anything more than a bad cold. This disease could kill Zach. He could actually die.

At the cabin, I sat on the porch and allowed the thought of losing Zach to really penetrate my mind. It was the first time I let it go down deep and fill my whole being. My head felt numb, and my chest felt like a hundred-pound rock was resting on it. Breathing required thought and concentration.

I thought about what it would be like to sit on the porch of that cabin without Zach there. To know he was gone and would never be back. I wondered if home would ever feel like home again and if life would ever feel whole again. Or did losing a child mean that life would always be wrong, like a puzzle without all the pieces?

It was a strange thing to grieve a son whom I could see building sand castles with his little cousins on the beach in front of me. Images of him emaciated, sick and dying, flooded my mind. It felt like betrayal, like I was somehow giving up by allowing these thoughts to play out in my mind. Grieving the living was a skill that took practice, and this was my clumsy start. I would eventually learn to be pragmatic about it, allowing grief to dwell in a little closet that I tucked back in my mind and only opened the door to at specific times throughout the day, releasing it to run freely.

Over the next days, I became obsessed with reading CaringBridge posts of families who had battled osteosarcoma and lost. I focused on the stories where the cancer had shown up in the lungs and would follow it through to the end. I wanted to see the pattern and compare it with ours. I wanted to see the future and know what was going to happen. I was tired of surprises.

It was a horrible week. The stories I read went one of two ways: no cancer in the lungs meant survival, or cancer in the lungs meant a long battle followed by death. It was a grim way to spend time, but I couldn't stop. I needed to know.

It was finally Friday: thoracotomy day. We checked in, and Zach was taken to a room to get ready. He always amazed me with how upbeat he was when we checked in for surgery. There were times he was nervous, but he never seemed frightened. We joined him in the pre-op room before they took him to the operating room. The mood was light as we watched *Man v. Food* on the Travel Channel. The nurses, doctors, and surgeons all came in to introduce themselves and go over the procedure. We walked with Zach to the kissing corner and told him we loved him.

An hour and a half later, the surgeon found us. "The procedure is done, everything went well, and Zach is being moved to the recovery room," he reported.

"Did you find anything?" my mom asked. She and my dad had come to the hospital to keep Rob and me company as we waited.

"Yes, I found a couple of spots that I removed," he replied in the same matter-of-fact way he had described the procedure to Zach a week earlier.

"What do you think it is?" my mom asked, expecting to hear good news.

I didn't want to know until the results came in from pathology. I wanted one last weekend to hang on to that last little bit of hope.

"It felt like osteosarcoma, and given Zach's history, there is no reason to believe that it isn't."

Our last hopeful weekend was lost. The enemy had returned, and denial wasn't an option. Life had changed. Again.

ZACH BARELY MADE IT TO MY SISTER'S WEDDING, JUST FIVE DAYS after his thoracotomy. The day was a mixed bag of joy for the happy couple and worry about Zach's recovery and his future. Zach had planned to go on a pilgrimage to Madrid, Spain, the following summer for World Youth Day, a huge event where millions of Roman Catholic teens and young adults from around the world gather to celebrate their faith. He had been looking forward to this event as an opportunity to be inspired by kids who were all on a journey of faith. He was ready to answer the call to take his faith to the next level and start sharing it with the world. Months earlier, it seemed like a reasonable goal when the plan had been hatched. But then cancer showed up in his lungs, and now I wondered if we should scrap the idea.

Before the lesions appeared in Zach's lungs and he signed up to take part in a study that required weekly infusions, I mentioned the trip to the oncology doctor to see if she thought it would be possible. I was concerned about disrupting treatment. Before I could get the full question out of my mouth, the doctor stopped me and looked squarely at Zach.

"Go," she said emphatically. "Don't delay anything. Just go. We'll figure out a way to manage it."

So we signed him up for the trip. Being cooped up in a hospital for weeks made him antsy; he needed to stretch and take on some adventure.

Now I wondered if the trip was in jeopardy.

ZACH STARTED BACK AT SCHOOL IN SEPTEMBER 2010 FOR HIS sophomore year. He was ready to make a fresh start as he rejoined old classmates and hoped to make new friends. He was also anxious to return to the routine of school life. As much as he hated to admit it, he missed school.

The pathology report came back with news that the nodules that had been removed from one lung had, in fact, been osteosarcoma, but the nodule on the other lung was not—a little silver lining. Since there were no visible nodules left that were thought to be cancerous, Zach was considered NED (no evidence of disease). We would simply keep a close eye on Zach's lungs with CT scans every three months.

So Zach would be able to live the next three months without thinking about cancer. The miracle of normal was upon us, and it was glorious! Cancer was never too far from our minds, but we didn't have to think about it every day, and that was enough.

Zach enjoyed high school life. He did all the typical stuff: homecoming, parties, studying. In my mind it was all a huge gift, and my heart was content. All my children were well and safe. I felt whole.

Zach loved having his friends over, and the basement was often full of kids watching movies or hanging out and talking. One new friend in particular caught my eye. Mitch was just a few inches shorter than Zach and had almond-shaped, hooded blue eyes and dark blond, neatly trimmed hair. He was the kind of kid who was interested in everything. He wanted to know and understand how things worked, and loved to research and talk about what he'd discovered. Zach was the same way. They always seemed to have some fascinating discussion going on, and many of those conversations resulted in an experiment that usually involved something from my kitchen. If he and Zach weren't at our home, they were out doing something together.

Zach had a lot of friends, but he needed a close friend who could talk openly with him about cancer and wasn't afraid to be pragmatic about it, but who didn't define Zach by it. Mitch opened up a world of scientific and spiritual inquiry that was new for Zach.

One day I walked into the kitchen and found the two of them

frying up a can of beets, one of their many culinary experiments. As I walked out into the hall, I heard Mitch asking Zach about his thoughts on cancer.

"So, Zach. We should do some research on osteosarcoma," he said enthusiastically. "I really want to understand the mechanism that causes the cell to malfunction . . ." Then he went on to use words that were over my head. Mitch loved the science behind everything and had a way of making it comfortable for Zach to look at cancer objectively, from a scientific perspective.

Mitch wasn't afraid to explore spiritual things either. Though he did not consider himself a person of faith, he welcomed hearing about Zach's perspective and was open to engaging in dialogue about spiritual matters.

Another mutual love they had was music. Mitch played cello, and it was not unusual for he and "Ella" to show up at the door together. He and Zach would spend hours together in our family room collaborating on different pieces.

While Zach had several close friends who spent time with him and treated him like a normal kid, Zach found Mitch's approach of openly talking about his cancer refreshing. He related to Zach as more than a kid who was sick with cancer; he saw how much more interesting Zach was because of it, and in turn Zach was able to be just Zach.

Mitch provided a springboard for Zach to jump back into normal life.

I DETERMINED THAT I WOULDN'T THINK ABOUT SCANS UNTIL THE month they were scheduled. When November hit, the familiar stress began to creep back in. But the scans were clear! Another three months of bliss were ours, and we got to have our Thanksgiving, Christmas, and New Year's without cancer!

A year earlier, not long after Zach had been diagnosed, Rob and I lay in bed one night and talked about what was ahead of us. I told him that when we were through with the horrible year the doctor had warned us we would have to endure, I wanted to take the family to Mexico for a relaxing vacation on the beach. Now that Zach had a clear scan and three more months until we needed to worry about cancer again, it was time to take a family trip.

In January, we took the kids to Mexico and spent a week of leisure on the beach, swimming in underground cave pools and taking a zip line through the tropical forest. It was glorious. I watched Zach and Rob play volleyball with a group of other resort patrons in one of the several pools. It was so fun to watch him enjoy being athletic. His competitive streak unleashed as he pounded the ball over the net. I took out my camera and captured a shot of him as he jumped out of the water, arms above his head ready to whack the ball, a look of concentration on his face. Later, after looking at the picture, I realized that everyone who was in or sitting around the pool was looking at Zach. I knew it was silly, but I was proud of him, my boy who had endured such horrific suffering was out there playing like a champ. But it was one of those bittersweet moments as I allowed my mind to touch briefly on how it could have been—Zach running down the basketball court, all eyes on him. It was a petty thing, I knew, so I brushed the thought aside.

I loved this boy, and I would be satisfied even if I was the only one in the world who knew what a wonderful spirit he had.

FEBRUARY SCANS CAME AND WENT, AND WE WERE HANDED ANOTHER three-month pass to normal life. I had started back at work at the dental office a few months earlier, after Zach had recovered from his thoracotomy and was back at school. We were in a routine that felt like the old days, but cancer hung in the corner like a cobweb, annoying but easy to ignore.

Until one day in late April when Zach came home from school and called me at work to tell me that something didn't feel right in his chest. I knew it was bad because Zach didn't complain unless he was concerned, and every time Zach was concerned, he was right.

I told the ladies in the office I needed to pull some files from the warehouse and excused myself. I hadn't cried in months, but the impact of what Zach had just told me was like being unexpectedly shoved from behind. I wasn't prepared, and I needed a private place as I scrambled to get back up. I sat down on the floor of the warehouse and sobbed. All sorts of frantic thoughts ran through my head. Maybe his backpack was too heavy and he had strained a muscle, or maybe he picked up some kind of virus and he was being overly conscientious. But I knew deep down that wasn't the case.

I so desperately wanted to cling to our normal lives, but something was wrong and we needed answers. I forced myself to call the oncology clinic and explained what was going on to the nurse practitioner. We scheduled an appointment, and she did an exam, listened to his lungs, and ordered some blood tests. Everything sounded and looked good, but if we wanted to see if there were new lesions on Zach's lungs, she thought perhaps we might want to think about moving the pending CT up a few weeks—it was up to us.

We moved it up.

Cancer was back.

Eleven

I DON'T LIKE PREACHY PEOPLE WHO DUMP THE TENETS OF THEIR faith in your lap, knock the dust off their hands, and walk away. It might make them feel better, but it doesn't help anyone else. They can talk about God and Jesus all they want, but it's how they live day-to-day and how they confront suffering that really tells the story. I cringe as I write this because I'm not a graceful sufferer. I complain. A lot. But I know the people who have taught me the most about what it means to live a faith-filled life are those who live it and then wait for people to ask how.

I grew up in a home where I witnessed daily the silent but loud example of what it means to preach always but use words only when necessary. My father supported our family of nine by operating a little auto repair shop in my hometown of Lake Elmo, Minnesota. For over thirty-five years, he spent his days under the hoods of cars, arms submerged in their inner workings; his strong hands with their thick fingers were grease stained and scarred. He was an educated man who gave up going to college to pursue his dream of becoming a mechanical engineer in order to support his ailing father who could no longer work and to help his overworked mother.

Over the years, he saw a need in our community to help those who were struggling through difficult times. For over twenty years on the second Saturday of each month, he opened the doors of his shop and, with the help of volunteers, repaired vehicles free of charge. It was his humble way to share what God had given him.

I witnessed other actions of faith over the years too. I remember when I was in my early teens, an immigrant couple from Lebanon had a van that needed repair so they brought it to my dad's shop. When my parents found out that the couple was living in their van with two toddlers and a baby on the way, my folks invited them to live with us. With seven children of their own and limited income, they converted our garage into a living space so this family would have a place to stay through the winter. For seven months we had sixteen people living under our roof since my grandparents also lived in an apartment in our basement.

My parents formally trained us in the tenets of our faith. They sacrificed to send all seven of us to a Catholic school. We attended church weekly, received all the sacraments, and had nightly devotions and prayers. But it was how they lived their lives, the sacrifices they made to help those who God brought to them, and the story they created that laid the solid foundation that informed my faith. They lived what they preached and, in doing so, preached by living.

This example of faith coupled with formal teaching was how I hoped to raise my own children. I wanted my children to see how a life lived in faith could bring hope to the world around them, that acting out of love rather than fear would allow Christ to shine through them without ever having to say a word. And to know that joy—not just happiness, but true joy—comes when we give up our own agenda and let God work through us. Then we can begin to see the bigger picture, the eternal picture, rather than just the tiny brush stroke of our own lives.

May 2011

HERE WE WERE AGAIN, WITH CANCER CRASHING BACK INTO OUR lives. It was devastating news, especially after Zach had so many months of a normal life of school and friends. He'd been looking forward to a carefree summer and maybe even to finding a part-time job as a barista. He loved the idea of working in a coffee shop, and he was hoping to end the summer with the trip to Madrid for World Youth Day.

But instead he started out the summer by celebrating his sixteenth birthday, May 3, 2011, in the hospital receiving his first of several new rounds of chemotherapy in hopes of knocking the cancer back. The infusions required him to be in the hospital for five days at a time with a couple of weeks in between, which meant the summer was shot. I asked the doctors if they thought there was any way Zach could salvage the trip to Spain, if maybe we could pause the chemo so he could still go. They advised that we not stop chemo for anything; the cancer was very aggressive, with five new lesions in one lung and six in the other. The trip was lost. Zach was disappointed but turned his attention to gearing up for the battle that lay ahead.

ZACH HAD BEEN GROWING BACK HIS HAIR FOR MONTHS, AND IT WAS to the point where it was getting obnoxious, but he refused to cut it.

"You're beginning to look like Animal from the Muppets," I told him. "At least let me trim it up a little." It was driving me crazy, how shaggy he looked.

"Nope," he refused. "I'm going to let it grow until it's down to my butt."

Now that the cancer had returned and the new chemo would cause him to lose his hair again, he wanted it gone.

"Mom," he said to me the morning after we found out the cancer was back, "will you shave my head this weekend?" He'd been through this before and didn't want the process to drag out.

"Sure," I said with an upbeat tone, trying desperately not to reveal how much I didn't want to do it.

That Sunday afternoon I got the clippers out to shave Zach's head. I laid my hands on his head and kissed his hair, then picked up the clippers and started in. Alli, Grace, and Zach decided to play with it a little, first cutting it into a Mohawk before shaving it completely off. I fought tears as I laughed. I didn't want to do this again. I didn't want to give up the "normal" life we'd gotten back, and I certainly didn't want to watch Zach have to suffer through chemotherapy again. But most of all, it was the reality that we might not win this war, that cancer might actually kill Zach, that was beginning to sink in.

As I swept the hair up off the floor, Rob took me aside.

"You should probably save that," he said in my ear.

I'd already taken a Ziploc bag from the pantry and pointed to where it lay on the countertop. I put his hair in the bag, sealed it up, and hid it in my closet, then sat on the bed and sobbed as I imagined having only some old hair clippings to hold on to.

I HAD NEVER HAD OUR FAMILY PROFESSIONALLY PHOTOGRAPHED (IT seemed extravagant), but now I felt an urgent need to capture our family as it was, right now. Alli was already in college, Sam would be leaving home soon too, and Grace was growing up fast. And there was no certainty that Zach would make it. I decided I would pay any amount of money to capture this moment in time. The day before we checked in to the hospital for Zach's second treatment, I called a photographer named Jeff Dunn. I had seen a stunning photograph he had taken of my close friend Anne. She is an author and needed a photo for her latest book. Jeff managed to capture a beautiful image not just of her but of her spirit.

"We really need to have this session now," I told Jeff. "As the chemo builds up in his system, Zach won't feel well. His eyebrows and eyelashes will fall out. I just need to remember him as he is now," I explained.

Jeff rearranged his schedule to get our family in right away, and we spent an evening at a local park, splashing around in the water-fall that ran through it as Jeff snapped countless photographs. I was amazed and relieved at how beautifully he captured Zach's spirit and the spirit of our family as we interacted. He became a family friend and would take several photographs over the coming years as Zach's life took each interesting, and sometimes scary, turn. He ensured that no matter what, we would always have Zach's image close to us. It gave me a measure of peace as we stepped back into fighting the war.

THE NEW AMPLATZ CHILDREN'S HOSPITAL AT THE UNIVERSITY OF Minnesota opened two days before Zach checked in. The rooms were luxurious compared to the old hospital. They were single occupancy with all sorts of amenities, including a large-screen television with movie and game options along with an outdoor camera that would allow the patient to see what was going on in the outside world. The rooms were also large enough to accommodate several guests, and parties were encouraged.

So we took advantage and threw a little surprise birthday party with a few of Zach's closest friends. They surprised Zach with special presents, fake mustaches, and a plastic coconut bikini top (which Zach ended up wearing for Halloween—horrifying). They also came with a giant card that had been signed by at least a hundred of his classmates who wished him well. He would not be finishing the school year and would likely still be going through treatments at the start of his junior year.

The treatments made him extremely sick for days. Over the course of the infusions, he got progressively worse each day to the point where he couldn't even raise his head when people came to visit, let alone sit up and play the guitar he'd insisted on bringing to the hospital. Even after he got home, it would be days before he would start to feel well again—just in time to go back in and do it all over again.

I remember coming home from a movie one night. It was a comedy that had me rolling with laughter. When I peeked in Zach's room to see how he was doing, he was lying on his bedroom floor with a bucket beside him.

"Zach," I said as I kneeled down beside him, "honey, why aren't you in bed?"

"I don't want my bed to remind me of being sick," he whispered. "I'll go back in when I feel better."

I felt so guilty for going to that movie and laughing harder than

I had in months while Zach was so sick he wouldn't sleep in his bed. I didn't sleep that night. I felt like I had failed my son and had no way of making things better.

When I checked on him the next morning, though he still looked pale and sick, he was already up and getting out of the shower.

"What's up?" I asked.

"I'm going to hang out with Mitch and Sammy today. They're coming over in a little while," he answered. "I figure, if I'm going to be sick, I might as well be having some fun too." Somehow he managed to look forward to each day even though he knew it would likely bring with it periods of misery. He refused to let what he suffered define and contain him.

He endured each suffering with patience, and when it was through, he didn't dwell on it. It was what it was, and there was no time to be wasted feeling sorry for himself.

After his third infusion of six, we packed up his things to leave the hospital for home. I rolled up Zach's comforter and packed it into a backpack, and he grabbed his pillow and guitar and headed out the door. I watched as he walked down the bright green hallway with twinkle lights embedded in the ceiling; he hobbled back and forth with a hitch in his step. I marveled as he cheerfully smiled and waved good-bye to the nurses as he passed their station even though I knew he was so sick he could barely walk. He was telling the story of his faith by being joyful in the midst of suffering, and he was doing it without uttering a word.

We drove home in silence as Zach rested his head on his pillow against the window and napped while I quietly contemplated the crazy life we had been given. With this last recurrence of cancer, I had begun to shift my thinking from battling through the disease to accepting the possibility of losing Zach. My heart ached at the thought. But I could see the grace that God was bringing into my life through Zach and his humble acceptance of the cross he'd been given. His life was unfolding as an answer to every prayer my heart as a mother had ever uttered for my child: that his life would emulate Christ and thereby bring Christ to others.

As we exited the highway and entered our neighborhood, Zach opened his eyes and raised his head.

"How are you feeling?" I asked as I stroked his stubbly cheek.

"I'm okay. Glad to be home." He rested his head back on the window.

"I'm really proud of you. This thing is really hard, and you've handled it with extraordinary grace. Thank you."

We circled the roundabout and headed down our street. He closed his eyes and thought for a moment.

"Physical pain is a joke. It's just Satan's way of messing with you and trying to get you to feel sorry for yourself," he said. "Mental and spiritual pain are different. That's the real battle where faith and prayer come in."

I took in a deep breath, puffed up my cheeks, and exhaled slowly. There was so much going on in his head that he worked through on his own. So much wisdom that should be heard as he walked his road of suffering.

"Ya know, Zach, most people have to wait decades to build a story that people would want to hear. You have something real and solid you've lived through with grace. It's your story to share, and you might want to start thinking about how you want to tell it."

We pulled into the garage. Zach waited a moment before he opened the door to get out of the car and turned to me.

"Who do you think I would tell it to? Who would want to hear it?"

"I don't know. Just be ready when they start asking."

July 2011

ZACH HAD COMPLETED THREE CHEMOTHERAPY TREATMENTS. IT had been a grueling cycle of a few days in the hospital, a few days of being extremely sick at home, a few days of feeling better, then back in the hospital. A CT scan of his lungs came back inconclusive. The lesions had not obviously shrunk, so before they moved forward with the last three treatments, protocol dictated that the lesions be removed to see if the cancer had been affected by the treatment— they needed to see if the cancer was dead. Two thoracotomies later revealed it hadn't worked. The nasty beast survived the most powerful poison we could throw at it. The treatment was stopped.

It was a good news/bad news kind of thing. Zach was thrilled that the new therapy was outpatient and he wouldn't have to spend more time in the hospital. But as we sat in the exam room at the clinic, I flipped through the pages of information about the new treatment. I'd been doing this long enough to know what I was looking for—response statistics, those magical numbers that become a cancer patient's crystal ball. They weren't good. It was clear we had run out of treatments that would cure the disease, and we were onto treatments that could only extend his life.

Zach was so focused on the summer he had regained that I knew he didn't understand things had taken a sharp turn for the worse. And I knew it was time that he start facing that reality. He needed to start preparing to die.

I hated what I had to do.

"The numbers aren't good," I started out slowly as I turned the last page over.

"Yeah. Well, I'll just deal with stuff as it comes," he replied nonchalantly as he flipped through a worn copy of *Car and Driver* he'd already read a couple of times. His only other reading choice from the rack that hung on the wall was *The Potty Book: For Boys*.

"Zach," I lowered the collection of packets to my lap, "this stuff won't get rid of the cancer. It will only delay it from coming back for a while. If we're lucky." I looked him square in the eye to hold his attention. "Honey, you're not invincible."

He finally set the magazine down and looked at me. I held his gaze and watched as the understanding played out in his big green eyes. He was silent for a moment, then sighed.

"Okay. Well, it sucks that I just spent two months being sick for nothing. But I'm glad I don't have to waste any more time in the hospital." He was doing it the best way he knew how. He confronted the future, then left it there and came back to the present where he had a life to live and enjoy. I really loved that about him. As his mom, it made me proud. As a human, it inspired me.

Twelve

. . . .

ZACH HAD HIS SUMMER BACK. IT WAS LATE JULY, HE WAS FEELING great, he wasn't in the hospital all the time, and he was living as carefree as he possibly could. The new outpatient treatments, which he started several days after we'd found out the previous chemo wasn't working, were a dream in comparison to the excruciatingly long hospital stays from earlier in the summer. His friend Mitch often came with us to help the time go a little faster.

The first time Mitch accompanied us to the clinic, he and Zach wore Forever Lazy adult "onesies"—huge, blue, fleece suits that made them look like Teletubbies. We received more than a few strange looks. Mitch proceeded to grill the doctor about his knowledge of cancer and the various biological failures that happen when a cancer forms. A very serious conversation ensued between the man in the lab coat and the teenage boy in a onesie. Zach looked on with a huge grin on his face.

For Zach's second infusion, Zach and Mitch filled rubber gloves with water and drew faces on them to create a family of water glove people. (One exploded all over me on the way home.) I put a stop to things when Mitch pulled a syringe and tourniquet from a drawer and threatened to give one of the water glove people an IV.

For the third infusion, they brought their instruments: guitar and cello. A little three-year-old boy, whose six-year-old brother was receiving an infusion in the next room, stood in our doorway, mesmerized as he watched them play.

Another day they got jars of bubbles out of the toy cabinet. They walked down the hallway, Zach pulling his IV pole behind him, and blew bubbles into each room as they passed. When they got back to our room, they were both excited to tell me that after several attempts, they had gotten a teenage girl to smile at them. She had been lying on an exam table, looking very ill. To them, her smile was a victory over cancer.

August 2011

IT WAS THE WEEK I HAD DREADED FOR A COUPLE OF MONTHS. WORLD Youth Day in Madrid was all over the news, a constant reminder of what Zach was missing out on. Pictures popped up on Facebook every day as his youth group traveled through Rome, Italy, and then Madrid with a little "Flat Zach"—a picture of Zach they brought out for group photos to assure him he was with them in spirit if not in person.

The last day of the event, I overheard Mitch and Zach talking. They were having a lazy day hanging out downstairs. Neither one of them had the energy to motivate the other to go out and do something.

"So, who do you think was the first person to be on this land where your house is right now?" Mitch asked.

"I don't know," Zach said, pausing for a moment. "Probably a Native American. It's close to the river, so I'm guessing they hung out in this area."

They both got quiet for a while as they let their minds travel to other places and other times. It was the kind of thing they did often.

"We should just go," Zach blurted out.

"Where?"

"Rome. We should just plan a trip to Rome ourselves. Think about all the people who walked around that city for thousands of years. All that history. It would be so cool to walk the same streets as those people."

"We should plan it," said Mitch. He pulled Zach's computer off the coffee table and sat down on the floor. "Where should we start?"

"Well, Rome, obviously. I'd like to see Paris too."

They spent a lot of time this way, fantasizing about the what-ifs of life. But this time the tone of the conversation sounded as though they thought they could make it happen. An hour later, when they plopped down on the stools at the kitchen counter, I had a pretty good idea of what was coming.

"Mitch and I want to travel around Europe," Zach started right in. He knew I was just as devastated by the lost opportunity to travel with his youth group to Madrid, and he played on it.

"And where do you think you will get the funding for the trip?" We hadn't been financially devastated by the two years we'd spent battling cancer, but we didn't have the disposable income we had before Zach got sick. I looked out the window above the sink where I stood and washed dishes from the night before. A bee lumbered from one blossom to the next on the shrub outside.

"We'll figure out a way," he replied, then turned to Mitch. "Let's go figure out a way to make some money." And the two of them made their way back downstairs.

I wanted them to go to Europe. And I wanted to take them. In fact, a few days earlier a strange thought had popped into my head that we should take Zach to Lourdes, a place in the south of France where Jesus' mother, Mary, appeared to a teenage girl named Bernadette in the 1800s. I don't know where the thought had come from. It wasn't the sort of thing I was usually interested in, traveling across the world to visit a shrine in search of a miracle. I figured God had His reasons for allowing Zach to get cancer, and if He wanted to heal Zach, He would do it wherever Zach was. I had quickly dismissed the thought and moved on with my day. But it kept coming back.

I began to think about how we could actually make the trip happen. Where would the money come from? We didn't have the funds to work in a trip. *If God wants us to go, He'll send us*, I thought.

One month later while I was at a Bible study, a woman I had not met before approached me and asked, "Have you ever thought about taking Zach to Lourdes?"

"Actually, the thought just popped in my head about a month ago," I answered.

"My husband and I have been following your CaringBridge site for the past two years and have been very moved by your story. We would like to send you, Rob, and Zach to Lourdes," she said. "Would you be willing to accept?"

I was stunned. I had prepared all sorts of answers to other questions, but not this one.

"Okay," was my brilliant response.

We were going to Lourdes.

Later that evening I told Rob about the offer. Rob was not one who liked to receive help from others, but this was Zach we were talking about, and even though it was hard to accept the help of another family, he would do it.

A week later I met my lifelong friend Lisa on a warm, sunny afternoon on the patio of a restaurant that sits on the bank of the St. Croix River. We hadn't been together in a while, and she wanted to see how I was holding up.

"I was thinking," Lisa said. "I have really wanted to do something to help you guys for a while." She lifted her glass to her lips and took a sip of her mojito. "I know that you have people bringing meals, and I know you keep saying you guys don't need financial help, but I think it would be really fun to throw a big party. A benefit that could raise a little money for Zach to do some things he's always wanted to do."

I took a long draw from my own drink. Rob would have a hard time with it, especially right after accepting the trip to Lourdes. We had resisted offers to have a benefit in the past because we hadn't really needed the help. But now that we had been fighting the disease for two years and I had quit my CPR job and had taken periodic leaves of absence from my dental office job, the extra money would ease some of the financial stress . . . and a party could be fun. Since it looked like that "we kicked cancer's butt" party wasn't going to happen, this could take its place.

"Let me talk to Rob about it. But I am open to the idea," I said, setting my glass on the table between us.

I wasn't sure how to present the idea to Rob. We hadn't talked much the past several months, two proverbial ships passing in the night. With the exception of the Lourdes trip offer, I'd gotten into the habit of keeping things to myself, and I'd taken Rob's silence as confirmation that he wanted it that way. But he needed to be part of this decision.

"It might allow us to take the whole family to Europe, and maybe even Mitch." I laid out my way of thinking to him. "And we could use some of the money to give to other families who we know are in need as well."

"Yeah," Rob said after a few seconds of thought. "I think it sounds like a good idea. If it will allow Zach to do some things that he wants to do, I'm all for it."

Lisa was elated, and the benefit planning began. I was apprehensive but excited. People had been so generous to us over the past couple of years, and it would be so wonderful to have them all together in one place. And I knew Zach would love the idea of throwing a huge party. He loved a good celebration.

November 5, 2011

OVER SIX HUNDRED PEOPLE FLOODED THE HALL. THE ROOM WAS full of high school girls in party dresses with full hair and makeup that must have taken hours. High school boys walked through the room with plates heaped with pasta and salad and squeezed in together at tables to carb load before heading out to the dance floor. Lanky middle school boys dressed in their best dress pants and colorful shirts with snazzy ties hung in packs out on the patio until they gained enough courage to join the much older-looking girls who stood in a circle in the corner.

Families from our church, coworkers, fellow firefighters, family, and friends filled the room, having come from all over the Twin

Cities to join us in the celebration. As I stood by the door and greeted them, I was overwhelmed and humbled by the outpouring of love.

"We are so grateful to finally have a way to support Zach and your family," I heard over and over again. The room was buzzing with excitement and a spirit of joy as it filled with people who were genuinely happy to be there.

I saw Zach flitting around the room greeting people, a huge smile on his face as he doled out one hug after another. Grace had found her pack of friends, all decked out in their finest dresses and shoes with heels so high I was certain they'd had to beg their mothers to wear them outside of the house. Alli and Sam hung out with their cousins who'd come up from Indiana for the occasion. They all sat at a table together, laughing and catching up with one another, and Rob sat at a table talking with a group of coworkers.

When the band started, a couple of the high school boys jumped up from the tables and formed conga lines that snaked their way through the hall, inspiring the little ones to fall in line. The dance floor filled, young and old rubbing shoulders it was so packed. There were lines of enthusiastic bidders walking the tables of silent auction items that had been donated from people and companies from our community. The place was buzzing with conversation and laughter. Then the room went silent as Zach, Mitch, and Zach's lifelong friend Sammy Brown, who was the daughter of my best friend, Anne, were introduced and took their places onstage.

Zach and Sammy loved music. Sammy had been singing for several years, and Zach had become a skilled guitarist. They found their styles complemented each other, and they enjoyed collaborating in their love of music.

The crowd on the dance floor came to a halt, and those on the periphery of the room pulled in to listen. I stood toward the back of the room and proudly watched as Zach stepped up to the microphone.

"Before Sammy, Mitch, and I play a couple of songs for you, I just want to thank you all for coming out tonight and supporting me and my family," Zach addressed the crowd. "Your support means the world to me."

Sammy stepped up to the mic as Zach slung his guitar strap over his shoulder. When he was ready, he glanced back at Mitch, who was seated with his cello, and then looked up at Sammy and gave a little nod. She gave him a wink, and Zach began to play. They sang Jeremy Messersmith's "A Girl, a Boy, and a Graveyard" (ironically a favorite of hers and Zach's), as well as the Beatles' "Blackbird." It was only the third time I had seen Zach play for a big audience; the others were high school affairs for an audience a fraction of the size. All that time spent in our basement practicing over and over again paid off; they sounded amazing. The smiles on their faces showed a sort of comfort they had with one another. They trusted one another. After the songs, Sammy turned to Zach and gave him a fist bump. She turned to Mitch and gave him a high five. The crowd was alive again, people jumping and clapping, whistling and cheering. It was an explosion of love.

I felt a hand rest on my shoulder and I turned, hoping it was Rob. I wanted to be with him at this moment, soaking in the spirit of the room.

"You must be so proud of Zach." It was Lisa. She'd been standing in the back near me taking in the show. She'd spent practically every waking moment of the last several weeks (along with the help of several other wonderful women) putting this beautiful night together.

"I am," I said, a little disappointed it wasn't Rob but incredibly grateful for this woman who had managed to throw the party of the year for my family. "He has a lot of people who love him," I said, motioning to the crowded room. An iPod had been plugged in, and thirty preteens had taken over the stage dancing to Maroon 5's "Moves Like Jagger." The dance floor was overrun with teenagers and their mothers, all of them pulling out their best moves. I spotted Rob standing with a group of friends across the room.

The night was a giant success. Our family had been loved and supported by all these people over the past couple of years, and having so many of them in the same room was overwhelming. It was a night of pure blessing. There was only one thing about the whole night that wasn't perfect. I was worried my marriage was falling apart.

Thirteen

I SOMETIMES LOOK BACK AND WONDER HOW ROB AND I DID IT. HOW did we manage to go through our all-out war with cancer and come out together? There were so many different battlefields on the cancer front, some trickier than others. Marriage was one of them, and cancer almost left us in ruins.

I started seeing the signs two years after Zach was diagnosed, but I ignored them. It was August 2011 and Zach had already had two recurrences of cancer in his lungs that required four thoracotomies on top of months of chemotherapy and a hip replacement. Zach had been through so much, but it hadn't been enough. We'd just found out that the most recent chemotherapy he'd spent half the summer enduring hadn't worked, the cancer was still growing, and we were running out of options.

Our family was participating in our local American Cancer Society Relay for Life fund-raiser, held overnight at the high school. It was Zach's first year participating; the previous year he had been in the hospital recovering from his first thoracotomy. He was thrilled to be there and was having a fantastic time with his closest friends and about thirty other kids who had joined the team. They had set up a little commune of tents earlier in the day and planned to take turns walking the track throughout the night. Between shifts they tossed a football around and played Frisbee, some dressed in ridiculous costumes for various theme hours. They were all having a great time enjoying life, enjoying one another, and enjoying being sixteen.

As Rob and I walked the track, we stopped occasionally to look at the different decorated paper-bag luminaries that had been set up on either side. Each bag had been dedicated to someone who was fighting cancer or in memory of someone who had died from the disease. It was overwhelming to see all those faces of people from our community who were affected by the disease. But even more impressive were the numbers of people who were there either walking or running the event. I was especially moved to see all the bags dedicated to Zach. There were whole stretches of the track with bags decorated with Zach's name and picture. I was beginning to see how many people truly cared for Zach beyond our family and friends. It was a profound and humbling thing to take in.

The sun was setting and a pink glow cast on the field. The smell of freshly cut grass hung in the warm and humid air. I looked up from the luminaries just as Zach ran across the field, arm stretched out to catch a Frisbee. His pronounced limp from the hip replacement more exaggerated as he ran—his left leg would swing out and his upper body would bob back and forth. But it didn't hinder him at all. He was just another carefree kid having a great time. The huge, signature smile spread wide across his face and the sparkle in his eyes could be seen from where I stood several feet away.

And he was running. Running!

I hadn't seen him run for over two years and hadn't dared to let myself hope to see him do it again. It was another one of the things we had lost that I'd closed up tight behind the door of the closet tucked in the back of my mind where things to be mourned were put to be visited at some later time.

Complete joy filled me to bursting as I stopped dead in my tracks and soaked it in. I filled my lungs with the sweet evening summer air and watched with a smile on my face as this boy, who eighteen months earlier could barely walk without crutches, ran across the football field! He was happy and full of life. Tall and tanned from the summer sun, he looked so healthy. So miraculously normal.

I reached up and grabbed Rob's arm. "Look. He's running," I said with a sound of wonder in my voice that is normally reserved for parents who see their child do something amazing for the first time.

Rob stopped for a moment and watched with me. I grabbed his hand and looked up at his face, sure that I would see the same joy on his face as I felt on mine. My heart sank as I saw instead a look of utter sadness that bordered on anger.

"Too bad he'll never be able to play sports again," he said. I dropped his hand as he turned to continue the walk around the track.

As quickly as the joy filled me, it drained away. I stood there on the track, feet planted, as I watched Rob walk away. Why couldn't he be happy with this moment? Why wouldn't he allow himself to be grateful for what was right in front of him? I was frustrated, disappointed, and angry, but I wasn't completely surprised.

When we were newly married, twenty-two years earlier, I learned quickly that Rob planned thoroughly before he did anything. No decision was made without first researching and accounting for all possible outcomes. He believed if he planned well, bad things would be avoided, and with enough research he could be armed and ready for anything. There should be no such thing as the unexpected to catch one off guard. This was especially true when it came to protecting his family. His greatest fear was to have tragedy strike with no preparation.

He was also a man who required structure. Every day there was a plan, and that plan was not to be altered unless fair warning had been given at least a day or two prior. Spontaneity was problematic; it was a thing left for those less responsible types. He operated at home much like he did at work, where he was employed, not surprisingly, as a planner.

This planned and structured way of life served him well for years. Then I came along and threw a bit of a wrench into the works.

I had a more carefree, let's-dive-in-and-see-what-happens approach to life. I enjoyed the moments in life and the meaning that could be found within them. I was interested in what was around the next corner but not so much about the one after that. I wasn't a reckless person, just more focused on what was directly in front of me rather than what lay far ahead. Something like balancing the checkbook was not terribly high on my priority list because it didn't really affect the present, and it could always be dealt with later. I liked the idea of planning things out and living a structured life, but it just took so much time and thinking. It was a job left for someone more suited. Like Rob.

For the most part, I was happy, and Rob and I worked well together. He was a good balance to my more spontaneous side and provided the stability I wanted and needed from a husband and the father of my children. Likewise, I softened Rob's rougher edges by encouraging him to relax a little and experience the joy of the moment where he actually lived rather than spend it planning for a future that may never happen. We complemented each other, but there were times we drove each other crazy.

I remember when I was due with our first child, Alli. It was a Saturday, and I'd started having contractions early in the morning, so we spent the day together and watched college football (a sport Rob adored but I couldn't care less about). He had decided to keep track of each contraction by writing it down in a notebook so he would know when it was time to take me to the hospital. According to the childbirth class, we should go when the contractions were about three minutes apart and lasted around a minute.

It became evident as the day wore on the contractions did not follow the pattern correctly. Frustrated, he brought his notebook to where I lay on the couch.

"I thought the contractions were supposed to get longer and closer," he said as he flipped through multiple pages. "You're all over the place!"

I glared at him as yet another contraction took hold. "I. Don't. Care."

He let me be until I told him it was time to go.

Later, in the hospital, as things got more intense and the contractions became nearly unbearable, I asked for something to help with the pain. As the medication took effect, I expressed my relief, to which Rob replied, "Yeah. But, you know, it's going to get worse."

"Not. Helpful," I said with a glare. When I questioned him later about the point of his less-than-encouraging words, he explained that he knew I had a long way to go and he didn't want me to be caught off guard. He was trying to protect me.

There were times my indecisive nature and lack of preparedness annoyed him too. Drive-thru windows at fast-food restaurants were a source of great tension in our marriage—still are, actually. All those choices would leave me in a bit of a quandary. It always took a couple of minutes to decide what I was in the mood for, and the moment could get very awkward for Rob, who of course knew what he wanted miles earlier. After telling the worker on the other end of the intercom for the second or third time he wasn't ready to order yet, he would get a little cranky. Now he asks me what I want before we leave the house; if I'm not sure, he tosses the keys to me.

We had our conflicts throughout the years, but we were steadfast in our vows and devoted to each other. We were also very committed to our faith. We understood marriage was more than just an arrangement for two people to hang out together and be happy until the happiness died. It was about changing ourselves to become better people and to grow in love and serve each other. In short, it was about being a reflection of Christ in the world.

We had grown to respect each other as the years of living together had revealed our shortcomings and how they were balanced by the other's strengths. We could see how God had brought us together because we were the perfect fit. Rob learned to go with the flow a little more, and I learned to run a tighter ship. We worked better together than apart.

So when Zach was diagnosed with cancer, we started out on the right foot and managed the logistics as a team. We went to all Zach's important appointments together. Rob would take diligent notes and research as I focused on the daily needs of the family, such as meals, housekeeping, and making sure the kids were all doing okay.

But this was more than just another project or minor dilemma we needed to work through together. This was our child, and he was sick with a deadly disease. We each had our own agony as we battled with despair, and we chose the weapons we each knew best. I focused on what was right in front of me and searched for any joy that could be found, while Rob armed himself by planning for a future of grim possibilities.

As the two of us stood there that summer night and watched our son run barefoot across the green football field, we saw and felt two very different things.

I saw triumph that filled me with joy.

Rob saw loss that filled him with sadness.

I decided then that I needed to keep those precious moments of joy to myself. I couldn't share them with Rob anymore because his heart was so burdened by what he knew was coming and his sadness was so deep for what was lost and would be lost, he had no room for an intrusion of joy. He seemed so heavy with the burden, I didn't know how to talk to him anymore and couldn't trust that he would be able to hold me up should I need to lean on him.

I lived one day at a time, unable to take on more. I didn't want to be reminded of a future I knew we would likely have to face soon enough and couldn't understand why Rob seemed to want to live there. We still had time, precious time right now, and I didn't want to waste it by living in that lonely place where Zach was no more. It was too awful.

So I lived several months by a subconscious rule to keep the joys and heartaches to myself—both potential burdens to Rob. I was afraid that if I leaned on him, the weight would cause him to sink into total despair, and if I shared those pearls of joy with him, the contrast of their beauty to the darkness he suffered would be too much. And I needed those little pearls to stay pure, unmarred by that darkness, because sometimes they were all I had to get me through the days.

As I pulled away, Rob closed in on himself. We lived together and slept in the same bed, but we were in different worlds. The most important part of our lives at that time was off-limits to discuss, so we spoke of nothing deep, only of those things that were neutral and mundane. I would ask, "How was work today?" and he would answer, "Okay." It was the same day after day until I finally quit asking, and he didn't notice.

I started to become angry. I knew this wasn't how I wanted our marriage to be—it wasn't how it should be. I began to think that it would be so much easier if Rob wasn't there, if I didn't have to think about him too. I didn't know how to make things better and wasn't sure I had the energy to try. I would play out different conversations in my head trying to figure out a way to make things better, but they all led to the same problem: we simply dealt with things differently, and there seemed no way of getting around it. I felt like I was walking through quicksand; each attempt in my mind to step forward just seemed to drag me down further. I didn't have the energy to deal with a dying son and a dying marriage.

The night of the benefit I finally reached my limit. As Zach got up on the stage to play a song with Sammy, I looked across the room to where Rob stood talking with some coworkers. We hadn't spent any time together that evening; he'd gone his way, and I went mine. In the midst of all these people who loved and cared for us, I realized the one I wanted to be closest to was the one who was farthest away. I wanted Rob to be standing next to me laughing and talking like he was across the room. I wanted him by my side to cheer Zach on as he got up on that stage and played for the biggest crowd, at that point, he'd ever played for. If we couldn't come together now, how would we manage when things got worse? I began to pray fervently that God would somehow bring us together. I knew God wanted our marriage to be more than this emptiness.

After the party, I did some research and found a marriage counselor who came recommended, and I found a marriage retreat that focused on communication skills for couples who were struggling. The thought of either one scared me. I didn't like the idea of laying out all the emotional baggage and trudging through it when we were already so emotionally fragile. But I realized this thing was bigger than the two of us, and the usual methods weren't going to cut it. We needed help.

A few weeks later, a couple of weeks before our anniversary, Rob came into the living room and sat down on the couch across from me.

"Do you want to get away for a couple of nights for our anniversary?" he asked.

I set the book down that I was reading and thought for a moment. "No," I finally replied. "We haven't talked in months. I can't imagine spending a whole weekend together." He didn't say anything and looked a bit stunned. "I think we should get counseling or go on a marriage retreat. I'm worried if we don't work on things now, we aren't going to have anything left when we really need it."

Rob sat quietly for a moment, looking out the window into the darkness.

"I don't want to go to a counselor," he said. "I think the experience would rely too heavily on the quality of the counselor. But I'm willing to do the retreat. Do you have the website address? I'll sign us up."

I felt as though a weight had been lifted. I hadn't been sure how Rob would respond, but I didn't expect him to be as willing and open as he was. I was so relieved because in my mind his response was the make-or-break point of our lives together. It was the point where we would decide whether we would live separate lives under the same roof or would come together and build a relationship that was stronger than it ever had been.

A floodgate was opened and we began talking again. I told him how much I had wanted him by my side at the benefit and that I missed him. He told me that he thought I wanted to be left alone and that he didn't want to burden me with his fears and struggles. We both recognized the need for something better, and while Rob wasn't thrilled about going on the retreat (what guy is?), he knew I needed it, and that was enough.

We spent a whole weekend together at the retreat. It was the first time in several months that the two of us spent more than just a few minutes together in the same room. And we were learning how to communicate again without fear of being misunderstood. We were given the tools to rebuild our relationship and make our marriage a safe haven from the storm that brewed around us.

The emotional work of learning to communicate again was hard. Rather than go our separate ways after dinner, we made time each night to talk about the hard stuff, the scary stuff.

"I need to see the joy in our lives if I'm going to get through this thing," I told him one night, "but I can't share those moments with you because they just seem to make you angry."

He thought a moment and then spoke. "I've spent my life trying to do things right. I've lived a moral life. I pray every morning on the way to work. I beg God to cure Zach. But He doesn't. Zach just keeps getting sicker," he opened up. "I try to see the joy in life, but every time I do, it just reminds me of what we are losing if Zach dies, and I'm filled with sadness. Then I get angry at God because

I see so many people who don't live faithful lives who have it much better than we do. I just don't get it and sometimes I wonder, what's the point?"

There was a time when this revelation would have scared me. I would have thought I could somehow make things better. But now, after more than twenty years of marriage and years of intense suffering under our belts, I had finally learned that no pep talk was going to help the matter. I couldn't wipe Rob's sadness away. But I could simply love him.

"I get it," I said. He was a man who believed in order, and there was nothing orderly about our son dying from cancer. God made Rob that way, and He was the only one who could help Rob. I silently begged God to pour out His grace on my husband who would gladly have given his own life ten times over to save the life of his son.

As we peeled away the layers of callousness we'd built up over the years, and especially the last few months, it left us both feeling a little raw. But as we continued to make ourselves vulnerable to each other, a whole new level of love began to grow. I didn't resent Rob for how he struggled; I fell deeper in love with him because of it. We learned how to lay out our sadness and grief in a way that didn't burden each other, but rather drew us together. Our marriage became a safe place to settle in when the storm of life got too scary to face alone. And it became a source of grace that fueled us and kept us strong so that we could step back into that storm together.

Fourteen

January 2012

DO YOU REALLY WANT TO GO TO PARIS?" I ASKED ZACH AS I SAT ON the hotel bed with my laptop while he and Rob watched a football game on the television.

"Yeah. I think Paris would be cool. Who wouldn't want to go to Paris?" he responded.

It was two months after the benefit. We had traveled to MD Anderson Hospital in Houston, Texas, to get a second opinion on Zach's course of treatment. It was from a Houston hotel room that I started planning the Europe trip. Planning for our trip was a nice distraction from the future the doctors were painting for us, but frankly, the closer our departure date came, the more I dreaded the decision to go.

The last two and a half years had left me drained, and the thought of being "Julie, your cruise director" for the travel group left me feeling a bit weary. But I knew Zach needed this trip. Like many teenagers, he craved to be part of a bigger world than the confines of his shel-tered life. For Zach, the yearning to bust free for a little while was probably stronger because he'd spent much of his teen years cooped up in a hospital room. And there was the added urgency, knowing that cancer would pounce at any moment. The dream needed to be realized before it was too late. We had no idea how much time we had left. But God knew.

We wanted the whole family to go and any other friends or rela-tives who wanted to join us. In the end, eleven of us made the trip: Rob, Sam, Zach, Grace, and me; Mitch; my mother, Nancy; my sis-ters, Amy and Lee; Lee's husband, Jon; and my travel-loving friend Stephanie. Alli was heartbroken she couldn't make the trip with us, but she had some big things brewing in her life.

She had been asked to go on a cruise with her boyfriend Collin's family. She and Collin had been close friends in high school. After a year of college, Collin decided to enlist in the navy and, just days before leaving for boot camp, called Alli to reveal that he had secretly loved her for years. Based on years of friendship, she knew that Collin was the kind of guy she could spend the rest of her life with, and the switch from friendship to romance was an easy transition. Now, after a year apart and seeing each other only on a computer screen, he'd asked her to join him on the cruise. She couldn't wait to see him and suspected he had a big question he wanted to ask her.

March 2012

AFTER THREE MONTHS OF RESEARCHING AND PLOTTING OUT OUR trip, we were finally off! We gathered in the driveway and said our good-byes to Alli as she headed off to meet up with Collin's family. We hopped on our plane and eight hours later landed in a whole other world. Rome.

Rome had a way of making us feel like we could link hands with the ancients. It inspired a broader perspective of time. It also gave us a sense that we belonged to something greater than ourselves. A legacy. I wondered if Zach thought about leaving a legacy and what it might be.

We spent three days in Rome. Zach, Mitch, and Sam shared a room at the monastery where we stayed, which meant mischief was to be had. One evening, after a long day of sightseeing, the adults all gathered in Rob's and my room. We bought a bottle of wine that we shared on the balcony that overlooked the monastery's courtyard. Walls divided our balcony from the adjoining room, so we couldn't see what was going on next door. As we hashed out our adventures, we all lifted our glasses in a toast to the success of the day. As we put our plastic cups to our lips, a hand reached around the dividing wall with a paper cup filled with red wine. Mitch peeked around the wall with a huge grin on his face.

"Cheers!" he exclaimed.

"Mitchell! Where did you get that?" I scolded.

"I just walked down to the grocery store. They have boxes and boxes of the stuff! And it was only two euro," he replied happily.

I never saw Zach's face, but I heard him echo, "Cheers!"

I sat back in my chair on the patio, lifted my glass, and shrugged; Sam was eighteen, and Mitch and Zach were sixteen, old enough to drink in Italy. "When in Rome . . . why not?" There was no assurance Zach would have the opportunity to enjoy a glass of wine on a balcony in the heart of Rome as an adult. Parenting a teenager with a deadly disease is fraught with decisions about the usual boundaries. Within the context of limited time, sometimes experience trumps protocol.

While in Rome, we visited all the usual sites: the Colosseum, the Vatican, and the catacombs, but one unusual stop we decided to make was to the Capuchin Crypt. It is a six-room crypt that was decorated with the bones of Capuchin monks that had been moved from Jerusalem to Rome in the 1600s. We were reminded by the ticket taker as we entered the crypt that this was a holy place and there was to be silence as we walked through.

The bones lined the walls in peculiar and intricate patterns, each room with its own theme. One room was decorated with skulls, another with pelvises, yet another with leg and thigh bones. One room had various bones arranged around a picture of Jesus as He commanded Lazarus to come out of the tomb. This room was known as the Crypt of the Resurrection. A sign on the wall read "What you are now we used to be, what we are now you will be."

For some reason, I hadn't considered what effect entering the crypt would have on Zach. For a second I had a flash of worry that the experience would be too morbid. I was wrong. Zach reacted to the experience the same way we all did, with fascination mingled with horror and more than a little humor. Still, I stayed close to him as we walked down the hallway and gazed into each room. There were a couple of times he nudged me to point out a chandelier made of pelvises or a delicate ceiling design made from vertebrae.

"So, that was creepy," Zach exclaimed as he exited the crypt, the bright light of day hitting his face.

"Yeah. Strange way to decorate," Sam replied. "I wonder how they got started. I can just see these monks moving all those bones up from Jerusalem and pulling into Rome. 'So, what do you think we should do with the pelvises?' And the head friar points to a room and says, 'Why don't you start decorating that room over there? It could use a little brightening up.'"

We all laughed. "Did you see all that dust?" Mitch asked. "Think about it. We were breathing that in. We were breathing in dead human dust."

"Yeah. I guess I'd rather think about the dead in a spiritual sense rather than have them laid out and in my face like that. That was just weird," Zach responded.

"Okay." My sister Lee clapped her hands together to rally the troops. "That's out of the way. Now let's get back to the land of the living and have some fun!"

We thanked the dried and dusty bones for their morbid reminder. But for now, we would shake the dust off our shoes and leave the dead where they lay. Our time hadn't come yet, so we would fill it with the wonder of life that awaited us.

AFTER LEAVING ROME, WE SPENT TWO DAYS NESTLED IN THE Pyrenees Mountains and the town of Lourdes. The shrine was open year-round, but the official season, when all the daily Masses and processions took place, wouldn't begin until the first week of April, two weeks after our visit. So as we stepped off the train onto the platform, I felt as though we had stepped from a chaotic and busy street into the tranquility of a beautiful church. Or . . . a ghost town.

"It feels like we should expect zombies to come around the corner at any moment," I joked as we walked around the town the first evening, but I couldn't deny how cool it was to have the whole town practically to ourselves. It was perfect.

The summit and main purpose of our visit to Lourdes was to dip into the healing waters at the baths. They were fed by a spring that had been miraculously revealed to Saint Bernadette in a vision. Mary, the mother of Jesus, appeared in a vision to Bernadette several times in 1858. In one of the visions, Mary directed her to dig, with her bare hands, at a place where Mary indicated. Bernadette obeyed, and as she dug in the mud amidst the mockery of her fellow villagers, water bubbled up from the ground. Since that time, people from all over the world have come for various reasons to wash in the healing waters of Lourdes. The miracles associated with the spot are too numerous to count.

The day we visited was a gorgeous, unseasonably warm day. The sky was clear and the air was crisp, but the sun was strong and warmed us as we walked from our hotel to the Grotto. Before we made the trek down the steep road to the Gave de Pau River, we stopped at a bakery that had the most decadent pastries I'd ever seen and bought some, along with coffee. We walked a short distance along the narrow river until we reached a bridge that would take us to the Sanctuary of our Lady of Lourdes and the Grotto.

Mitch and I walked leisurely behind the rest and stopped for a moment to lean against the rail and watch the river roll by.

"I love this place," Mitch said.

"Why? What is it that you love?" I asked.

"It's so peaceful," he said as he rested his chin on his hand. "I just love the sound of the water, and the air is so fresh and clean. It's perfect."

Mitch was a restless soul who had questions and wasn't afraid to seek answers. He wasn't interested in organized religion, and he was ambivalent when it came to matters of faith. But there was something about this little town nestled in the mountains, with a river that flowed through it, that soothed him.

"Yeah. It is a beautiful place," I agreed. "It feels like a place to heal."

We lingered for a moment more, then continued on to catch up with the group.

Outside the baths were two locker rooms, one for men and another for women. A nun gave each of us a cape to drape over our shoulders and a large blanket to wrap around our bodies for modesty. There were several helpers at each bath to aid and direct, and there were signs posted in several languages that explained how to prayerfully prepare for the experience.

This was the primary reason we had traveled thousands of miles, so I really wanted to savor the moment. I spent the time waiting in line remembering those at home for whom I'd promised to pray. And I prepared my own heart to ask fervently for my own request. The one I'd been so afraid to ask for so many years.

I wanted Zach to be healed.

I was next in line. The moment I had planned for, waited for, and prayed for was here. I entered the anteroom and read the sign posted on the wall. It advised each person to take a moment on the first step down into the water to prayerfully offer up all the deepest desires of their hearts. I had decided I would take my time and really pour my heart out to God. I stepped through the curtain and into the bath room—a small room not much bigger than a walk-in closet with stone steps that led down into a deep, square tub and sparkling clear water. A nun took the cape from my shoulders and instructed me to make the sign of the cross. Another attendant held out her hand to guide me down the step and into the water.

I imagined this moment would be like stepping into heaven as the soothing water enveloped me in God's grace. I couldn't wait. I took a deep breath as my foot submerged into the water, and all I could think was . . .

It's.

So.

COLD!

The water took my breath away and turned my feet into blocks of ice. Two women grabbed my arms and dipped me backward, up to my ears, and then immediately stood me up. It was all they could do to unwrap the wet blanket from around me and get the cape back on before I was sprinting out of the water!

One by one, we all met in the warmth of the sun, mysteriously relaxed and dry. We each had our own embarrassing story to tell. Jon had been offered a jug of water before he entered the bath. Because of the language barrier, he wasn't certain what he should do with the jug, so he took a swig of water. Only after a more seasoned man stepped in did he realize the water was for washing faces, not for drinking.

There had been a little confusion in the women's baths as well. As each of us removed our bras and hung them on a hook, a helper (mine was a portly French matron) grabbed them off the hook and shoved them back in our hands, then hid our hands—bras and all—under the folds of our capes. What were we supposed to do? Take them in the baths with us? It turned out, the bras were taken along with the cape by an aid before we each entered the water, and "re-braing" was a part of their service. It was all a bit stressful but made for great storytelling.

Despite all the comical errors, we shared one thing: we were all left feeling more relaxed and tranquil than when we entered. Afterward, I walked with Zach back toward the Grotto.

"How was it?" I asked.

He'd already told his own step-by-step story of his dip into the water, but I wanted to know if he felt anything beyond the cold, beyond the physical. There had to be a reason we'd come all this way. His knowing glance told me he understood what I really wanted to know, and he took a moment to reflect.

"Peaceful."

I closed my eyes and turned my face to the sun, then took a deep breath of the clean, fresh air.

"Good," I replied. "Peace in the storm."

I cupped his face with my hands and pulled it down to kiss his forehead. Whatever God chose to give us, peace was the real miracle.

As Zach and I watched the sunlight glinting off the water, Mitch joined us on the bridge. "We should do that more often," he said. I couldn't agree more.

WE LEFT THE SERENITY OF LOURDES AND HOPPED A TRAIN TO PARIS. After six hours, we rolled into the Montparnasse train station in the heart of the city.

We spent a few days walking the city. On the third day, as we crossed the Pont Alexander III Bridge, Zach and I took a moment to admire the bronze statues of lively cherubs and nymphs lining the bridge.

"Well, is the trip everything you hoped for?" I asked Zach. I hadn't seen him much over the past few days. We had allowed the boys to have some freedom and go off by themselves. It was important they make the experience their own.

"Yeah, it's been a perfect trip. I loved Rome. It was so cool to see how the past intersects with the present," he started in. "And Lourdes was so amazing. I didn't really know what to expect, but it was just so peaceful. I thought the baths were the best part. It was so weird how I just felt like my whole being was clean and refreshed afterward. If I lived there, I would go in the baths every day." He lifted his gaze from the water and panned the city. "The culture in Paris is so different," he said. "It makes me want to be more refined." He straightened the collar of his plaid flannel shirt and ran his hands over his sleeves as if to remove the wrinkles, a look of mock sophistication on his face. Then his expression became thoughtful as he turned his gaze to the city. "I got everything I came for, and I'm ready to go home."

I regarded him for a moment as he looked at the water that churned below us. I was grateful to have this chance to see a little piece of the world through his eyes.

We continued across the bridge, then headed down the Champs Elysees toward the Louvre on our way to Notre Dame Cathedral. Stephanie joined me and we fell back, leisurely walking as we enjoyed the sites and conversation. Zach, Mitch, Sam, and Grace marched on, determined to get past the Louvre (they'd had enough of museums) and back to our hotel. I looked up to catch a glimpse of them; even though they'd surged far ahead of us, they were easy to spot. But something wasn't right.

Zach's usual hobble was suddenly more pronounced. He glanced over his shoulder at me. His eyes held a familiar shadow of pain.

My heart sank.

Fifteen

. . . .

WE RETURNED FROM EUROPE RENEWED. THE EXPERIENCE HAD satisfied Zach's restlessness and had allowed me the peace and satisfaction that comes with knowing I'd provided what my child needed. I also came back with a new sense of hope. Our visit to Lourdes had been a taste of heaven in our hectic and frantic battle against cancer. It left me knowing that no matter what was ahead, God would be there too.

Alli returned as well and had exciting news. During an evening walk along the deck of the ship, Collin had gotten down on one knee and pulled out a ring. Alli was elated! She was getting to marry her best friend. They set the date for May 31, 2013, a little over a year away, and she was excited to start planning the wedding. I wondered how I would manage giving her the attention she deserved while being at the ready for whatever cancer threw our way.

I called Zach's orthopedic surgeon the day after we got home and told him about the pain Zach experienced toward the end of the trip. He thought it was likely caused by all the walking Zach had done and encouraged him to rest for a few days. The pain eased, and by April Zach was feeling pretty good.

Spring had made an early appearance. The buds on the trees came almost a month early; winter already seemed far away one evening in mid-April, about a month after we returned from Europe. Zach was playing Ultimate Frisbee with a group of friends at a park across from his friend's house a few miles from home. He reached to grab the Frisbee out of the air when he slipped on the wet grass, fell on his left side, and heard a loud *pop*. By the time Rob and I got to the park, he was in extreme pain so we took him to the nearest emergency room to have his hip X-rayed. The X-ray showed the prosthetic was in place and the joint looked good. The ER doc sent us home but told us to follow up with the orthopedic surgeon.

The pain persisted so I scheduled an appointment with the surgeon the following day.

"It could be that the cup needs to be replaced, though we don't usually have to do that for at least five years," the surgeon said after looking at the X-ray. Zach had the head, neck, and about six inches of his femur replaced, but not the cup that the head fits into. "It's hard to know what is going on without proper imaging; an MRI would be difficult to read given the distortion to the image the hip prosthesis will likely cause. At this point, I would recommend a lidocaine and steroid injection to help ease the pain, then see what happens."

Zach was looking forward to a weekend spent with friends. His birthday was coming up, and given his newfound interest in Frisbee, I'd ordered a set of Ultimate Frisbees he mentioned he wanted. Now I wondered if he would have to wait until next summer to get the chance to use them.

We scheduled an appointment for the injection to help with the pain, but on the recommendation of the doctor we had seen in Houston earlier in the year, Rob insisted that we also do a PET scan of Zach's hip and pelvis. PET scans offer a more definitive picture of what is occurring on a cellular level than an MRI, and given that the MRI would be almost useless anyhow, Rob thought it best to try something new. He had a gut feeling something more was going on.

"How are you doing?" I asked Zach as we headed home from the meeting with the orthopedic surgeon.

"I'm okay. The pain stinks, but whatever I need to do I'll do. I just want to get on with life and have a fun summer," he said in a nonchalant, almost distant way. I'd noticed he'd seemed preoccupied lately, and I wondered what was going on. He wasn't down, just distant.

Eventually, the last weekend of May—a couple of days before Zach was scheduled for his regular three-month CT scan of his lungs and the PET scan—I found out where his mind had been. Zach had confided in Sammy that he was interested in a girl named Amy and asked her to find out if the feeling was mutual. Whatever was going on with his hip, Zach had decided romance wasn't taking a backseat.

ZACH HAD ALWAYS BEEN A BIT OF A FLIRT.

He would tease and charm everyone he met with his wide, toothy grin and mischievous looks. He'd had a few girlfriends throughout his high school years. All of them started as friends, and somehow they all remained friends. I was never sure how things transpired. He didn't tell me much. I suspect each relationship simply ran its course and, in the end, the decision was made that they made better friends than a couple. There never seemed to be any real heartbreak on Zach's part, and based on the fact that the girls all stayed in his life, I assumed the same was true for them.

Zach hung out with a core group of about ten friends. Amy was close with some of the same kids who traveled in his circle. She ate at the same lunch table as Zach, and they had a few classes together. But they hadn't spent much time together outside of school.

Amy had attended the benefit thrown for Zach and our family the previous fall. Though she didn't know Zach very well at that time, she came with a few of their mutual friends to support him and celebrate all he'd overcome. As she was dancing on the packed dance floor, she began to feel a little sick and had a sharp pain on her right side. In fact, she barely made it home she was so ill.

Early the next morning she ended up in the ER having her appendix removed. Zach was worried about her and wanted to cheer her up. And he didn't mind being on the other side of a hospital visit for a change. Since Amy had already been released from the hospital, he and Mitch, along with a few other friends, visited her at home. They all dressed in big blue Forever Lazy adult onesie suits and danced around the living room until they made her laugh. It was the start of Zach and Amy's friendship.

In the weeks before we left for Europe, during the spring of their junior year, Zach, in his teenage boy way, began to show signs of his interest in her by showering her with his affectionate and incessant teasing.

But as with so many things in Zach's life, the two realities of being a teenage boy and being a teenage boy with cancer would somehow have to intertwine.

Sammy, ever the loyal friend, told Amy of Zach's affection and interest. Amy had picked up on the heightened teasing over the past several weeks and figured Zach had taken an interest. She liked him and how she felt around him, but she had a hard decision to make. Should she enter into a relationship with a boy who had been through so much? Or would it be better for her to step away and protect herself from possible heartbreak? It would not be until much later that she and her mother, Mary, would tell me their stories of the remarkable beginning of her relationship with Zach.

It started the Tuesday after Memorial Day weekend. Amy and a friend sat at Amy's kitchen table after school with our CaringBridge page up on her laptop. Mary walked in as the girls spoke to each other in hushed tones as they read the words on the screen before them.

"Hi, girls. What's going on?" Mary asked as she observed the forlorn looks on their faces.

"We're waiting to hear how Zach's scans turned out," Amy replied as Mary stepped behind her and read the post over Amy's shoulder.

The CaringBridge post I wrote explained that Zach was experiencing intense pain in his hip and we hoped the PET scan would reveal that there was simply a problem with his prosthesis and not that the cancer had come back in his bones. We were also waiting to hear if the CT scan had revealed any new lesions on Zach's lungs since he hadn't had any new ones in over a year.

Mary had met Zach. She was aware of his battle with cancer and impressed by his ability to stay upbeat and positive through it all. She didn't think much of Amy's interest in Zach other than caring and concern for a friend. Their whole family had followed Zach's story over the past few months and were all interested in keeping up with the latest news. But later that night Amy revealed a little more. "Mom, there's something else," she said as she settled on the couch next to her mom. "I found out this morning that Zach likes me as more than a friend."

A mixture of emotions flooded Mary. She was excited for Amy and had looked forward to sharing these kinds of moments with her daughter. But her enthusiasm was tempered by the reality of what her daughter might be opening herself up to if she chose to move forward with the relationship. Every mother wants to protect her child from heartache, and if this relationship was allowed to blossom, heartache was a likely ending.

"How do you feel about that?" Mary asked.

"I don't know. I guess I'm flattered that he likes me. We have a great time together, and I feel good when I'm around him," Amy replied. "I just don't know what to do."

"What would you do under normal circumstances?"

"I guess I would just take things as they came and see where they led."

"Then why don't you do that?" Mary asked. "Just take things as they come."

Amy laid her head on the back of the couch and cried. "I just don't know if I could handle having my boyfriend die. It would be so hard."

Mary sent up a silent prayer for wisdom as she considered how to guide her daughter. She knew Amy was a strong and levelheaded girl who wasn't prone to drama like so many teenage girls. Had God placed Amy in Zach's life for a reason? Or had maybe God placed Zach in hers?

"Honey, this is going to be hard no matter what happens. You and all your friends have a tough road ahead of you. It seems to me God put you in this place for a reason and that you and Zach could be a real gift to each other."

IT WAS MAY 31, 2012. ROB, ZACH, AND I SAT IN THE EXAM ROOM AT the pediatric oncology clinic as the doctors delivered the news: Zach had new lesions on his lungs. I was ready to hear that news; I had expected it. But they also found the left side of his pelvis was riddled with cancer.

I felt like I'd been shoved into a pool of ice water and was trying to catch my breath as the doctor began to explain to us that in order to surgically remove the cancer from his pelvis, they would have to remove Zach's left leg and half of his pelvis. He would not be able to sit up for several months, and it wouldn't guarantee the cancer wouldn't come back.

I looked at Zach, and he silently shook his head no. The ugly truth was that we'd used up all known effective treatment options. There was nothing left, no weapons left in our arsenal to win the war.

Zach was terminal.

We sat in silence for a moment as we processed the news. None of us betrayed the devastation, sadness, and fear that stormed inside of us; we'd had lots of practice by this point.

Rob had suspected for months that the cancer had been harboring at the primary site and had flown under the radar of the limited sights of X-rays and scans. He'd done his research and knew that if the cancer continued to show up in the lungs, it was likely there was residual cancer hiding out near the primary tumor site or in other places. It was why he insisted on the PET scan.

Rob diligently took notes as his questions were answered about our options and how we should proceed. There were some experimental studies that Zach might qualify for, but there was the more urgent problem of pain that needed to be dealt with, and we needed a plan of action.

Zach kept his emotions tucked away pretty tight. He never seemed caught off guard by the bad news, but I was never really sure if it was because he had planned for it or if he was just skilled at rolling with the punches. He was stoic as the news was delivered and was pragmatic as treatment options for pain management were discussed. He behaved as though we were at a routine appointment and the world wasn't crashing down around him.

I was blindsided. I'd been so sure there was no way the cancer could be at the primary site—the tumor had been removed with clear margins. How could this happen? The lungs I was prepared for, but not the pelvis. It was like expecting a punch in the face and getting socked in the gut as well. There was the part of my brain that tumbled around with emotion, and there was the side that was ready to move forward with the next practical step. *Okay, Zach is dying. Now what?*

We had to make some tough decisions. None of them led to the future we had fought so hard to gain for Zach. They all ended with him dying; it was just a matter of how soon and in what shape. Did we continue to hack at his body and remove the cancer, leaving him with more hospital time and weeks, maybe months, of recovery? Did we hunt for experimental treatments across the globe, taking Zach from home for weeks or months and possibly gaining nothing? Or did we simply declare "enough is enough" and walk away from the fight?

Zach joined in the conversation. He wasn't too worried about surgeries. "Thoracotomies, no big deal," he said.

But the idea of being cut in half and unable to sit up and still having no guarantee that it would buy him much more time wasn't worth the sacrifice.

Months earlier, we had taken Zach to the Mayo Clinic in Rochester, Minnesota, and then to MD Anderson Cancer Center in Houston, Texas, to seek second and third opinions from doctors. He hated being away from home for treatment and was not about to spend weeks away from his family and friends for treatment that may only give him the same amount of time back.

The doctor at the U of M offered an experimental option: radiation therapy to kill the cancer and reduce the tumor so the pain would stop. It was something to throw at the cancer and slow it down. But that was it. We were buying little pieces of precious time.

Zach made the decision. He would start radiation the following week and start on the experimental chemotherapy that could be taken at home. He wanted to spend his time living as normally as possible. He wasn't giving up, but he was tired of cancer elbowing its way into the foreground. Cancer would have to take a backseat.

As we walked out of the clinic, Rob stayed behind to talk with one of the doctors. I knew what he needed to ask. It was the question that had hung in the room but couldn't be uttered. How much time?

I walked ahead with Zach, my calendar in hand as I filled the space between us with mindless chatter about our next step and about how we would tackle the next couple weeks. As we waited for the elevator, Zach stood, legs crossed, his chin resting on the crutch tucked under his arm, and turned to me.

"When the time comes, I want to have another party," he said with resolve. I looked up at him. He looked back with a steady gaze. He knew what was coming, and he knew how he wanted to deal with it.

"Okay. We'll do it."

He was ready to take the lead and show us the way.

"HOW LONG?" I ASKED ROB WHEN WE GOT HOME.

"Six months to a year," he answered. I held his gaze as the news sank in.

It was what we expected to hear, but there was something about it being stated, out loud, that was so jarring. It wasn't some far-off possibility anymore. The meandering road of treatments and surgeries had become much straighter, and the end was coming sooner than we'd hoped.

Zach never asked how much time, but he had an idea. He had wanted a new phone and spent several days after the news of the reoccurrence in his pelvis distracting himself by researching phones and data plans. He had some money burning a hole in his pocket and intended to use it to pay for the plan and the new phone.

Infomercials had been a pastime for Zach from the time when he was little. He loved shopping online for quirky things like nightlights that could change color with the push of a button on a remote, or a flashy multicolored light that could be hooked up to speakers and would pulse to the music that was being played. Once, when he was four years old, he came to me while I was making dinner. In his little green bib overalls, wide-eyed with excitement, he exclaimed, "Mom! You need to buy Zoom 2000! It cleans everything!" Shopping was in his blood.

Once he'd decided on the best option, he came to me for permission to buy the phone. I was concerned about how he would pay for the phone. After years of medical bills and all the other expenses that came with cancer, I knew we couldn't afford it.

"Mom, can I buy this phone?" he asked, showing me a picture of the phone on his computer. "I found a pay-as-you-go plan that's a good deal too."

"That's fine, you can buy the phone. But how much money do you have left in your account for the data plan? The phone isn't any good if you don't have a decent plan."

He locked his eyes on mine. "I have enough money to cover ten months," he said with a knowing look that pleaded for understanding.

"Okay." I held his gaze and nodded my head. Message received.

He'd set his goal.

AROUND THIS TIME, I NOTICED ZACH HAD STARTED SPENDING MORE time with Amy, whom I'd only met on a few occasions when the whole group was over. She came by herself a couple of times to hang out with Zach and watch a movie or talk. I wasn't sure what was up, so I called Anne, Sammy's mother, to see if Sammy had told her anything.

"Zach told Amy that he likes her," Anne said. "I wondered if you knew about it."

"No. Well, not until recently. I've noticed the two of them are spending quite a bit of time together. Does Amy know how sick Zach is? Does she understand that he is going to die?" I asked.

"Yes. She knows. All the kids know," Anne answered. "She and Sammy have had many all-night talks about Zach. Amy is well informed."

"Do her parents know about Zach? I'm wondering if I should talk to her mom and make sure she understands Zach's condition and what her daughter is getting into. This is a tall order for a teenage girl, and she's going to need a lot of support."

I was concerned. Amy was entering Zach's life at such a complex juncture. Did she understand what was happening with him medically? And would she be able to handle the emotional turmoil that he was bound to go through in the coming months? I was concerned about Zach too. Was he in an emotional place where a girlfriend was a good idea? Teen love could be fickle, and I was afraid of the heart-break that might come—for both of them.

"I know Mary pretty well. Amy and Sammy have been close friends for a few years, and I know she is aware of Zach's prognosis, but if you want I can talk to her and let her know that you're concerned," Anne offered.

"Yes! Please. I would feel so much better if I knew there was full disclosure."

I found myself in this strange position of needing to respect the boundaries of trust and privacy that Zach needed while also protecting both him and Amy from the harsh reality of what was to come. It was not something I wanted to manage; until then I had maintained a pretty hands-off approach when it came to the kids' relationships. Unless I saw a glaring problem or they came to me, I tried to keep a watchful eye on things without opening my mouth too much. But this was different. I knew I had a responsibility to guide Zach, but I needed to make sure Amy had the same.

Anne got back to me the next day after she had talked to Mary. Mary assured her that she and Amy had talked at length about her dating Zach. She knew he only had months to live, but she also knew her daughter was a strong girl with a good head on her shoulders and she was stepping into this relationship for the right reasons. Amy cared deeply about Zach, and she simply liked being with him.

I was relieved. I wouldn't have to burden Zach with more sadness by discouraging him from pursuing her. And it sounded like Amy was exactly the kind of girl Zach needed in his life.

Zach hadn't said much to me about Amy other than a cursory, "She's a friend," when I would ask about her. One day, on our way home from the clinic, after I'd talked to Anne and knew they were more than just friends, I dragged it out of him.

"So, tell me what's going on with Amy. Are you dating or are you just friends? 'Cause I'm hearin' it's more than just friends." He looked at me for a moment, deciding how much to divulge, but he knew he didn't have a chance at keeping this kind of news from me. I had too many sources.

"She's more than a friend," he finally offered.

"Okay. Well, what do you like about her?"

"She's calm. No drama. And she doesn't hide from the truth, but she doesn't dwell on it either. I like being with her because she's steady and strong and willing to keep up with me. I need that right now."

I was thrown a little by his concise and immediate response. His mature approach to the relationship was a reminder that he wasn't like other boys his age who had all the time in the world to find the right girl. He knew he didn't have time to waste.

"Well, it certainly sounds like you've thought it through. I'm glad she's in your life," I said. "She's welcome to come for dinner to meet the family. I think it would be nice if we had a chance to sit with her and get to know her a little."

"She'll be out of town for a while for a family reunion, then a dance competition," he replied.

"A dancer, huh?"

"Yep. She's been doing it since she was five. I'm hoping I can see her perform sometime. Her team name is Topaz. I guess they're pretty good. Maybe in a couple weeks I'll invite her to have dinner with us."

"I look forward to it," I said. I was grateful that he was going to have someone special in his life. But I wondered what would happen when reality started to bang on the door. Did Amy really understand what was coming? Did she have it in her to be there when he would need her more than ever?

June 2012

EVERY MORNING FOR THE FIRST THREE WEEKS OF JUNE, I DROVE Zach the forty minutes to the hospital for his two-minute radiation treatment. His appointments were scheduled early in the morning, which meant that we would run into heavy traffic and had to add several more minutes to the commute. As the week went by, Zach became increasingly sick. The pain in his hip intensified with each passing day, and he was nauseated and extremely tired.

By the third morning, it took every ounce of energy he had just to get from the house to the car. Along with the pain, he was so weak that he was unable to pull his legs up into the car without assistance. As we traveled down the highway, Zach's condition worsened. His face turned white, and he thought he might pass out. A few miles from our exit, traffic came to a complete stop. Nothing was moving. We were stuck.

I didn't know what to do. If I called 911, it would take them just as long to get to us as it would probably take to get to the hospital ourselves. But if he passed out, I wouldn't be able to help him because I was in the middle of traffic. So I did the only thing I could do: I turned the air-conditioning on full blast and had it blow in his face, then turned the radio on his favorite station and told him to hang on. And I drove. Terrified and panicked, I inched along as Zach got worse and worse.

We finally reached our exit, and I pulled into the parking ramp where there was a special entrance for radiation patients. We had a handicap pass for parking, but all the spots were taken and they were too far for Zach to walk anyhow. I pulled the car right up to the door with absolutely no idea how I would get him from the car to the clinic and then get the car parked. There were no wheelchairs in sight, and my cell phone didn't get reception in the parking garage, so I couldn't call for help. And there was no way I could leave Zach.

It was the first time in two and a half years that I felt completely alone and utterly helpless. As I got out of the car to walk around to Zach's side, I whispered a simple but desperate prayer: "I can't do this alone."

I opened Zach's door, pulled his crutches out that were wedged between him and the door, and knelt down on the ground next to him.

"Can you walk?" I asked as I desperately tried to keep the panic at bay.

He did a slight shake of his head, almost imperceptible. His breathing was shallow and fast, and he was extremely pale. I hadn't noticed a car had pulled up behind us until a gentleman in a valet service uniform was standing next to me.

"Ma'am? Do you need some help?"

I felt like I could dissolve into a puddle of tears on the floor, I was so relieved. Sometimes God sends angels to do His work, but most of the time it's just ordinary, everyday people who are commissioned. And on this day, it was the valet guy.

"Yes!" I exclaimed. "I need a wheelchair, and I need help getting him to radiation."

Within minutes, this wonderful man had a team assembled. One brought a wheelchair, two helped get Zach into the chair, and one parked my car for me.

It was one of the countless moments when God reached His hand down and rested it on my shoulder. Like the rainbow we had seen on our way home the day of the biopsy two and a half years earlier, it was a promise that He would be there when I really needed Him. All I had to do was ask and watch.

We got Zach into the clinic and the doctor did an exam. After several minutes, Zach began to feel better, the nausea dissipated, and his color began to change from a dusky gray to a more natural pink. We considered checking him into the hospital, but Zach refused; home was where he wanted to be.

Sixteen

. . . .

IT WAS THE SECOND WEEK OF JUNE, AND THE SCHOOL YEAR WAS coming to an end. Zach hadn't been able to finish junior year with the rest of his classmates because of his radiation schedule and, frankly, he just wasn't well enough. He'd spent a good portion of the last two weeks sleeping and feeling really crappy. The day after he almost passed out in the car, the radiation had started to ease the pain, but the trade-off was that it left him feeling like a very old man.

I'd taken that Saturday afternoon to go visit my folks and spend a little time by their pool. I needed a break and was itching to get out of the house, and since Rob was home with Zach, I decided to take advantage of a few free hours. I figured Zach could use a break from my hovering as well. I was constantly checking on him and asking if he wanted something to eat; he hadn't eaten anything of substance in several days.

I came back home around five o'clock in the afternoon to find Zach lying on the couch in the living room, the afternoon sunshine draped across him. I set my bag down, kicked my shoes off into the closet, and sat down on the armrest at the end of the couch.

"Hey." I rubbed the top of his foot. "How are you doing?"

He glanced at me, then quickly averted his eyes and brought his hand up, resting his fingertips on his forehead to shield his eyes. He was fighting tears and couldn't speak for a moment.

My heart sank. I knew the physical struggle was getting to him, but emotionally he seemed to be handling things well. Over the years he'd had a few moments of doubt and sadness, but nothing that laid him out flat for long. Now, though, with the latest news, it seemed despair might have a better footing and the realities were finally catching up with him.

"Come on. Tell me what's going on," I coaxed. I was terrified of what I would hear. In my own struggle to figure out how to deal with the beginning of the end, I wasn't sure I would have any words of comfort left.

"I just don't know why my friends or anyone would want to waste their time hanging out with me," he said as he finally let the tears flow. "What's the point if I'm just going to die anyway?"

His friends had always been good about coming to visit him when he was too sick to leave home. But it was finals week, and they were busy with their studies and all the other activities that teenagers find themselves caught up in. Zach was stuck at home lying on the couch, feeling sick and lonely with plenty of time to think about what he was missing. His friends' busy lives stood in stark contrast to his.

Now despair tried to sneak its way in. I paused for a moment as I searched desperately for words to comfort and guide him. But no words seemed adequate. He was beyond all the life experience I had to offer. He was dying, and I couldn't soothe him with words of encouragement because there weren't any that didn't sound trite.

In the end, it was plain old parenting that took over. He didn't need me to come down into that hole with him. What he needed was a pep talk, something solid to pull him up out of the hole he was in so he could fight the lie that his life was worth nothing as it tried to worm its way into his heart.

"So, you think that because you're terminally ill your friends should just dump you?" I was in lecture mode. "Why? Are you less interesting than you were two weeks ago? Because I'm thinking the whole terminal thing makes your life a whole lot more interesting." I was building steam. "You aren't just some useless lump, Zach. You have just as much to offer them as they have to offer you. And even if you don't know it, they do."

The tears had stopped as he listened. The "snap out of it" tone in my voice had caught him off guard, but he was responding the way I'd hoped he would; it was what he needed to yank him back to who he really was. He wasn't the mopey kid who let cancer get him down. He was the kid who fought back and did things in spite of his disease.

Emboldened by his response, I continued.

"Would you jump ship if one of your friends were going to die?" It was a weak spot that I knew would seal the deal. He loved his friends dearly and was nothing if not compassionate, which was probably one of the reasons he was having a hard time bringing them down this road of suffering with him. But he needed to see that part of loving someone meant allowing him or her to stick with you, even in the darkest of days.

"No," he responded sheepishly.

"Okay. Then don't assume the worst from them. They don't deserve it."

I stood up and walked to the kitchen. As long as he was listening, I might as well get him to eat something. "You haven't been eating enough. What kind of smoothie do you want?" I pulled the yogurt from the refrigerator.

A moment later he joined me in the kitchen and sat down on a stool at the counter. I opened the cupboard door to grab the blender and paused for a moment. With the door blocking his view, I took a deep breath in and let it go. The emotional weight of what he was going through was huge. I felt like I'd caught him just as he was about to fall over the edge. He was sick and tired, but he was okay. I was exhausted.

"Blueberries sound good," he replied.

I smiled. They sure did.

"SO, IS AMY BACK IN TOWN YET?" I ASKED. SHE'D BEEN OUT OF TOWN for a week at the dance competition. Zach had stopped feeling so sick and friends had started coming over again, now that school was done, but I hadn't seen Amy stop over yet. We were on our way to the clinic for a CT scan of Zach's chest. He had completed three weeks of radiation on his hip and needed a follow-up physical, but he'd also been having some difficulty breathing so the doctors wanted to check out his lungs.

"Yep, she got home yesterday and we are going on a picnic today at eleven." It was eight o'clock in the morning. "When do you think we'll be done with this appointment?"

"It shouldn't be more than two hours. It's just a CT and checkup. What are you bringing to the picnic?"

"I don't know. She's packing it. We're going to a park by her house," he said. "They better be on time today or we're leaving early. I'm not waiting around," he threatened. "Why are we going to the U again? I don't get it. We already know it's bad. It seems like a waste of time." This picnic obviously meant the world to him. I'd never seen him this antsy; he was usually so laid-back. It made me smile as I remembered the excitement of new love.

We pulled up to the hospital like we had hundreds of times before. We had the CT first, then made our way up to the clinic on the ninth floor and waited for the doctor to come in to do the exam and give us the results of the scan. We'd already had a month to get used to the worst news we could expect, so I wasn't terribly nervous about the results; it was just another hoop to jump through. Whether the tumors had grown or not seemed irrelevant at this point; we already knew the worst was coming.

Zach sat on the exam table anxiously looking at the clock. He was especially irritated because he had forgotten his phone at home and had no contact with the outside world. The oncologist and the nurse practitioner opened the door to our room, and the expressions on their faces were serious.

"Well, Zachary. I'm afraid, dear sir, that you have a collapsed lung. A quite impressive one at that." She delivered the news as she pulled her stethoscope out of her white lab coat pocket.

"How do you feel?" she asked. "Your mom said on the phone that you were having some difficulty breathing." She tugged his shirt to indicate for him to take it off.

Zach peeled off the white T-shirt with "Pants" written across the front. He loved the irony. "It hasn't been that bad. Just a little shortness of breath when I do stairs or have to walk long distances. It's really no big deal. I feel fine."

She listened to his lungs, then stepped aside to let the nurse listen as she pointed out the difference in sound based on where the scope was placed. It was a teaching moment. Collapsed lungs didn't show up in the clinic very often.

"You'll need surgery to repair it, and we've talked to the pediatric surgeons. They have to work their schedules around a bit, but it looks like they can do the surgery early this afternoon. You can go right over to the hospital, and they'll check you in."

I watched Zach, the expression on his face betraying what was going on inside his head. He was in no mood to put up with silly things like collapsed lungs. He had a date he needed to get to.

"Can't we just schedule it for another day?" he pleaded. "I feel fine. It can't be that big of a deal."

"Actually, Zach, it's very serious. Your lung is leaking air into the pleural space, the space between your lung and rib cage. That air has nowhere to go and, as a result, is pushing your lung over and putting pressure on your heart. If we don't do the surgery immediately, the air will continue to leak into the space and could cause some very serious, potentially deadly problems. This is a medical emergency, Zach. I'm so sorry."

For the first time since his diagnosis, Zach was angry. He had finally started to feel better after spending the first month of what was probably his final summer in pain and feeling sick. He just wanted to spend the rest of it enjoying life. Now he would have to endure another surgery and days in the hospital. But worst of all, he'd have to miss his picnic with Amy.

He was devastated.

Zach couldn't remember Amy's number, so he had me call Sammy who, in turn, called Amy to tell her the news. On the other end of the line, Amy broke down into tears. It was real now. Cancer. There was no more pretending it would quietly take a backseat in their lives. It had crawled up and planted itself firmly between them, a nasty little thing that refused to be ignored.

Amy would have to learn how to live and love while letting go.

So would I.

Seventeen

June 2012

THE HOUSE WHERE I GREW UP WAS SITUATED JUST A FEW YARDS from the railroad tracks that ran through my hometown. The loud rumbling and the *click, clack* of the racing train made the whole house shake. I remember waking up to the blaring horn and the deep rumble that reached all the way through my body as the six o'clock train would roll by. It wasn't a pleasant way to wake up, but it was something I had grown used to.

In the days that followed the devastating news that Zach was terminal, I would wake up in the morning and, for a few seconds, feel the peace and contentment of our home. But it didn't take long for the rumbling to start. I would first feel it in my chest, then it gradually made its way to my fingertips and toes. It felt like the six o'clock train from my childhood. The rumbling would gradually change over to tension as the nightmare I was waking up to would slowly enter back into my consciousness.

I relished those few moments at the beginning of each day, when sleep hadn't quite given way to the new day, before I remembered what it was we would have to face. The moments before the rumbling would start.

I'd been through this kind of thing before, at different points in Zach's battle. When we would get disappointing results, it was like being shoved from behind by a bully who lurked around the corner. We never knew which scan would hold bad news, and it always seemed to catch me a little off guard, and I'd have to pick myself back up from the blow.

I began to get used to it after a while, recovering from the enormous stress of the horrifically bad news. But there was always a physical response that faith and prayer couldn't head off or take away. When bad things happen, your body responds: your heart rate goes up, your mouth tastes like metal, and you get very tired but have a hard time falling asleep. That's just the way it is; you simply don't have much control over it.

I remember early on in our battle, I had posted a message on our CaringBridge site about feeling this stress before going in for a thoracotomy. I noted that Zach was pretty nonchalant; he'd had the surgery before and knew what to expect and knew he could manage the pain. "Thoracotomies. Meh. They're no big deal," he would say.

But his sixteen-year-old-invincible-boy way of thinking didn't allow him to see the bigger picture. He didn't see the war, only the battle. I was more concerned about the results than the actual surgery. Was the new chemo working? Was it killing the cancer? If it wasn't, then we were running out of ammunition, and that meant losing the war.

A woman who had read the post made a comment in our

CaringBridge guest book implying that because I was feeling the stress of the situation, my faith was inferior and less genuine than Zach's. I was furious! How dare she make that implication? I didn't disagree that Zach was strong in his faith, but to suggest that mine was weak because I was stressed about my child dying seemed utterly ridiculous, and cruel. For Pete's sake, Jesus was more than a little stressed when He was faced with death. Was my response that much different? I deleted her guest book message and blocked her from visiting our site again.

But her message caused me to reflect. Not so much on my faith—I had lived most of my life believing in a loving God who sent His Son to redeem us and show us the way to heaven—but on where to place my hope.

I had gotten messages from people through CaringBridge and from family and friends that they were fervently praying Zach would be cured. They had their hearts set on a miraculous healing that would glorify God, and they prayed daily for it. Their hope lay in the healing power of God.

I wasn't so certain.

I knew God wanted us to pray for what our hearts desired, but I had witnessed others who had walked a similar path to ours and had placed all their hope in a physical cure. They spent all their energy praying for a miracle, and when their loved one still died, it left them with their faith shaken. They had been so convinced that if they had enough faith, they could move God to conform to their will.

I wanted desperately for Zach to be cured. I wanted him to have a future where he would graduate from high school, go to college, marry, and have children. I wanted his children to crawl up onto one of my kitchen chairs and ask, "Grandma, why is this chair all scratched up?" And I would tell them the story of how their father had to wear a special brace after he had his hip replaced and it scratched the chairs. I wanted to tell them about the miracle God performed. That God had touched their daddy's hip with His mighty hand and there was so much love in that touch it caused their daddy to limp, just so he would never forget that powerful love.

But I struggled with praying for a miracle of physical healing because I wasn't sure that was God's plan for Zach. I believed that a person's suffering is a powerful thing when it is united with Christ's, and that it can become a powerful channel of God's grace into the world. I knew God must have allowed cancer into our lives for a reason, though I wasn't certain what it was.

I wrestled with what to pray for, and I wrestled with where to place my hope. I knew God was asking me to trust Him, but that meant giving up Zach. How could I do that? I felt like Abraham preparing to sacrifice Isaac. While I wasn't wielding a knife over my bound son—cancer had already done that—in my soul I still had to choose.

Let God do it His way, or beg Him to do it my way.

Trust God or not.

Place my hope in something higher. Or not.

So, there I was, at that moment in time. We had run out of chemotherapy. There was nothing left. Without a miracle, Zach would die within a year.

I sat, gliding slowly back and forth in the comfort of my favorite rocking chair. I had lulled babies to sleep and dreamed of their bright futures in this chair, and now I had to contemplate what it would be like to lose one. All the memories of years filled by the spirit of that beautiful boy swam in my mind and left my heart to ache like arms that clutched a weighty treasure for a long time. How could I let go of this son who brought so much joy into our lives and into our home? What would our family be like without the child who made everything run smoothly just by his peaceful presence?

They were a team, these children of mine, and they worked best when together. Zach was the hub, the touchstone in the family whom everyone could connect with. It wasn't that Alli, Sam, and Grace didn't get along—they did—but it was Zach who brought them together. He brought an enthusiasm for life into a room that drew the rest of us out of the daily grind to join him.

The morning sun shone through the windows that lined the wall. The dappled sunlight danced on the floor at my feet as I contemplated the hole that would be left in our family when Zach was gone.

Who would hash over life's big questions with Alli? Who would Sam talk to about physics and the mysteries of the universe, and who would share life's secrets with Grace? Who would walk in the door at the end of the day and yell, "Ma! What's for dinna?" in an obnoxious and poorly executed New Jersey accent? Or sit on a Sunday afternoon and watch the game with his dad?

How could God ask this sacrifice of Zach, who loved Him more and better in his short life than most who are given a lifetime? And how could He take Zach from Rob and me? We had done things the right way; we had done our best to live faithful lives by serving Him. Wasn't that enough?

My heart was raw from the struggle. I was tired and broken with tears streaming down my face.

"What do You want from me, Lord?" I questioned. "What do I pray for? How do I pray?" I begged.

And then, a scene I had contemplated hundreds of times as I had prayed the rosary over the years filled my mind. It was a vivid image of Jesus in the Garden of Gethsemane. He was kneeling and in agony. He turned His face to heaven and opened His mouth and prayed, "Father, if you are willing, remove this cup from me. Nevertheless, not my will, but yours, be done" (Luke 22:42).

That's when it hit me. Christ, in His most extreme suffering, had given us the perfect prayer. The most loving and perfect being to walk the earth, God's own Son, wrestled with God's will, just as I had. He saw what was coming and asked to be spared. But He knew His Father's will was greater than His own, and He surrendered His will to the Father.

So I took that prayer, and with all that was in me, every part of my being and from the very depths of my soul, I made it my own. As I sat there alone, I spoke to God.

"Okay, Lord. You can have Zach. I want him, but You see a bigger picture. If Zach must die, please just let it be for something big. I want it to be for something big. Just one soul changed forever."

At that moment, my soul was freed. I wasn't in charge of this thing, and in the depths of my being, I truly understood the meaning of hope.

Hope is something much bigger than anything physical we may desire. It is about raising our eyes from a point on the horizon to the heavens and into eternity. And it's about relying on God's grace to do it, no matter what the cost.

God knew that what I wanted most of all was His will to be done. And if that meant watching my son suffer and die as He watched His own Son suffer and die, then so be it.

We would walk that road. We would pick up that cross.

In the silence of that early morning, with the sound of the breeze rustling the leaves on the trees, I stood and wiped my eyes. The wind through the open window caressed my face and pushed the abandoned swings hanging from the backyard play set. *Life moves on*, I thought, *and we move with it.*

I took a deep breath and tossed my tissue in the trash can as I grabbed the dog leash by the door.

"Come on, Daisy. We're going for a walk," I said as she happily bounded behind me, bopping my ankle with her wet nose. We were doing this thing, and we were going to be okay. Life would be okay.

I had no idea as I stepped out the door the big plans God had in mind and the answer to my prayer He was about to unfold.

Eighteen

. . . .

WHEN DEATH IS ON THE HORIZON, THE SPACE BETWEEN YOU AND IT can be a dark and scary place. Zach's summer had started out hard. Radiation and surgery for his collapsed lung had taken up the first half, but in the end it had been salvaged. He was feeling good and spent most of his days doing what he wanted, living like a teenager should, and enjoying the last days of summer before his senior year of high school. It hadn't been easy, for sure, but he packed in as much as he could and started back at school.

He'd survived the tough start of the school year and had worked his way back to finding his purpose again, learning to live in the present and to embrace the beauty of each moment. But he knew what was coming; dying was the backdrop of his life, and that stark view of reality, of life and death, gave him clarity. And then the reality of that was made even clearer by a former hospital roommate's death.

I remember when Zach, Mitch, and I walked into the infusion room at the clinic a year earlier, at the beginning of Zach's junior year. Lance, Zach's one-time roommate from his first regimen of chemotherapy, and Lance's mom, Laurie, were there too. I had enjoyed the brief time we shared with them over a year earlier; Laurie and I had a lot in common, and it was nice to talk with someone who understood what we were going through. For a split second I was excited to see them again. But then my heart sank; the infusion clinic is not a place where you want to run into old acquaintances.

Lance was not doing well. His cancer had spread faster than Zach's and was no longer responding to treatments. Though he knew his time was short, Lance continued to live a pretty normal life. At nineteen years old, he was working as a chef and taking care of his beautiful little daughter who was born not long after he was diagnosed with osteosarcoma. His approach to dying was very simple: just live.

Zach and Mitch were impressed. They decided they wanted to reach out and do something special for Lance in some way. The opportunity came when the biannual National Honor Society's Coffee House (a fund-raising event that showcased the musical talent of several high school students) committee was looking for suggestions on where to donate the funds. Zach and Mitch proposed Lance. On Lance's twentieth birthday, December 9, 2011, he and his family attended the event.

A local news station picked up on the story, one boy fighting cancer helping raise money for another. It was the first time Zach's battle with cancer had been covered on the news, and the folks at Children's Cancer Research Fund saw the story. They wondered if this boy with the generous heart would consider helping raise money for pediatric cancer research. Maybe do a radiothon interview the following year? They tucked his name away for future reference.

Now, ten months after the Coffee House fund-raiser, Lance had taken a sharp turn for the worse. The cancer had spread to his brain, and his lungs had filled with tumors.

On October 6, 2012, Lance died.

Zach, Sammy, Amy, Mitch, Rob, and I went to his funeral. I wasn't sure how it would be for the kids, seeing Lance. But I knew death was a reality that each of them needed to confront in a real way, not just as an abstract possibility. As each of the kids stood by the casket and looked down at Lance's body, now looking like the simple shell it had become, it finally hit all of them. Zach would be there soon. His body, too, would become an empty shell. It was the first time I saw the kids really cry. They mourned Lance, but they were also mourning Zach.

We waited in line to offer our condolences to Lance's parents, Laurie and Brent. They both looked so strong as they greeted each person in line. I wondered if I would be able to contain my tears as my son lay in a casket behind me. As I got closer to Laurie, my own emotions forced their way to the surface. I'd been so concerned about the kids, I hadn't taken the time to work through how I might feel. It was my turn.

Laurie and I made eye contact. She pulled me into an embrace, and we both melted into tears. We were simply two moms who'd been through the same agony.

"It was just so fast," Laurie whispered in my ear. "I knew it was coming, but it was just so fast."

She was on the other side now. She'd been through the worst. My legs shook uncontrollably, but her embrace steadied me.

Zach was next in line. I stepped aside and watched as Laurie held him. She pulled back and looked up at him.

"Just live, Zach," she said. "Just live your life."

As we drove home from the funeral on that gorgeous fall day, I couldn't get over how beautiful the leaves were on the trees. They were obnoxious with showy, contrasting color, and it was glorious to see. I'd been obsessed with the fall colors for the past few weeks and found myself distracted by them as I drove through the countryside.

Why? I wondered. *Why was I so entranced?* The colors were pretty much the same every year, so what was different this year? I realized that it wasn't the colors that had changed; it was me. The years of fighting cancer and the struggles that came with it had a way of winnowing the chaff of life away and revealing the good kernels left behind. The beauty in life is more visible when the clutter is gone, the colors of life more vibrant against the backdrop of death.

I reveled in the wonder at this strange and unexpected phenomena. I realized as I turned memories of the past years over in my mind how often I saw this effect. There were so many times that the sorrow and agony of a particular moment was punctuated by something intensely wonderful and beautiful. Laughter was always sweeter through tears, and joy was more potent when born out of suffering. It was like a rope that had been dropped from heaven. I prayed that Zach, his friends, all of us would be able to grab on.

After we'd dropped the kids off at their homes and Rob at work, Zach and I headed for home. We made small talk about the Stillwater Area High School Ponies homecoming game a few weeks earlier, and we discussed the upcoming annual Friedrich Family Booya, a family tradition that involved camping at my parents' house with aunts, uncles, and cousins and making a huge cauldron of soup that would be served to guests the following day. Both subjects were lighthearted, normal things to discuss. But the obvious topic, the one we were avoiding, lingered in the space between us. I pulled the car into the garage, and we walked in the front door.

"How are you doing?" I finally asked as I pulled off my pumps and tossed them into the closet. "That had to be hard for you." It was easier to keep emotions in check when we weren't face-to-face. It was best to keep it casual.

He paused and thought for a moment as he took off his coat, then turned to me, a far-off look in his eyes, and said, "Yeah. It was." He took a seat at the kitchen counter and crossed his hands in front of him. "But I really realized I need to live life to the fullest. I don't want to just hang out downstairs and burn my time away. I want to do as much as I can with the time I have left. I just want to live the best life I can, and I really want it to count for something."

"You're right. I think that's really the only way to do it." I pulled a loaf of bread out of the cupboard and sandwich meat from the refrigerator. "What do you have in mind?" I asked.

"I don't know yet. I guess I just want to experience things I've never experienced before. I just feel like I'm supposed to leave the world better than it is now," he said. "I just want to get out there and do some crazy stuff."

He had come away from Lance's funeral with a solid understanding of the limits of time, and rather than fall into despair, he had chosen to be inspired. It freed him to see the worth and beauty in his life and to be ready for something big.

Nineteen

October 2012

ZACH WAS POPPING NINETEEN PILLS A DAY, A TASK HE WAS QUITE proud to have mastered; he would show anyone who was willing to watch how he could swallow nine pills at a time . . . with no water. It made me gag. Part of the regimen included massive doses of a drug that is also used for controlling acne—his face never looked better! But it had the unfortunate side effect of making his hands peel, and thick callouses formed between his fingers. It drove him crazy, especially when he was playing the guitar. He was constantly slathering on lotion.

It was a couple of weeks after Lance's funeral. Zach was scheduled for another CT scan of his chest to see if the therapy he'd been on since July was holding the cancer at bay. We checked in for the CT and took our usual place in the waiting room. Zach was playing with his phone and I was engrossed in a book when Zach started to laugh. I looked up to find out what he was laughing about, but he just shook his head and lifted his phone up in front of him. I realized he was taking pictures of me. So, to fight back, I pulled out my phone and started taking a video of him.

He began laughing so hard he doubled over and had to wipe the tears from his eyes. He'd been doing his best to take the most unflattering pictures he could of me and then used a Fat Booth app to make me look hundreds of pounds heavier. It was horrifying, but he was very pleased with himself and couldn't stop laughing.

He had a way of bringing joy into everything, even the scary times when we were waiting to find out how much closer death had come.

After the CT, we headed up to the clinic where the doctors would view the scan and deliver the news. It was a busy day in the pediatric wing. Kids played at the computer station, watched the obnoxiously loud cartoons on the television (why do we have to have televisions everywhere?), and played in the little playhouse kitchen.

In the middle of the room was a small, round table with little chairs to match. A mother and father sat there with their child who was maybe ten or eleven years old. The mother had spread out a variety of foods on the table, despite the signs that said "No Food Allowed in Waiting Area." She didn't care about signs; she was attempting to entice her child to eat. It became clear rather quickly that the child was not well mentally; he was angry, was easily agitated, and began to yell obscenities at his mother, then started to throw the food.

I sat there feeling uncomfortable as I watched the chaos of this poor family's life unfold, and I just wanted to get away. I looked over at Zach who was sitting quietly flipping through screens on his phone with his thumb. He didn't seem disturbed at all. After his name was called and we were walking down the hall, he tucked his phone in his pocket and said under his breath, "Things can always be worse."

We took our seats in the exam room. The medical assistant took Zach's vitals and entered updates in the computer. "I like your T-shirt," she commented as she finished typing. The shirt read "Cure Childhood Cancer" with a yellow ribbon printed in the center. He'd purchased it online several months earlier along with some pink fabric dye. He had planned to wear it for the high school–sponsored breast cancer awareness day when everyone wore pink. It was his way of reminding everyone there are other cancers out there too. He was a little jealous of the breast cancer awareness success and wished there was more for pediatric cancer. He never did get around to dying the shirt pink.

As she finished up and left the room, she assured us the doctor would be in soon. We had learned over the years that the longer it takes for the doctor or nurse practitioner to come into the room, the worse the news is. Ten minutes went by. Then fifteen. Then twenty.

"You ready for bad news?" I asked, looking up from an article about the art of making homemade soap in a worn-out copy of *Real Simple* magazine.

"Yep," he responded without looking up from his *Car and Driver* magazine. He loved fast cars; they looked cool and could get you where you wanted to go in style and quickly. He adored the engineering, a trait he got from his grandfather, the mechanic. Researching them was one of his favorite pastimes and had kept him occupied for many hours in the hospital after visitors had gone home.

After several more long minutes, the doctor and nurse practitioner walked in together. They wore forced smiles as they greeted us, but their eyes were full of apology and sadness. And they were teaming up—a sign of bad news.

"Well, things don't look good," the doctor dove right in. We were seasoned veterans; there was no need for pleasantries. "There are several new lesions in both lungs, around ten on each side, and the old ones have grown significantly. I'm afraid the treatment you've been on doesn't seem to be doing much good."

And there it was. We'd made a huge leap closer to that point on the horizon. It seemed it would take less time than we'd expected to reach it, and the road was revealing itself to be pretty straight and narrow, with not much left to slow us down. The cancer would fill up Zach's lungs, and he would die. Both Zach and I nodded our heads as the doctor delivered the news. The cancer bully took another shove, but this time it wasn't as effective at knocking us down. The surprise factor was no longer part of its reliable tactics. We continued on with the appointment and discussed the next treatment option, the next rock we would pick up and throw at our tormentor.

We wrapped things up, a new plan of action in place to slow the cancer, and said our good-byes to the team of caregivers who had learned to love Zach over the years. As Zach and I walked down the hall toward the waiting room, he looked over at me and, with a smirk on his lips and in his eyes, said, "Well, I guess I won't be doing home-work anymore."

We both burst out laughing as we made our way past the waiting area and check-in desk. People looked up at us and smiled as we passed by. Those people probably thought we just got great news. Seeing ourselves through their eyes, it made me happy to know the outside was reflecting what was going on in the inside: we were okay.

As the valet driver pulled our car up, Zach turned to me and said, "Let's start planning that party. It's time to have some fun."

Cancer was still a bully, but we'd learned to live with it, and we were stronger because of it.

A FEW DAYS LATER, ON ONE OF OUR GORGEOUS MINNESOTA OCTOBER days, I sat downstairs in the family room with a rumpled piece of paper spread out on my lap. The lyrics to a beautiful and heartbreaking song scribbled in Zach's crazy, chicken-scratch handwriting spilled across the page. I'd found it a few minutes earlier and was quietly staring at the page with tears spilling down my cheeks.

I heard Zach come in the front door of the house, set his backpack down, and make his way into the kitchen. I wiped away the tears and waited for him to come down. I didn't want him to know I'd been crying. He rustled around in the snack cabinet a bit and thumped down the stairs, doing his best to keep pressure off his left leg.

"Hey," he said as he pushed the door open. "What's up?"

I held up the sheet of paper. "Zach," I said, "this is really good."

He looked at the paper, opened a bag of chips, and popped one in his mouth.

"I didn't know you were writing songs. Have you got others? Do you have music?"

"Yeah. I'm working on some other stuff too. I couldn't really write letters like you said I should. I tried it, but nothing really came out right, so I thought I'd try writing songs." He leaned back on the couch and pulled the phone from his front pocket. "I recorded 'Clouds' on my phone." He placed the phone on the old painted chest that served as a coffee table between us and tapped the screen.

For the first time ever, I heard Zach play and sing a song that he had written.

Well I fell down, down, down
Into this dark and lonely hole
There was no one there to care about me anymore
And I needed a way to climb and grab a hold of the edge
You were sitting there holding a rope
And we'll go up, up, up
But I'll fly a little higher
We'll go up in the clouds because the view is a little nicer
Up here, my dear
It won't be long now, it won't be long now
When I get back on land
Well I'll never get my chance
Be ready to live and it'll be ripped right out of my hands
Maybe someday we'll take a little ride
We'll go up, up, up and everything will be just fine
And we'll go up, up, up
But I'll fly a little higher
We'll go up in the clouds because the view is a little nicer
Up here, my dear
It won't be long now, it won't be long now
If only I had a little bit more time
If only I had a little bit more time with you
We could go up, up, up
And take that little ride
We'll sit there holding hands
And everything would be just right

And maybe someday I'll see you again
We'll float up in the clouds and we'll never see the end
And we'll go up, up, up
But I'll fly a little higher
We'll go up in the clouds because the view is a little nicer
Up here, my dear
It won't be long now, it won't be long now

As his raw but soft voice came through the tinny phone speaker, I bit down on my bottom lip and tried to clamp down on the tears that were forcing their way out. I was stunned at his ability to articulate such a deep and painful thing in a way that somehow lifted my spirit. Those beautiful words mixed with the melody, so heartbreaking yet joyful—so much like his life these past three years. A mix of deep sadness and awe mingled inside of me. This boy, my boy, who had been through more pain than he could ever deserve and who had to wrestle out his own private battles with God, had taken it all and turned it into something beautiful.

He had gone from seeing beauty in the midst of suffering to creating it. He had taken this thing that could have suffocated him with despair and stripped it down until all that was left was hope.

He had taken his eyes off that point on the horizon and lifted them to the heavens, to eternity, to the clouds.

Twenty

. . . .

"WE NEED TO GET THIS RECORDED," I SAID. I WANTED TO HOLD ON to this song forever.

Zach said he had a time set up with his guitar teacher who had recording equipment and that he and Sammy had some other songs they'd worked on together. This was news to me. I didn't know they had been working on anything, but it made sense. If anyone knew Zach, it was Sammy, a redhead with beautiful green eyes whose quirky sense of style often included wearing old men's sweaters coupled with a big bow in her hair. She was an Irish dancer and singer whose voice could just as easily fit into a church choir as a jazz lounge. Zach and Sammy had always been close friends and understood each other in a way only people who have grown up together do.

Seventeen years earlier, as desperate moms sometimes do, Sammy's mom, Anne, and I had joined a church group for mothers with young children, and we got together regularly for playdates. Zach and Sammy met on a picnic blanket in our backyard at a playdate I hosted when they were a year old.

My friendship with Anne emerged after a playdate she hosted. I'd gotten a look at her hideously outdated cupboards and knew she couldn't possibly like them. So hoping she had a sense of humor and wouldn't be offended, I told her that I knew she secretly hated them and offered to help her paint them.

Thankfully, she laughed, agreed wholeheartedly with my assessment, and took me up on my offer. Our friendship solidified during a long day of painting. After we became dear friends, our husbands and children naturally followed suit.

For years thereafter, the Sobiechs and Browns, along with two other families, went on annual Labor Day camping trips. The "Last Hurrah," so to speak, before the kids went begrudgingly back to school. When they were eight years old, Zach and Sammy stayed up late around the campfire and talked in hushed tones about the stars and what it might be like to hop from one to another. As they got older, the conversation turned to the bigger things in life like creation, their places in it, and heaven.

They were in the same class at St. Croix Catholic School, and for the second-grade Halloween party Sammy dressed as a beauty queen and Zach as a ninja. He decided that Sammy, being a beauty queen and all, should probably have a bodyguard. He knew just the guy and spent the day protecting her from evil and guarding her life, should it be threatened. That same protective instinct spilled over into their high school years. Zach was fiercely protective of Sammy, always suspicious of any guy who would try to persuade her with his affections. He didn't trust them.

Sammy tolerated Zach's overprotectiveness, along with his goofy and annoying sense of humor, not to mention his insatiable need to tease. Sometimes he drove her crazy! Like when he programmed her cell phone to autocorrect "choir practice" with "fartface poopy-pants." (It's still programmed that way—a problem, now that she's joined the college choir.)

Before cancer, Zach was prone to being a bit showy of his athletic ability. He would never let anyone else win a race, and he felt the best way to display his incredible aim was to pelt a girl as hard as he could with a ball. Later, after cancer stripped him of strength and agility, he turned to self-deprecating humor and would show off his "wimpy" skinny leg. He became more introspective and quiet, moving away from the boyish reveling of how powerful his body was and reflecting on the bigger things in life, just as he did when he was with Sammy. He needed more and more to be with people who were calm and peaceful. He needed people who could sit in silent reflection while he strummed on his guitar. Sammy understood that part of him too. She became skilled at reading his face and knew that when the talk among his friends turned to more childish or gossipy things, a glance at Zach would solicit an irritated rolling of his eyes. She would steer the conversation in a more neutral direction. Their friendship was something precious and sacred.

Music became the thing that filled the empty space that words could not. They spent hours together, Zach strumming out a familiar tune and Sammy singing along. They decided, along with a few other friends, to take a stab at songwriting and planned a meeting to get started. Everyone assembled hoping to get something together for a Battle of the Bands event at the school, but the meeting didn't go as planned. They all had different interests and ideas, and by the end of the night their enthusiasm for the songwriting endeavor had waned. The group moved on to other topics of conversation.

But Sammy still wanted to make a go of it. She grabbed a notebook and pen and quietly tucked herself away at the end of the couch next to Zach. She began scribbling down a couple of lines:

Dandelions have goin' to seed, it's my soul I need to feed
Trees stand so tall and bare and here I stand without a care . . .

She nudged Zach and turned the notebook for him to see. He read it and nodded his head. He liked where she was going with it. After the group disbanded, Sammy stayed. By the end of the night, she and Zach had written their first song together: "Blueberries."

I knew they were working on songwriting together, and I was glad the two of them had a hobby to collaborate on. Sammy had a way of keeping Zach steady in turbulent times.

A week later, Sammy and Zach were hanging out downstairs in our family room working out an arrangement for the National Anthem they were asked to perform with a couple other friends at their high school's homecoming game. After they worked on it, he told her he'd been writing something new, a song he'd had in his head for a while. He pulled a sheet of paper from a notebook.

"I wrote a song," he said, handing it to her as he stood from the couch.

"Another one?" she asked.

"I've actually been working on it for a while, but things weren't forming in my head the way I wanted them to. But after we got 'Blueberries' down, I knew I could finish this one too."

With that, he walked out of the room and left Sammy alone on the couch to read the heartbreaking yet strangely joyful words on the page. No tune. No melody. Just words. Zach's soul laid out bare and raw. He was ready to deal with death. And Sammy knew he was okay.

If Zach was dealing with death, then she would have to as well. It had been there, lurking in the background, but they hadn't ever really invited it into their conversations. It was a topic left for another day. Zach hobbled back down the stairs and opened the door. She looked up, an unruly strand of red hair escaping the confines of the big green scarf tied in a bow meant to keep it in line.

"Are you crying?" he asked, incredulous.

"No." She wiped a tear away and laid the sheet of paper down. "This is good."

Maybe they didn't need to talk about it. Talking wouldn't really fix anything.

Sammy pulled a notebook out of her backpack and a pen from behind her ear. "Let's try this songwriting thing again." Zach sat next to her as she wrote across the page:

Tell me something you've never told before
Before I walk through the door,
I adore you, I adore you
I do . . . I really do

Zach took the pen from her and added a line. It was the beginning of their song "Fix Me Up." They would say the things that needed to be said in their own way.

WE HAD BEGUN MAKING PLANS FOR ZACH'S PARTY IN DECEMBER. Anne and I thought it would be great if we could have a CD of a few of their songs made by then. We could either give them away as party favors or sell them to raise money for pediatric cancer research.

With three original songs ready to record, they went into the guitar teacher's little studio. Every week for about a month they would get as much done as they could in a three-hour session.

A few days after their first recording session, Zach e-mailed me the recording of "Clouds." I loved everything about it. I loved the soft, raspy sound of his voice and the way it cracked at certain spots in the song. I loved the nervous swallow at the beginning as he laid out his soul in such a vulnerable way. It reached the most tender part of my heart and grabbed on to the deepest sadness, but then rebounded and soared up to a place of hope. It did what a song should do. It spoke to the soul.

The tune was catchy too; it stuck in my head, and I'd find myself humming it throughout the day. I knew I was biased. I loved the song because it was Zach's, and I knew it was born out of years of struggle and heartache.

Eventually I shared it with those closest to us, our family and close friends. I figured they would enjoy it because it would mean something to them as well. They'd been part of the struggle too. They all came back with the same response: they loved the song, and they were completely blown away that Zach wrote it. My favorite response was from my brother, Luke.

Luke was ten years old when Zach was born, more like a sibling than an uncle. Only now have my kids told me horror stories of the times Luke would babysit them. Like the time he chased them around the house with a stick he'd used to unclog the toilet, or when he let them watch *Child's Play*, a movie about a demon-possessed doll who runs around and slaughters people. (All of them slept on our bedroom floor for days afterward, terrified to sleep in their own beds, but refused to tell Rob and me why.) They all look back now and laugh; it was fun having an uncle so close in age. Zach especially loved and admired him and was inspired by Luke's musical talent as a drummer, guitar player, and lead singer. Luke was a seasoned musician and in a couple of local bands, one called Squares that had recently released their first record of haunting and beautiful songs that Zach and I both loved.

After Luke listened to "Clouds," he sent me a text with a simple two-word expletive.

It was my favorite endorsement.

EVERY YEAR AROUND CHRISTMASTIME, KS95, A LOCAL RADIO STA-tion, hosts a radiothon to raise money for the Children's Cancer Research Fund (CCRF) and Gillett Children's Hospital. In July 2012, Mindy from CCRF called to see if we would be interested in participating in the fund-raising effort by coming to the radio station and recording an interview with the morning show team, Ryan and Shannon. Aware of Zach's musical interest and talent, Mindy asked if Zach would be up for playing and singing a song.

My reaction was to tell them that Zach was a strong guitar player but he was a little shy about singing. I'd heard him when he was down in the family room as he played the guitar and experimented with singing. He had a nice voice, but it wasn't strong. To me he sounded best when he was backing up Sammy; she was really the singer of the pair. In truth, I had no idea how comfortable he would be. All I knew was that I didn't want him to stress about it, and I really didn't want him to be embarrassed.

When I asked Zach, he jumped at the opportunity.

"Are you sure?" I asked, my tone imploring him to really think about it. "Have you ever sung alone in front of people before? I mean, I'm not saying you shouldn't, I just don't want you to do it if you think you'll be too nervous."

"I don't know. I guess I figure, what have I got to lose? If I screw it up, it's not like I'll have to live with it for a long time. Besides, I'll kick myself later if I don't try this," he responded.

He was right. Zach had the end in sight. If he couldn't jump in and try something crazy now, then he never would. When it came down to it, I was afraid that he would fail and didn't want him to be devastated by it. I was learning that my fears weren't for Zach. They were my own, and failure only happened in the lack of trying.

So we headed into the interview with his guitar in tow. We didn't know what to expect; this was the first time we talked publicly about cancer and dying. It was a hard interview for me. I broke down several times and cried. We were still getting used to the idea of losing Zach, and I was pretty raw. It's hard when your child passes you by in life experience, and you realize you have no wisdom to draw from to help him on his way. I was candid about how difficult it was to see my son suffer because I wanted people to understand that suffering.

Zach kept his emotions in check. I was proud of his ability to articulate his view on things. When they asked him if he'd ever gotten angry because he had cancer, he said he'd never really thought of it that way. He said that his cancer was so rare that he "may as well be proud of it—one in a million." He explained how he lived one day at a time and focused on what was immediately in front of him.

When we were done with the interview, we headed to the studio to record Zach playing and singing. He chose "I'm Yours" by Jason Mraz because it was a song he knew he could play. They printed up the lyrics because he wasn't sure he would remember them all. I was a nervous wreck as I stood in the hall and watched him through the window. I could tell he was nervous too, but he got through it and sounded pretty good. As we walked out of the station, Zach beamed.

"That was awesome." He opened the back door of the car and shoved his crutches in. "I could do that every day!" It was his first taste of the rock star life, and he liked it.

In October I got a call from Mindy. The radio station was wondering if Zach had another song that might fit better with the interview. "I'm Yours" had turned out well, but the upbeat tone of the song didn't mix well with the content of the interview. As a second option, I sent them "Clouds." Within four hours it had been mixed with the interview and e-mailed back to me. The producers loved it.

Two days later, Friday evening, I got a call from Dan Seeman, the general manager of Hubbard Radio Broadcasting, the radio station where we'd done the interview. He'd heard "Clouds" earlier that day and would later describe in a letter to me the effect the song had on him.

"What I heard was a song that made me cry. A song that was personal and poignant. A song about faith, friendship, family, and hope. I heard a song that made me sad, yet inspired and hopeful. But most of all, what I heard that Friday morning was a really good song—personal and poignant, yes, but also catchy and popular, with a melody that stuck in my head. The lyrics contained a message that needed to be heard, a message that was wise and mature, yet delivered with innocence. But it was melody that drew me in. It was the melody that took an incredibly sad message and gave it hope.

"My eyes filled with tears, but my spirit was filled with hope. My mind filled with a clear understanding of the desire to embrace every single day. My heart was aching, yet longing for the opportunity to get to know Zach better. To help him tell his story."

He offered to get Zach into a professional studio with professional musicians to record "Clouds." We accepted, and by Monday evening Dan had a studio and a group of musicians lined up and ready to work on the project. The studio session was scheduled for Tuesday.

Dan asked if I would like the studio session videotaped; he knew a videographer who had some time that day and could spend it with us. I was thrilled at the prospect of capturing this unique experience on video. I wanted as many pictures, sound recordings, and videos as I could get.

When kids are little, it's easy to video them. It's a natural thing to do. But as they get older, unless they are doing something important like graduating, performing onstage, or playing in some sort of sporting event, there really aren't opportunities to capture them on video without it being awkward. It's especially awkward when your teenage child is dying. Every time I videotaped Zach in those final months, he was painfully aware of why I was doing it. He knew it was for our family to watch after he was gone. I could see on his face the moment when he would realize what I was doing. It was a heart-wrenching look of resignation.

The next day I drove Zach to his first big studio session. We entered the studio, and it was like Zach had stepped into Willy Wonka's Chocolate Factory. He was in awe. The room was filled with instruments and high-end mixing equipment, and it was painted black with huge panels of purple acoustic foam throughout. He stood there leaning on his crutches and looked around, a huge grin on his face. Karl Demer, the studio owner, a big guy with a shy demeanor—the kind of guy you knew could give an awesome bear hug—introduced himself and welcomed us. Zach reached out and shook his hand and thanked him for such an incredible opportunity. One by one, the musicians arrived. Zach, the drummer; Matt, the electric guitarist; Sean, the bassist; and John, the pianist. Some of the guys had played together for a couple of theater productions, but none had worked together in a studio and especially not on something they hadn't had time to prepare for. They'd been e-mailed the acoustic version of "Clouds" just a day or two earlier. Each had some ideas of what he could contribute to the song, but they all wanted to hear what Zach had in mind.

Once everyone was settled, instruments ready to go and lyrics handed out, they sat down in a circle and listened to the song together. It didn't take long, and the ideas started flowing.

"What do you think, Zach?" asked Karl as he used his whole body to get a feel for the song. His foot tapped the floor, his hand slapped his leg, and even his shoulders and head were fully engaged. He loved a good song. He didn't just listen to it; he became a part of it. "Do you have a direction you want to take the song?"

"I don't know," Zach said. "I guess I was sort of thinking I'd like it to be upbeat. I don't think it's a sad song." Everyone nodded in agreement. Zach reached over the armrest of the couch and grabbed his guitar that was leaning against the wall. He started playing the chords. Zach Miller, the drummer, picked up his sticks and joined in as he tapped out a rhythm on the coffee table. Sean plucked a few notes on the bass, and Matt strummed on the electric guitar. John sat down at the electric piano and played along. It was an incredible thing to watch all that talent as it came together in a unique and crazy way. There was a sense that something outside of that room was weaving it all together.

After toying with a few different sounds, they had a good idea of the tone the song would take. Zach, who was just thrilled to be there and work with professionals, was willing to let them lead the way. As they refined the sound, Zach liked what he was hearing and was ready to start recording. Karl grabbed Zach's guitar and led him into the soundproof room. Zach leaned his crutches on the wall and took a seat at the microphone. Mike Rominski, the videographer, followed them into the room, and so began the recording of "Clouds" and the "Clouds" video.

One after the other, each musician went into the soundproof room and laid down his track. With each new layer, the song emerged. It became fuller and richer and something entirely different from the version Zach had already done. There were a few times a track would need to be redone or tweaked, but it really just sort of came together. I was so amazed by these guys who didn't know Zach and didn't really know one another before that day and who had all taken time off from their day jobs to come together and make this wonderful thing happen.

It was one of those magical days that don't happen very often, when people are brought together for something bigger than themselves, by something bigger than themselves.

As the recording wrapped up, I asked Karl if this was how it usually happened, meet for a day and hammer out a song. As newbies to the whole production process, it was fascinating to watch how effortlessly the whole thing had come together. He chuckled. "No. Something like this should have taken at least two, probably three days."

I knew that was probably right. The day simply felt blessed.

After the musicians packed up their instruments, we all stood around, exhausted but elated. One of the guys leaned over to me and said, "I am so happy to be part of this. It's been an incredible day."

(top) Zach, age three, holding Grace for the first time. He referred to her as "my baby."

(right) Zach, age four, dressed as a farmer for Halloween.

(left) Grace and Zach in January 2000. Zach had this photo in mind when he wrote the song "For My Grace."

(bottom) Zach, age ten, and Rob on the field in 2005 at the Vikings' stadium after winning the championship game.

(top) Zach, age eleven, holding his first guitar on Christmas Day.

(right) Zach after the tumor resection and hip replacement surgery in February 2010. Four days later he was home and walking.

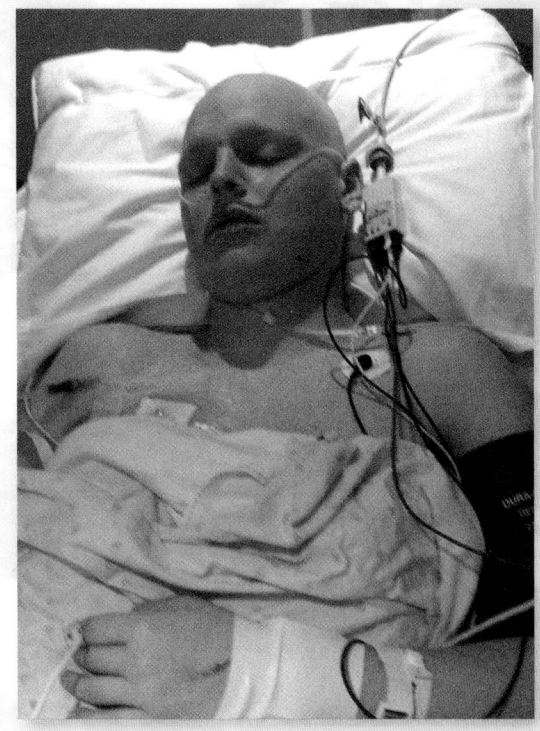

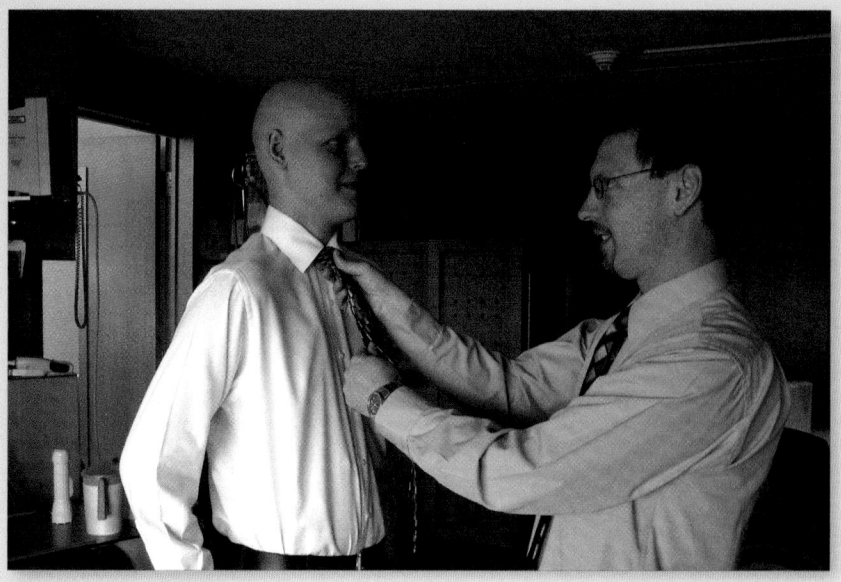

(top) Rob helping Zach with his tie the morning of Confirmation. Zach was feeling sick and had to be hooked up to a backpack with fluids, but he still made it!

(left) Zach, age sixteen, with his Mohawk haircut. The cancer was back, and Zach's future was uncertain, so I saved the clippings in a plastic bag.

Jeff Dunn—J Dunn Photography, Inc.—www.jdunnphotography.com

(top) The Sobiech clan in the Willow River, Wisconsin, in June 2011.

(right) Zach and his little cousin Calvin goofing off at the cabin. Zach adored kids and was a favorite of the little cousins.

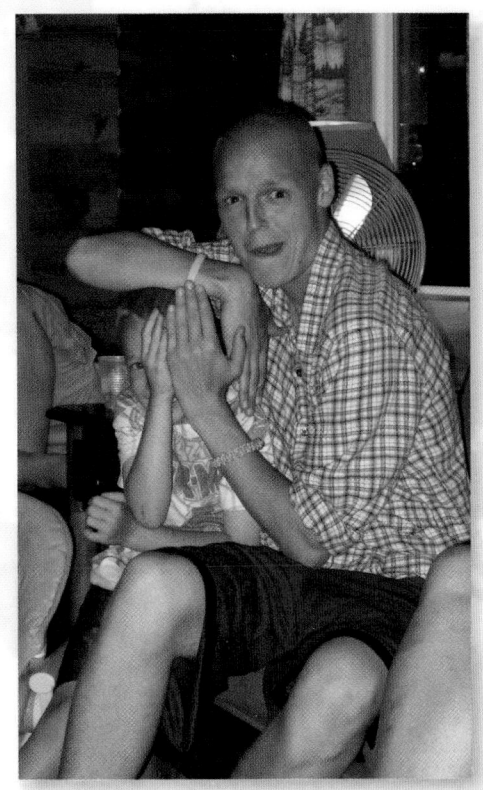

Zach, age sixteen, running across the field at the Relay for Life in Stillwater, Minnesota, in August 2011.

Uncle John, Grandpa Jim, Grace, Uncle Luke, Alli, and Zach at the Friedrich Family Booya in 2011.

(*top*) Sam, Grace, Zach, and Mitch looking into the Seine River in Paris at the Pont Alexandre III bridge.

(*right*) Zach on stage at the benefit in November 2011.

The Seeman and Sobiech families at Times Square in January 2013.

Daisy taking her place in the interview chair during set up with the *My Last Days* crew. Oh, the stories she could tell if dogs could talk.

Jeff Dunn—J Dunn Photography, Inc.—www.jdunnphotography.com

Reed, Sammy, and Zach, age seventeen, playing at Studio C at Cities 97 in March 2013.

Zach on stage with 4onthefloor at First Avenue in Minneapolis.

Zach, Reed, and Sammy during the filming of the "Star Hopping" video the day after he returned from Florida on March 27, 2013.

(top) Moon, Zach, Amy, and Staci from KS95 after Zach asked Amy to the prom on air in April 2013.

(right) Amy and Zach on the beach in Fort Meyers, Florida, for Zach's last taste of summer on March 26, 2013.

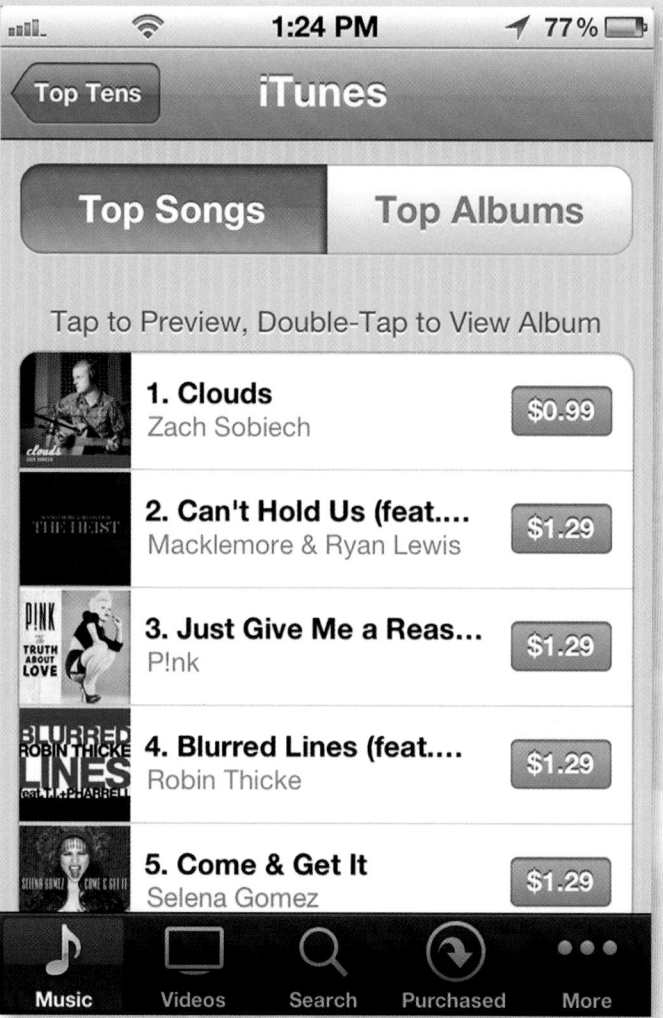

Clouds at #1 on iTunes on May 22, 2013,
two days after Zach died.

Sammy, Austin, Kelly, Andreas, Amy, and Reed in Duluth, Minnesota, in August 2013. The Z-shaped cloud can be seen above Amy's head.

© PeggySue Photography, PeggySue Imihy 2013

The Sobiech family at Alli and Collin's wedding on May 31, 2013.

As we left the studio, I noticed Zach, the drummer, and Karl go into the soundproof room with a glockenspiel, an instrument similar to a xylophone but with metal bars rather than wood. I'd heard them talking earlier about adding the instrument and how it might have a cool effect somewhere in the song.

The next day Karl e-mailed me the mixed version and wanted to know what I thought. I was so used to the acoustic version and its understated and folksy sound that the more pop-sounding version took me awhile to get used to. And honestly, the glockenspiel was a stretch. I couldn't help but think of Christmas music. But when Karl told me that he was trying to give the song a music-box sound to give it a childlike quality, I understood. He was right; it was a perfect fit.

When Zach got home from school, I played him the finished recording. The glockenspiel started, and his eyes lit up. "That's so cool." He laughed.

As the song progressed, he made comments about each part that he loved, especially the echo in the bridge that gave the lyrics a forlorn and introspective feel. He was ecstatic. That's when Grace entered the kitchen.

"Hey, Grace," called Zach, "did you hear the super awesome song I wrote?" He danced around her as she walked into the kitchen. "Did ya? Did ya hear it?" He goaded and poked her in the ribs until she yelled at him to knock it off.

"Yeah, I heard it," she said. "It's okay." She popped a gummy worm in her mouth and walked out. She had a way of putting him in his place when he took things too far. If he was going to get a big head over this thing, she'd be there with a big needle ready to pop it. He was cool. But he wasn't that cool. About an hour later, she asked if I would upload the song from my computer onto her iPod.

"It's a good song," she said with a tinge of resignation in her voice.

I e-mailed the song to Rob, who was at the nursing home with his mom. Her health had been failing for several years, since before Zach got sick, and had recently taken a turn for the worse. She'd had a heart attack the night before and was in very serious condition. She wasn't expected to make it to the end of the week. Rob played "Clouds" for her, and she wept. After eighty-four years of hard work and good living, she wasn't sure she was ready to die. Now here was her seventeen-year-old grandson teaching her how to.

Now that the song was finished, the video could be produced. Mike e-mailed me the first version with a question: Would I like to put slides throughout the video to explain Zach's story? Initially I thought, why bother? Everyone who would want to watch the video would likely already know Zach's story. Who else would be interested in Zach and his song? But as I thought about it, I decided maybe people outside our circle of friends and family would want to check it out. It was a good song, after all. Maybe if we put in slides that explained what Zach had been through with a link for CCRF at the end, people would be interested in donating. It would be nice if "Clouds" could help raise a few dollars to help pediatric cancer research.

I sent Mike a few slides that briefly summarized Zach's story along with the link to CCRF for the last slide.

Two days later, Rob's mother passed away. I held her hand as I hummed "Clouds." She was the first to bring "Clouds" to eternity.

No one had any idea that in a matter of days the song would be brought to people around the globe and would change the hearts of others who were burdened with anger, fear, and despair.

No one could guess how big this thing was about to get.

Twenty-One

· ·

December 2012

WE WERE THRILLED TO FIND OUT THAT KS95 PLANNED TO PLAY "Clouds" in steady rotation during its two-day radiothon. The event would take place all day Thursday and Friday. We were excited, primarily for the live interview, but also to be part of the fund-raising effort. It was a big event, and we were thrilled to do our part. In his short life, Zach had gotten to do some incredible things: play football in the Hubert H. Humphrey Metrodome to win the championship, win his championship basketball game, and get a nibble of the rock star life. Not to mention he got to travel to some amazing places like Mexico, Italy, and France. But this! This was a whole new level of incredible. He was going to have a song that he wrote and performed played on a major radio station in a major market. It was crazy!

The week started with a couple of interviews. A reporter from a local newspaper, the *Pioneer Press*, and an affiliated videographer followed Zach, Amy, and Sammy around for a couple of days. The newspaper was going to run a front-page story that focused on Zach, his battle with cancer, and the writing of "Clouds" in that Sunday's edition. The video would take a different approach; it would be a more intimate look at Zach, his personality, and his relationships. It would be posted on the newspaper's website the Saturday before the article was printed. We also spent a good deal of time preparing for the upcoming fund-raiser/party in Zach's honor. By the end of the week, all the media attention and party planning had us all exhausted.

When radiothon day arrived, we were excited. We figured we would get through it, enjoy the novelty of hearing the song on the radio, and move on. Once the radiothon was over and the video and article were published, interest in the song and Zach's story would die down, and we would move on and be just another family with a child dying from cancer.

The live interview went well, though there was a moment I thought I would choke when Ryan, the DJ, put the mic in my face and asked, "Laura, why is it so important that people call in and donate to help fight childhood cancer?" My mind froze for a split second; it seemed like such a no-brainer: because kids will keep dying if we don't have money to figure this thing out. I recovered and explained in more eloquent language than what ran through my head.

"If we don't raise money to fight this horrible disease, it doesn't go away. We can all hope for a cure, but what it boils down to is that it takes money to fight this thing. Plain and simple."

Zach made me incredibly proud with his poise and eloquence. This boy, who just moments before he was called for the interview was playing around on the escalators and reenacting the scene from *Elf* where Buddy steps on an escalator for the first time and ends up doing the splits the whole way up, stepped up to that mic and spoke with incredible maturity.

"It's not just about me," he said, "it's about the kids who will be diagnosed tomorrow. Or the kids who are lying in a hospital bed right now. Let's work together to help them."

The station played our prerecorded interview from several months earlier along with "Clouds," and the phones rang as people called in to donate what they could. We were encouraged to know that we were helping to make a small difference. It felt good to do our part in the fund-raising arena, especially since it was completely outside my comfort zone. I'd secretly put this kind of thing on my I-Never-Want-To-Do List. Asking people for money had always seemed so bold and intimidating. I simply had never had the confidence to do it.

We spent hours listening to the radio over the course of the two days. The station played the interview and song several times. Friends, family members, and coworkers texted us to let us know they'd heard the song, and we were receiving e-mails, Facebook messages, and guest-book messages on our CaringBridge site from people all over the Twin Cities who wanted us to know they had heard Zach's story and "Clouds." The outpouring was overwhelming and quite unexpected.

Zach and Sammy were scheduled to perform at Winter Coffee House, a biannual fund-raising event put on by the high school's National Honor Society, on Friday night, the last day of the radiothon. Each event raised money for a charitable cause that had been voted on by NHS members beforehand. A year earlier, Zach and Mitch had nominated Lance. This time around the NHS voted to give the funds to Zach.

He was about to step onstage to perform his music in front of two hundred classmates who had gathered to support him, and a song he wrote and recorded was playing in rotation on a local radio station. It was bigger than he could have imagined. He was exhausted and nervous, but he was on top of the world.

That night Zach, Mitch, and Sammy performed "Blueberries" for the first time. They sounded great and ended the song with fist bumps. The crowd loved it! And after a few more acts, Zach got back up onstage, stepped up to the mic, and performed "Clouds" for the first time in front of a live audience. With a huge grin on his face, he pointed across the room to Amy and dedicated the song to her.

That simple act had a big impact on a lot of people, but not in the same way. For Amy, it was a turning point. People who weren't close to either her or Zach suddenly understood what was going on. They realized that she was dating Zach. There was no mystery anymore. For Amy, it made things a little easier. She didn't have to deal with the wondering looks in the classroom or hallway anymore. Her classmates understood that she was Zach's girlfriend.

For other people in Zach's life, that dedication came off a little different. While Zach had previously made it clear to everyone he was close to—his family, Sammy, and Mitch in particular—that "Clouds" had been written to thank them for sticking by his side over the past three years, now people thought the song was all about Amy, a relative newcomer to his life. Feelings were hurt.

Things got even more difficult when the newspaper website posted the video.

The video itself was beautifully done and remains one of my favorites because it revealed a vulnerable side of Zach that he didn't show to outsiders very often. He talked about Amy and how she had supported him and how much he relied on her. He loved her deeply, and it really showed.

But what the video didn't show was everyone else who'd been faithfully by his side. There were mixed feelings among Zach's friends and siblings. They felt slighted but knew that it was neither Zach's nor Amy's fault. We were getting a taste of the celebrity life and how limited media can be, focusing on one chapter of a book in order to draw an audience in, but missing out on the beauty of the whole story. It was a crash course in how to balance the outside attention with the inside reality.

Twenty-Two

IT WAS A GOOD TIME FOR ZACH AND AMY TO GET OUT OF TOWN, giving the stirred-up emotions a chance to settle. They were going to attend Amy's cousin's wedding in Kansas and would be back late Sunday night. Zach and Amy and her family got home safely Sunday evening despite having to travel through a nasty snowstorm that dumped around ten inches.

When he walked in the door around eleven o'clock that night, he found me up, listening to my iPod. I had "Clouds," "Fix Me Up," and "Blueberries" on repeat while I knitted a pair of socks to give as a Christmas present.

"Hey! How'd it go?" I set my knitting down as he took a seat on the couch.

"It was awesome. Her family is a lot like ours. Everyone gets along really well and just likes to have fun," he said with an exhausted but content smile on his face.

He went on to tell me that he had given Amy a special present, a topaz ring.

"I wanted to give her something nice, that she could keep always," he said. "She deserves it." Amy's dance team name was Topaz so he liked the symbolism. He got quiet, and his eyes took on a look of sadness.

"It was hard, too, being at the wedding." He looked down at his hands. "Just knowing that Amy and I will never be able to get married. It's not fair to her."

My heart ached. To love someone so much that you spend the rest of your life with her was a wish he wouldn't be granted. But he worried about Amy.

We sat in silence for a moment as we thought about a future that would never be. It was easy to fall into despair thinking about things that could never happen. It was best to focus on what was right in front of us.

"I'm grateful she is with you now," I said, trying to bring us both back to the present.

He stood from the couch and stretched. It was late, and he was exhausted. It had been a crazy few days, and he had school in the morning. He leaned down so I could kiss him good night on the forehead and then took a piece of notebook paper out of his pocket.

"I wrote a song when we were driving through Ames, Iowa. I thought you might like to see it." He handed the frayed paper to me and hobbled out of the room. "Good night, Ma. And thanks."

I unfolded the sheet of paper and started to read:

> *Well, the water trickles down the glass*
> *The first will never be the last*
> *At least, not here and not today*
> *The sharp sun's rays bite at my face*
> *And the howling wind begs me to stay*

But I really must be getting home

It might be time for me to go

But that doesn't mean you have to leave

And winter might be giving us snow

But who's to say we can't still believe?

The trees have all cut their hair

They've said good-bye and left somewhere

As a sea of fields greet us and push us onward

We've curled up and settled in

And in this life you can never win

Only hope and pray that you can keep what you have

Well, it might be time for me to go

But that doesn't mean you have to leave

And winter might be giving us snow

But who's to say we can't still believe?

Our sleep will become deeper soon

More beautiful than the sun, sea, the moon

That's ours and no one can take it

It might be time for me to go

But that doesn't mean you have to leave

And winter might be giving us snow

But who's to say we can't still believe?

Our engine will keep on turning

And the stars will smile on us

And even when we're torn apart

I will not lose this love

I rested my hands in my lap as I clutched the paper and closed my eyes. The heartache of having to let go poured out of him in the form of words onto paper. I just hoped the void would be filled with some measure of peace.

"Keep him close, Lord. Please, keep him very, very close." I tucked my knitting away, switched off the lamp, and headed up to bed. As I lay in bed and waited for sleep to come, I reflected on everything we'd packed into the past few days. I marveled at how much we had been given. How many seventeen-year-olds had been granted such extraordinary opportunities? His life had been tough, for certain. But the backdrop of his unyielding battle made his accomplishments all the more sweet. I was so proud of him and so grateful for all that God had done for him.

Now the media blitz would end, and we would fall back into our routine. I smiled as I nuzzled into my pillow. It would be nice to have a week of normal life ahead. I drifted off to sleep, completely oblivious that people across the globe were about to hear the story about a kid named Zach Sobiech and how he wrote a song to say good-bye, and that our lives would never be the same again.

THE NEXT MORNING ZACH AND THE REST OF THE KIDS HEADED TO school, and Rob and I went to work.

"So, that was amazing," my coworker Traci said as I walked into the office. The ladies in the office, five besides me, had listened to the radiothon and heard "Clouds" played several times over the course of the two-day event. "Your live interview was great! And I think we all cried a little when we heard the recorded interview."

The office ladies had been through it all with me. They'd been there when Zach was diagnosed and for each recurrence and surgery after that. And they were privy to all the latest news and excitement of what we were doing with CCRF and what was happening with Zach's song. They were nice cheerleaders to have in my corner.

I sat down at my desk, turned on my computer, and pulled out the stack of claims I needed to work on. Zach's party was coming up in a week, and there was still a lot that needed to be done, so I checked my e-mail during my lunch break to see if I needed to follow up on anything urgent. As the e-mails began to load onto the screen, I froze. What was happening? Fifty. One hundred. Two hundred. Where were all these e-mails coming from? They just kept coming!

I began to scan the subject lines; most of them said things like "Zach's song," and "Thank you," or "Alternative Treatment," but there were a couple that were different and gave me pause.

I opened one with a subject line that read something like "Stop chemo," and skimmed through a rather lengthy rant that started with, "You need to wake up and stop poisoning your son." It went downhill from there, eventually ending with an accusation of Rob and me being brainwashed by Zach's doctors.

There were several more e-mails from people who suggested I take Zach to various clinics across the country, or out of the country altogether. Some were kind in their approaches, others, militant.

Over the years I'd developed a distaste for thoughtless recommendations for various treatments from people who were not educated on Zach's disease or condition. In the early months of our battle, they left me questioning the decisions we'd made. Should I really spend three hundred dollars on a bottle of algae? Would it do any good? Maybe we should take him to that clinic in Houston . . . Eventually, after months of doing my own research, I was confident Zach was receiving the best treatment available for his disease. And that no spice, vegetable juice, mushroom, oil, or special diet was going to cure him.

Another e-mail looked a little suspicious. It was a long story by a man who claimed to have died and come back to life seven times. He begged me to please tell Zach that he should not "go into the light" when he died because it was a trap. That the light was really the gateway to hell, and that he would see images of his dead relatives who would beckon him to come, but it was all a trick, a way of trapping him. I was horrified and felt sick!

An audible gasp escaped my mouth, and I reached up to cover it with my hand.

"What's wrong?" Traci asked.

"I don't know what's going on. I just got a bunch of e-mails, and this one is creepy. It's making me sick." My heart sank as I read through it again, holding my head in my hands. What if Zach or one of the other kids saw something like that? We had worked so hard to teach our kids about death and dying and how it wasn't something to fear so much as to prepare for. We wanted them to know that when the time came, they would be at peace.

Zach was a teenager forced into a reality that most don't have to deal with until much later in life. He didn't have years to build his faith before he had to face death. There were times he wondered if God existed at all. In a letter he wrote to Amy he said, "I've been questioning if there is a heaven. Often times I'll 'threaten' God, saying, 'You better be real!' I'm sure He's just shaking in His boots."

He'd had conversations with his friends about what death would be like. They asked Zach to give them signs of his presence when he was gone. He said he would do his best.

He and I had talked about death on occasion, when the moments would present themselves. I'd shared my belief that we spend our lives preparing for it, making choices between good and evil, choosing the narrow path or not, every day. And that we can either enter eternity with the same grudges and angst that we have chosen to hang on to in this life, or we can enter eternity with the peace and holiness that a lifetime of grace and following Christ's narrow path can achieve. We choose.

And now, this person, likely mentally ill, was trying to reach Zach and plant some very strange ideas in his head. I went to the restroom and sat for a moment trying to get on top of my emotions. If this was the kind of thing that a little "celebrity" brought with it, I wanted nothing to do with it. Zach had been through enough, and he didn't need crazy people making things murky for him. I wanted so desperately to stuff the genie back in the bottle, but I had no idea how.

When I got back to my desk, a few new e-mails had popped up. One was a request for an interview with a radio station in Seattle, Washington. They wanted to talk to us about Zach's song and the story behind it. I looked through a few more and found that the overwhelming majority of them were from kind-hearted people who simply wanted to tell me how much they loved the video and the song. As I kept reading, I began to feel a little better. It was like anything else in the world, I supposed. Most people have hearts that are in the right place, and some people are just messed up.

As I finished my day at work, the picture had become clearer. Dan from KS95 texted me that Ian Punnett from the syndicated radio show *Coast to Coast* had made an appeal to his audience to visit the "Clouds" video on YouTube and had challenged them to share the video with everyone they knew in an effort to obtain a million hits by Christmas as a present for Zach.

People had also visited our CaringBridge site, which at that time had no restrictions, and my e-mail was clearly displayed. That explained the flood of e-mails from across the country. I guessed this genie wasn't going back into its bottle. We would just have to ride it out and see where it would go.

I WAS PREPARING DINNER THAT NIGHT WHEN ZACH WALKED UP from the family room and took a seat at the counter.

"I'm getting, like, hundreds of friend requests on Facebook," he said as he held up his phone. "And this old guy wants to know if I've been saved by Jesus Christ." He handed me the phone to show me the message.

I was irritated. Really? It was just like the militant, alternative-medicine people, but with religion! Why do some people think it's their job to swoop in without bothering to get to know a person and push their own agendas? Sure, I'm all for sharing your faith, just like I'm all for sharing a sure treatment, but build a little bit of a relationship first. I knew in my heart this man meant well, that he was simply concerned for Zach's soul, but had he even bothered to listen to the song? Had he even read our CaringBridge site? If he had, why were his ears so closed to the message? Of course Zach knew Christ. You had to be wearing a blindfold not to see it.

"Okay. No more friending people you don't know," I said as I handed the phone back to him. "And you can ignore messages like this. If these people don't know you well enough to see that your faith has gotten you this far, they have no business telling you what you need to do. You owe them nothing. If they'd bothered to really listen, they would already know your soul is just fine."

"Okay." He looked at me, relieved.

Was I overreacting? Maybe. But I'd seen what this poor kid had been through, and I knew if there was anyone who should be giving guidance on how to live the faith, it was Zach. He hadn't passively waited for someone to come along and save him. He had spent years working out his salvation, sometimes with fear and trembling, but always with hope. It was his understanding that to suffer patiently and with hope was to be a channel of grace, and to serve others in the midst of it all was a more effective example of faith than any number of words, no matter how true or profound.

Twenty-Three

December 11–14, 2012

IT WAS TUESDAY MORNING, DECEMBER 11. I HAD THE DAY OFF WORK and had planned to run some errands for the party that was on Saturday. Things were coming together, but I still needed to tie up a few loose ends. The house was in disarray, and we had out-of-town company coming on Friday, so I had a lot that needed to be done. I mentally mapped out my day as I made a cup of coffee and turned on my computer. As I was about to sit down, the phone rang. It was Kris from Children's Cancer Research Fund.

She told me that a woman who was familiar with CCRF and their mission had heard Zach's story during the radiothon and was so moved and impressed by Zach's song she decided to get in touch with her brother, Adam, who was a producer at CNN.

Adam liked what he heard and was interested in spending a day with Zach and our family for a story they wanted to run on Friday, December 14. I was excited that CNN was interested in doing a story about Zach, but I was also apprehensive about agreeing to do the interview without first checking with the rest of the family. Given all that was going on with party preparation and the media attention we'd already had, along with the tension that was already running high, I told Kris I needed to talk with the rest of the family first. She agreed, but we would have to give Adam an answer that evening because he wanted to do the interview the next day.

I called Rob at work to tell him the news.

"Are you serious?" he asked in a tone of disbelief. "They want to do a story about Zach?"

"I know! Crazy, isn't it?" I had a hard time wrapping my head around it too. "I think we need to talk with the kids about it. We need to decide as a family how to proceed."

We all knew how precious our time with Zach was, and we needed to decide how much of it to sacrifice and for what purpose. This wasn't all just about Zach; it involved all of us.

Later that evening, after we'd eaten dinner and were gathered around the kitchen table, we called Sam, who was at college, and put him on speakerphone. He would transfer to a college close to home at the beginning of the next semester so he could live at home and be close to Zach, but he had a couple of weeks left in North Dakota.

"CNN wants to send a crew to do a story on Zach and the song," I explained. "We need to decide if we want to do this because once CNN picks up the story, others will likely follow. So do we move forward with this, or do we stop it now?"

Alli, who was studying journalism and was well aware of the power of media, was apprehensive. What was the point of it? Grace was more relaxed; she didn't really care what we did as long as it didn't intrude too much on her life. Rob and I could see the value in the publicity. When it became apparent that Zach's story and his music had the potential to raise awareness and thereby a significant amount of money, the folks at CCRF set up a separate fund in Zach's name called the Zach Sobiech Osteosarcoma Fund. We were thrilled that all the money Zach helped raise would go specifically for research that could one day help eradicate his disease. Rob and I figured an interview with CNN was a good opportunity to raise awareness and money. Zach was pretty quiet about the whole thing. He knew it was about more than just him, and he seemed to want guidance from the family.

Sam was the one who chimed in with a reasonable plan that pulled everyone together.

"If it's just about Zach, then I don't see the point. But if we use what Zach's been through to help other people and the media attention ultimately has the point of raising money for the fund, then we should go ahead with it," he stated with certainty.

For the first time we all had a common understanding of what we needed to do. Sam, who had been away at school and out of the tempest that had kicked up around us, could see with clarity and was able to articulate our mission in a way that made sense to all of us. This wasn't about Zach and it wasn't about "Clouds"; it was about using his story and music to help others. Period. God had laid the groundwork for a plan to unfold, and we were beginning to see the bigger picture. All we had to do was take one step at a time.

We all agreed that we would do the CNN interview, but any other interviews, should there be interest, would have to wait until after Christmas and New Year's. We needed Christmas.

I called Kris and told her we would do the interview. I'd never had a television crew in the house before, so I had no idea what to plan for. Zach had interviewed with the videographer for the newspaper, but that was pretty casual. This was CNN. National news was a whole other ball game.

The next morning I called my sister Lee and my mom and asked them to come over and help me clean. We ran around the house picking up, dusting, and vacuuming. It was a mad dash of activity. As usual, Zach had papers, notebooks, instruments, and clothes lying everywhere in his room and around the couch where he would lounge. It was a disaster!

"I've got the garbage picked up, but where do you want all the miscellaneous stuff that's lying around downstairs?" Lee asked.

"Just shove it into Zach's room. Let's focus on the living spaces and kitchen," I said as I tossed a roll of paper towels to my mom who stood at the ready with a bottle of Windex in hand. "Can't have the nation thinking we're big slobs."

The plan was that the crew would spend the afternoon following Zach around at school, then come to our home afterward and set up lights for the interviews they would do after Grace's basketball game and before we ate dinner. It was mid-afternoon, and the house was looking good. Everything was dusted and polished, the floors were washed, the carpets vacuumed, and the windows sparkled. Zach texted me that he, Amy, and the crew were on their way to the house. As Lee and I carried out some finishing touches, rearranged the books on the coffee table, and wiped down the kitchen counter, Zach pulled into the driveway with the crew right behind him.

I watched out the front window as Ed Lavendera, a reporter and familiar face on CNN; the producer, Adam; and the cameraman hopped out of the SUV and began to unload the equipment. For some reason the garage door had been left open and that was the first place they headed. The garage was a mess! I popped out the front door.

"Hello," I called out. "Welcome to our home, but you can't go in the garage. It's the only place we haven't cleaned for you."

The crew turned from the garage and walked up the sidewalk to the front door. Lee ran up the steps from the family room with a tissue in her hand. "Daisy pooped downstairs!"

"Are you kidding me?" I said through the smile plastered on my face. "Toss it in the garbage! Quick!"

Ed and the guys stepped into the house; Zach and Amy followed. We made introductions and chitchatted about how things had gone at school. Then I invited them to choose where they would like to set their cameras up. Ed turned to Zach.

"So, Zach. Let's go check out your bedroom."

Seriously! Of all the places, it had to be the room we'd just used as our dumping ground. Gah! I busted up laughing and explained what we'd used Zach's room for and told them that, truly, the rest of the house—aside from Zach's room and the garage—was available. Having a news crew in your home can be a humbling experience.

They decided to set the cameras up around the kitchen table and down in the family room. (Right where the dog poo had been. Thank God Lee had done a once over.) It took about an hour, then we headed to Grace's school for the basketball game.

After the game I had a moment to talk with Adam and Ed as they loaded the camera and other equipment into the SUV. I asked them what angle they thought the story would take so I would have some idea what kinds of questions I should anticipate for our interview once we got home. They were thinking the focus would be on the relationship between Zach and Amy and how he'd written a beautiful good-bye song for her.

I had spent a good portion of the last several days doing my best to field the fallout of hurt feelings from the perceived neglect that came after Zach dedicated his performance of "Clouds" at the school event to Amy and the video that focused on their relationship. It had come at me from all different angles, and I had to explain that it wasn't Zach or Amy who was pushing the story. It wasn't even the reporters who were at fault; it was simply one true part of a bigger story that needed to be told.

"No. You can't do that. Amy is an important part of Zach's story, but she's a fairly new part of it," I explained. "That song, while inspired by Amy, was really written for more than just her. If you focus on Amy, it will cause problems, and we just don't have time to waste on hurt feelings."

"How long have Zach and Amy been dating?" Ed asked.

"Only for the past six months. His other friends, like Sammy and Mitch, have been by Zach's side much longer." Ed nodded his head in agreement; he understood what I was saying. I sensed that Adam was a little resistant. I'd just thrown a bit of a wrench into the plan, but once he understood the situation and that this wasn't some petty request, he agreed.

At home, the crew set up in the kitchen, and Ed interviewed each family member as we sat around the table. He asked questions like, "How have you handled dealing with cancer?" and "What does Zach's song mean to you?"

I was stumped. How could we adequately wrap up in a sentence or two how we were dealing with cancer or what the song meant to us? It was like the radiothon all over again, trying to stuff a huge answer into a couple of sentences. There was so much I wanted to say about how we had to wrestle with the agony of losing Zach while still trusting that God was with us. Or how the song made me want to smile and cry all at the same time. It can be a difficult thing to explain hope.

After Ed was finished with interviewing Rob, Alli, Grace, and me, they went down into the family room and interviewed Zach and filmed him playing guitar while Sammy sang and Mitch played the cello. After they had finished and were packed up and ready to leave, Adam told us he expected the segment would air early Friday morning, around six thirty central time, and that, unless a big news story broke, it would probably run several times throughout the day.

Everyone got up early on Friday morning to watch our segment. It was strange to watch ourselves on the screen, mostly because it wasn't that big of a deal. We all thought they had done a nice job covering the story and were pleased that they had mentioned the fund and our desire to raise awareness for Zach's disease. I was secretly relieved that the piece focused more on the music and how Zach turned to writing songs as a way to say good-bye to everyone than on his relationship with Amy.

My folks called to say they had seen it, and I was getting Facebook messages and texts from people throughout the morning who had also seen it and were happy to see the coverage of Zach and his story. As I was on the phone, I looked up to see the news coverage had switched to an event that was underway in Newtown, Connecticut. I hung up the phone and watched as reports came in that a shooter had entered Sandy Hook Elementary School and several children and teachers were thought to be dead.

I sat stunned as the pictures flashed on the screen of mothers and fathers who waited to see if their children were okay. My heart ached for those who had lost their beautiful babies, mothers, sisters, and brothers in such a violent and evil way.

They never got to say good-bye.

Twenty-Four

December 15, 2012

IT WAS THE DAY OF ZACH'S PARTY, AN EVENT WE'D PLANNED FOR several months. The weather was ominous; it was cloudy and rainy all day with temperatures threatening to dip below freezing, which meant icy roads and maybe snow. It was to be Zach's last hurrah—the party to end all parties. A sort of prom, graduation party, and wedding reception all rolled into one as a way to celebrate Zach's life while he was still here. We had bands scheduled to play throughout the night, all of them our friends, and most were Zach's high school friends. Loads of people came together to make the party a success. Everything from the venue to the soda in the coolers was donated.

Earlier, Sammy and Zach, along with their friend Reed, on percussion, had finished recording several songs for the CD that we'd decided we were going to use as a fund-raiser. We were going to burn the CDs at home and had a simple design planned for the covers that we would make. But when I mentioned our idea to Dan Seeman from KS95 and

Karl Demer from Atomic K Records, who had both worked on getting "Clouds" recorded, they wanted to get involved. Karl agreed to make a master of the CD and got in touch with Ron, a gentleman he'd worked with on different projects over the years, who was willing to help us with reproducing the CD. Dan engaged a graphic designer from the station to do the CD cover. What we ended up with was a beautiful and professionally produced CD titled *Blueberries* under the band's name, A Firm Handshake. The cover was a picture of Zach strumming his guitar with a smirk on his face, eyes turned downward, and Sammy singing. The CD featured a few cover songs by a couple of their favorite artists along with their own original recordings of "Blueberries," "Fix Me Up," the acoustic version of "Clouds," and the produced version. It was Zach and Sammy's first CD.

Before the party started, we did a quick interview with a local television news reporter who had picked up on the "Clouds" video, which had almost a million hits by that time, and wanted to run a story about the community coming out to support Zach. Once we finished, we opened the doors and let the party start. It was an open invitation, and people poured into the dance hall. All night there was a line out the door as people waited to get in. We couldn't see across the room it was so full, but everyone was having a fantastic time. There was no sadness in the room, just pure joy.

Zach was surrounded all night by new fans and old friends. I could see that he was exhausted. It had been a crazy couple of weeks, but he was happy. He was with people who loved him.

We told all the people who had helped us out with recording the CD about the event, but I knew it was a tough time of year, right before Christmas, to give up a Saturday night to attend a party for someone they barely knew. So I was thrilled to see Karl and his three young boys and wife walk in the door. Just a couple of weeks earlier, Karl's wife found out she had skin cancer, which made the fact they came out to join us all the more extraordinary. We both found it interesting that our first meeting took place just days before her diagnosis. Karl would tell me later, after Zach died, that Zach's example of facing down the disease had uniquely prepared him to handle his wife's battle.

Our attorney, Adam Gislason, who had volunteered hours of his time to help us get Zach's music registered and the song copyrighted, was there with his wife; and Ron, who had donated over a thousand copies of the CD, came out in the nasty weather to be with us as well. Melissa, Zach's nurse practitioner who had been with us from the beginning, came with her husband and three-year-old son. Her little boy loved "Clouds," and he was thrilled to have a chance to meet Zach.

Later in the evening, Rob worked his way through the crowd and found me by the photo booth as I waited in line with my brothers and sisters. All seven of us were determined to cram inside the thing.

"Scotty Herold is looking for you," he yelled over the din.

"Who's that?" I yelled back.

"He's the guy from Rock the Cause, the one who Kris from CCRF and Adam told us about. I'll go find him and send him your way."

We had so many people come together to work on getting the song recorded and the CDs out that I started to lose track of who was who. It boggled my mind how much time, talent, and resources these people were willing to give. But I wasn't quite sure what part Scott played.

As I stumbled out of the photo booth, a gentleman who looked to be in his forties and was dressed in a "Rock the Cause" T-shirt, jeans, tennis shoes, and a sport coat waited for me.

"Hi, Laura, I'm Scott Herold with Rock the Cause. I just wanted to introduce myself and tell you what an honor it is to be able to work with you and Zach," he said as he extended his hand. He must have picked up on the blank look on my face.

"We're a nonprofit organization that works with music artists to set up charitable digital music distribution through the largest digital distributor called The Orchard." My face was still blank. "I'm the one who got your son's music on iTunes yesterday and on sale in one hundred forty-six countries around the world," he said with a smirk.

The light bulb finally went on in my head. We had kicked around the idea with the people from CCRF of somehow figuring out a way to get "Clouds" on iTunes with all the proceeds going to Zach's fund. No one at CCRF had experience in the industry, but Kris had a friend, Scott, who had seen the video "Sharing the Load with Zach" posted on her Facebook wall. He was so moved by Zach and Amy's love for each other that he dug into the story a little more and found the "Clouds" video. He loved the song.

"Hearing 'Clouds' was like a lightning bolt of divine grace had hit me," Scott would later tell me. He knew immediately he wanted to do whatever he could to get the song out into the world. He contacted Kris, and within seventy-two hours the song was on digital music websites across the globe.

"Anyway, I heard about this party you were having for Zach and I thought I'd drop by and introduce myself," he said as he handed me a bag of Rock the Cause T-shirts. "I met Zach a few minutes ago. I have to say, I am astounded by your son's strength and grace. You must be very proud of him."

"I certainly am," I responded. It seemed God had some big plans for "Clouds," and Zach's story would reach a few more people than I could have ever hoped for.

"Well, I'm not usually the type to hang out at these kinds of things. I know, weird for a music guy. But the spirit of this thing is just amazing. I think I'll stick around for a while and listen to the bands."

"Zach's on after this next band. He'll be playing 'Clouds.'"

He definitely wanted to hear Zach, so he traveled off into the crowd to take in the energy that was onstage. It was finally time for Zach and Sammy. The two of them looked at home up on the stage; it was obvious they loved what they were doing and belonged there. They played "Blueberries" and "Star Hopping." The crowd loved it and let them know with cheers of approval. I looked across the room to see Karl, a seasoned music veteran, standing up near the stage with his three boys, who were up way past their bedtimes, with the same look of awe on all of their faces. And there were Ron, Adam, and Scott all cheering on this boy they had just met, but whose spirit had affected them in a profound way.

They came to the end of the set, and Sammy stepped up to the microphone.

"I'm guessing that most of you know a song called 'Clouds.'" The crowd cheered, and Sammy turned to Zach, who stood waiting with his guitar slung over his shoulder. "Well, he wrote it, and he sings it, and he's going to do it right now." She reached over and slapped Zach on the arm as she stepped away from the microphone.

Zach adjusted his capo on the guitar and strummed. Everyone who hadn't been on the dance floor squeezed forward until the place was a sea of faces turned toward the stage. Everyone stood still and silent as Zach played. It was like a spirit of peace rolled out of him and over the crowd. I looked back from where I stood up close to the stage and watched their faces as they listened to the song. It was like they were hearing a story, and Zach was the storyteller.

After the last note was sung, the cheers from the crowd were deafening. They had come to celebrate life with a boy who was preparing to die, and he had just sung them his good-bye song. It was a moment that defined what our lives had been the past several months, the joy and sorrow of watching a boy live while dying.

I snuck away for a few minutes after the performance. I needed a little time to let my emotions settle before I went back out to field the congratulations from the crowd. These moments of joy were so tightly woven with the sadness of the long good-bye, and sometimes the potent emotions needed to wrestle it out in private.

The crowd began to dissipate, and the cleanup began. I was out on the dance floor letting loose with a couple of friends and a group of teenagers after a long night when Dan Seeman walked in. I was mortified. The general manager of one of the largest radio stations in the Twin Cities had just witnessed me doing my best Zumba dance moves out on the floor. I sheepishly walked over to where he stood, pushing my sweaty bangs off my forehead.

"What an amazing party," he greeted me, the slight gap between his two front teeth exposed by his wide smile.

"You should have seen it a half hour ago." I laughed as I extended my hand. "The place was packed wall-to-wall!"

"Ah! I know! I wish we could have been here earlier, but I had a work party that we had to attend," he said, regret on his face as he turned to the pretty blond woman with an open, friendly face next to him. "Laura, this is my wife, Cyndy."

"Hi, Cyndy, so nice to meet you. Thank you so much for making your way all the way out here, especially with the crazy weather we had today." I was impressed they had driven an hour out of their way just to come for a few minutes and show their support for Zach. I called Rob and Zach over.

"Zach." Dan reached a hand out and pulled Zach into a hug. "So good to see you again! Looks like you had an amazing night. I wish we could have been here to watch you perform."

"Yeah, it was pretty amazing. I'm totally blown away by all the people that came out tonight." One of Zach's friends tugged on Zach's arm; he was wanted across the room. "Thanks for coming!" he called over his shoulder as he was led away.

Rob and I chatted for a bit with Dan and Cyndy. We talked about the party and what a grand success it was. We laughed at the energy Zach still seemed to have as he danced out on the floor.

"So, how would you feel about heading to New York City?" Dan inquired. "The folks at BMI have heard about Zach and are interested in signing him as one of their artists."

My jaw dropped. "Are you kidding?" I knew Zach would love it and would jump at the opportunity. "I guess we're headed to New York!"

THE BIG PARTY WAS OVER, ALL THE ANTICIPATION AND EXCITEMENT of the night behind us, but the memories were sweet as we talked about them over the next several days. I'd been so busy planning the party that I hadn't spent much time thinking about Christmas. I was looking forward to spending some quiet time with just our family.

We had decided before the CNN interview that we would keep the weeks around Christmas sacrosanct and block out the outside world. We didn't want anything to intrude on our last holiday with the whole family together. It was a special time, but also bittersweet. It was another "last" on the list, so the cheerfulness was mingled with equal amounts of sadness. It can be a hard and sometimes awkward thing to balance the two.

Zach felt it too. He had asked for recording equipment and a mixing program for his computer. He wanted to be able to record songs at home. But he knew he wouldn't have much time to use it and felt a little guilty asking for something so big. As he opened the gift on Christmas morning, I watched a range of emotions play out on his face. He exuded a sense of childlike joy as he pulled out the pieces of equipment, but at the same there was a deep sadness in his eyes.

We all felt the same thing. Each happy moment was tainted with the sadness of wondering what it would be like next year, after Zach was gone.

As we did our best to live in the moment and focus on the joy that was present, Zach's story began to make its way around the globe, and people were listening.

Twenty-Five

··

January 2013

AFTER THE NEW YEAR, MEDIA INTEREST PICKED UP STEAM. WE received calls almost daily with some type of interview request for television, radio, blog, or newspaper.

Most of the Internet coverage was repurposed from the newspaper articles that had already been published, as well as from the CNN and local television stories. All the calls were small intrusions into our normal daily routine, but they required energy and time. Zach and the rest of the family ran low on both.

Every day when Zach got home from school, I would list off the new requests of the day. Eventually, when things got to be too much to handle on my own, the folks at CCRF worked with us to vet the calls. That left me spending my evenings perusing the Internet for the latest media coverage. It was easy to tell which countries had recently seen the story based on the comments that would be posted on the "Clouds" video website. We started to get messages on our

CaringBridge and Facebook sites from people all over the globe who wanted us to know what an impact Zach's song had made in their lives. Brazil, Poland, Czech Republic, Russia, and Japan were a handful of the countries we received comments from.

"I burst into tears having watched this video. It's so grossly unfair!!! I'm at a loss for words . . . Poland's with you, Zach."

"People from Czech Republic are with you too. I will pray for you every day—I promise. Remember that hope dies last!"

"Zach, I am from Russia and I have listened to your song . . . It is stunning, magnificent . . . We can only admire your soul's strengths. I am sure your song enforced all listeners to feel what you feel and to understand the situation."

I was touched by the wide range of people who were affected by the song. Children, teens, men, and women all responded in very similar ways. They were moved by a sad song that somehow inspired hope. Even the critics noted that the song's catchy melody drew you in to hear an incredibly sad yet hopeful message. But there were, indeed, critics.

The first negative message we received after "Clouds" was posted on YouTube was from an anonymous writer (the most hurtful comments always come anonymously) on our CaringBridge site. It read something like: "Zach, you're just another kid with cancer. You're not that big of a deal and you don't deserve all the attention you are getting. But I like your song.—anonymous"

It made me laugh. For a moment I thought how funny it would be if Grace had been the one who had posted it. She'd always had a way of admiring Zach but making sure he kept things in perspective. I thought it was funny, too, that despite the obvious jealousy, Mr. or Ms. Anonymous couldn't help but admit that the song was good.

Cover versions of the song began to pop up on the Internet as well. Days before Christmas, the sixth-grade class from a local grade school posted a video of themselves singing "Clouds" as a tribute to all those who lost their lives at Sandy Hook Elementary in Connecticut.

"My students love this song! We sang it as a tribute to the kids in CT. We have been tracking the view numbers for math class and praying it will hit a million by tonight. Look for my students to sing it for their 6th grade graduation in Minnesota. The students also get excited reading comments from around the world. Keep spreading the LOVE!"

A few days later, a group of girls from the same class stood on a street corner in downtown Stillwater, a beautiful river town just a few miles from where we live, and caroled to raise money for Zach's fund. They raised over five hundred dollars. The girls came to our home the next day and presented Zach with the money.

I loved watching Zach at times like those; it was where he really shined. He was genuinely grateful for what the girls had done and was gracious about letting them know just how much he appreciated their efforts.

"Whoa! You guys didn't have to do this, but you did and that's awesome," he said as he gave each one of the girls a hug. The girls were obviously thrilled. He had a way of lighting up a room with his presence but always made the others who were there feel like all attention was on them. "I mean it, you guys. This is really awesome."

Tributes began popping up from around the world too. A group of about seventy ninth graders from Japan who studied English sang "Clouds" for Zach and our family as a year-end project. Another group of high schoolers from Poland did a tribute where several of the kids spoke about how Zach's story and song inspired them.

They ended the video by releasing mini hot air balloons into the night sky.

Boxes and large envelopes filled with cards, letters, and special presents from children across the country started showing up on our front step. One group even sent a Bible with all the children's favorite verses highlighted. Every day I would bring down the letters and packages to Zach as he was resting after school. There were grocery bags full of them around his nest on the couch, and I often found him sorting through them.

The media attention to the story and the YouTube tributes were humbling and amazing, but the personal responses and messages that we received were what really blew me away. I remember one message from a veteran who suffered from post-traumatic stress disorder. He had struggled with the disorder and depression for a number of years and was ready to give up. He woke up one morning in early January and decided it was the day he would commit suicide. Then he saw the "Clouds" video. Somehow the message and spirit of the song penetrated his soul, and he realized his life was worth something. This was not the only message received from people who were considering killing themselves but heard the song and decided not to. They credited Zach with saving their lives.

We received hundreds if not thousands of messages like these from people who struggled with depression. The song really seemed to resonate with people who were in a dark place and weren't sure where to find hope.

There was another message from a soldier who had been physically and emotionally injured in battle. He hadn't left his house in years, but after hearing Zach's song and story, he decided enough was enough! He would go back out into the world again.

Another soldier, not much older than Zach, had recently returned from a difficult tour of combat. The day he saw the "Clouds" video was the first time in several months that he smiled. He thanked Zach for living every day with a positive attitude and ended his message with, "Zach, you saved me."

God's plan unfolded before our eyes. He was using a midwestern boy with a simple song to deliver hope to damaged souls and soothe the brokenhearted.

Justin Baldoni was one of those who received that message.

Justin, twenty-nine, was the producer of a series called *My Last Days* that ran on YouTube's SoulPancake channel. The series followed people who were terminally ill and focused on what it means to "live while dying." Justin wanted to inspire people with a message of hope and share with the world how the dying process can be a beautiful, rather than a fearsome, thing.

He had traveled with his girlfriend, Emily, from their home in Los Angeles to Milan, Italy, to meet her family when he fell quite ill and needed to stay back while the rest of the group went out to enjoy the city. He was frustrated. Of all the times to get sick, why did it have to be now?

"It was there, as I lay on the couch, bored, annoyed, and feeling sorry for myself, when God granted me one of the greatest opportunities of my life," Justin wrote to me. He picked up his phone and randomly tapped the News tab on the screen. The headline read: "Dying Teen Writes Farewell Song" above a picture of Zach. "There he was: Zach. With those deep yet playful eyes and that incredible, captivating smile.

"Suddenly everything made sense, and I felt an eerie sense of calm. I clicked on the link, read the story, and watched the YouTube video. That was it. I knew right then and there why this had all happened. It was like I had been guided to fly around the world, get sick, and slow down just for this moment."

After reading Zach's story, Justin knew instantly that Zach should be his next subject for the series. He immediately began searching for a way to reach us.

First Justin turned to Facebook, but Zach had too many friend requests and Justin's didn't get through. Next Justin tried tweeting Zach. But Zach had received so many tweets that it was buried. Finally, Justin saw a tweet Zach posted, "A perfect Friday watching *The Office*." He immediately got in touch with his friend and partner Rainn Wilson (Dwight Schrute) to tweet Zach. Surely Zach would notice a tweet from the actor who played a character on his favorite television show!

In the end, it was actually Kris from CCRF who saw Rainn's tweet, and then Justin's message. She e-mailed me their messages and the links to the SoulPancake videos about other people who had been featured in the series. Rob and I watched all the *My Last Days* episodes and found them to be beautifully done pieces. They articulated so well how we felt about the way Zach had chosen to live out his last days. Each episode was a message of hope meant to inspire, not just another sad story in a world full of sad stories.

We knew that our family was a good fit for the project. We would be able to tell a piece of our story to a world that needed to see how hope could be found in suffering. But if I'm being really honest, my main motivation was to have a beautiful video of Zach that we could find comfort in when he was gone.

The rest of the family needed to be onboard as well, and I wasn't sure how they would feel. The media attention brought a new stress into the house that was starting to tax us emotionally. Practically speaking, the media had not intruded all that much on Alli's, Sam's, or Grace's lives. They had only been present for a few interviews. But the exposure made them feel exploited, and they thought it was an unnecessary distraction from what our family really needed: time together.

After everyone had a chance to see all the *My Last Days* videos, we met in the living room one evening after dinner to discuss the pros and cons.

"I like what I've seen. The videos are certainly well done. But is it right for our family?" Sam asked, starting the discussion. "All the media attention that's come from the song already . . . isn't that enough?"

"And do we really want a house full of people for a week?" Alli questioned. "Our lives are stressful enough without that intrusion."

"I don't think having people around will be that big of a deal," Grace said. "I think it could be kind of fun."

"I guess I just want to make sure we stay focused on why we decided to do this thing in the first place," Sam picked up. "Does it stay within the parameters of our mission, to raise awareness about osteosarcoma, and will it help raise money for the fund?"

Zach remained silent on the topic as he sat on the couch. Amy was over, and he really just wanted to get back downstairs to hang out with her. He also knew it was a decision that would have to be made as a whole family. He would accept whatever conclusion we came to.

"Okay. Well, let's talk it through," I started in with caution. I didn't want my own agenda to steer the conversation, but I really thought we were called to do this.

"Zach, do you want to do this?" Rob asked.

"Yeah. I think it would be cool. But I know it's not all about me, it's not even really about us. But we have to decide as a family," he responded from the end of the couch where he was tucked in the corner with Daisy curled up next to him.

"I can say from my conversations with Justin that he's a genuine guy," I said. "He seems to have a higher mission than just making money or a name for himself. He truly wants to change the world with his work, and he thinks our story can help do that. So, Alli, I understand your concern about his motives, but I think his work speaks for itself."

Alli looked skeptical, but she was willing to listen.

"I know it will be tough having a crew here for so many days. And it will be emotional. Justin made it clear that if you don't want to be interviewed, you don't have to be. You can participate as much or as little as you like," I explained. I knew Alli was under tremendous stress. She was in her last semester at school and was working two internships, not to mention planning a wedding. "But I think it could be an experience that draws us together as a family if we let it."

Sam sat on the hearth, an elbow resting on his knee and his chin in his hand. "But will this Justin guy help us with our mission?"

"The link for the fund will be placed in the video so people can donate," Rob said. "And the story will lead people to download 'Clouds.' So, yes. The documentary will help us with our mission."

"Okay," Sam said, "then let's do it."

I called Justin and told him to pack a warm jacket and head to Minnesota.

Twenty-Six

. . . .

AFTER PLAYING AT THE PARTY, ZACH GOT THE ITCH TO PLAY IN FRONT of more live audiences. One night when Sammy was over, they came to me as I was relaxing by the fire in the living room.

Sammy knelt at my feet and looked up at me, her eyes fixed on mine. I knew I was in trouble. Zach stood off to the side, happy to let Sammy dive in with her powers of persuasion.

"So," Sammy started in, "Zach and I were thinking . . ." She paused for effect without breaking her stare.

"Okay," I said with caution, "what's on your mind?"

"We were thinking it would be fun and an amazing life experience"—another pause—"to take a road trip to Duluth and see if we can get some gigs."

I about choked. Duluth is the get-out-of-town-for-a-couple-days place to go in the late spring, summer, or early fall for many Twin Citians. But January in Minnesota is brutal. And this particular January had even the hardiest of Minnesotans crying uncle. We'd had one snowstorm after the other, and the temperatures were bone chilling. And that was just in the Twin Cities. Duluth was a hundred sixty miles north of us.

"A couple concerns," I said. "Where would you sleep once you got up there, assuming you even make it up there, and how are you planning to get gigs?"

"Well, we're very good drivers, Laura. You shouldn't worry about that," Sammy said with a touch of sarcasm. "And we'll get gigs by just walking into coffee shops and asking if we can play."

Zach didn't say a word. He just stood and watched with a look of hopeful amusement on his face.

"What about the sleeping part? You guys are minors, you can't rent a hotel room."

This time Sammy looked to Zach for help.

"We'll just sleep in the car," he jumped in, trying to save the plan that was quickly falling apart.

"Sorry, guys. The answer is no. Nice pitch, though, Sammy. That stare almost brought me down." I hardly ever said no to Zach, but this was a no-brainer. Zach had been involved in three minor accidents and ended up in a ditch twice in the last few months. To make matters worse, Zach had confided in me that Sammy's driving was downright terrifying. There was no way I was going to let him drive the icy roads up to Duluth. We had worked too hard to keep him alive these last three years.

Zach and Sammy left the room dejected, their dreams dashed. Daisy hopped off the back of the couch and followed them out. She didn't like my decision either. As the kids made their way back down the stairs to the family room, I heard Zach say, "Maybe we could play somewhere around here."

ATTENDING A CONCERT AT FIRST AVENUE IN MINNEAPOLIS IS A RITE of passage for pretty much anyone who grows up in the Twin Cities. The Varsity Theater in Minneapolis is another. Both venues have hosted some of the most celebrated musicians in the country, and for most local musicians, performing at either one could be considered the zenith of their careers.

A couple of the local radio stations had been playing "Clouds" on a regular rotation. The Current, a local public radio station that showcases local talent, was one of them. They were hosting a huge, multi-night, sold-out event at First Avenue that featured several local artists and bands. A band named 4onthefloor was the headliner for the event, and the lead singer, Gabriel Douglass, had gotten in touch with Scott Herold to see if Zach would be interested in playing "Clouds" with him on the main stage.

Zach was ecstatic! Just seeing a concert at First Avenue was on his bucket list. Playing on the main stage was something he didn't dare to even dream about.

I was terrified.

First Avenue, the stage made famous by Prince, was a place for seasoned artists. It wasn't a place for rookies. And now here we were, Zach, Amy, and I, along with our attorney (and now fast friend), Adam, in the green room of this legendary nightclub, waiting for my seventeen-year-old son to get up in front of twelve hundred people who expected something good. It's one thing to perform for people who already love and support you. It's quite another to perform for people who don't know you.

It was time for Zach to go onstage. I handed his guitar to a stagehand as Zach worked his way up the metal stairs with his crutches, doing his best to avoid the bundled cords that ran everywhere. He got to the top of the stairs, and the stagehand traded his guitar for the crutches as Gabriel gave a brief introduction, then stepped back from the microphone and welcomed Zach to the stage.

Once Zach was safely at the microphone, I turned my eyes to the crowd. From my position at the side stage I could see practically the whole venue. The crowd was made up of mostly middle-aged people, not many under the age of thirty-five, so different from the teenagers and families with young children who had made up the audience at the high school events and parties. All twelve hundred faces were aglow with stage light as they waited to see what this seventeen-year-old boy, too young to even get into the place as a patron, was all about.

Some people looked confused. Who was this kid taking up stage time? They were here to see 4onthefloor, not some kid they'd never heard of. I could feel my breath shorten and my gut tighten as my gaze landed on one face after the other that wore the same expression. *Oh, I hope Zach doesn't see those faces*, I thought. But then I began to see other faces that held looks of anticipation. They had obviously heard "Clouds" and knew a little about what Zach had been through. I started to breathe more freely when a couple of people yelled out their support.

"Go, Zach!"

"Yea, Zach!"

"We love you, Zach." Alli's voice came down from the balcony where she, Rob, and Sam sat.

There was a smattering of applause, then the room went silent as Zach began to play. I turned my attention to my boy, up there on the stage. He had always been so willing to put himself out there to try something new, whether it was a big risk or a small one. Unlike me, he was willing to make himself vulnerable and to make himself accessible to those around him.

Zach wrapped up the song and nodded his head in a brief bow. Then he turned to Gabriel to shake his hand, but Gabriel pulled him into a hug, then grabbed Zach's hand and lifted his arm in a victorious gesture.

"Let's give it up for Zach Sobiech," he yelled into the microphone.

The crowd yelled, clapped, and whistled with enthusiastic appreciation. Zach had done it. He'd played in front of a packed house at First Avenue, and he'd made them happy. He waved to the crowd as he left the stage and handed the guitar to me, where I waited breathlessly on the top step.

Zach grabbed his crutches from where they leaned on the stage rail. A wide, toothy smile spread across his face. He was elated!

"Well! How was it?" I yelled over the music. "Were you nervous when you got up there and saw all those faces looking up at you?"

He made his way to the green room.

"Yeah, at first it was really scary," he said with a chuckle. "But when I got started, all that scariness went away and it was amazing! I could go right back up there and do it all again."

At the end of the night when the various artists from the evening were invited to come back up onstage, Zach answered the call. I watched from the side stage as he walked out to mid-stage and stood victoriously with his crutches overhead as the crowd cheered them all on.

It was a dream come true. I was sure nothing could top it. And it was certainly better than some little coffeehouse way up in Duluth. But Zach was ready for more, and this time he wanted to take his band with him.

SCOTT HEROLD FROM ROCK THE CAUSE WAS A FORCE TO BE RECK-
oned with. He was a passionate man who believed that music should
change the world, and he believed that Zach's mission and message
just might be the thing to do it.

"So, I hear Zach and Sammy want to play a live show," Scott said.

"Yeah," I said. "They're thinking about lining up some local
coffeehouse gigs."

Scott nearly fell into hysterics. "You don't have any idea what's
going on, do you?"

"Don't I?" I knew he was more right than I was willing to admit
to myself at that point.

"Do you have any idea what would happen if the local media got
wind of Zach showing up to play guitar at Starbucks?"

"Um . . . guess not."

"It would be a media circus. Chaos! Just tell him to be patient.
I've got an idea. I'll talk to Dan Seeman and Hubbard Broadcasting.
Kris and CCRF too. I'm calling in the varsity string here, Laura. Tell
Zach to keep his guitar tuned up."

Twenty-Seven

January 24–27, 2013

THERE ARE A LOT OF PLACES I'D LIKE TO VISIT AROUND THE GLOBE. New York City was not one of them. Even though my first reaction when Dan mentioned at the party the possibility of taking a trip to NYC was positive, the more I thought about it, the less I wanted to go. Something about walking busy streets with hordes of people made this small-town girl cringe. Zach, however, didn't hesitate. New York was on his bucket list.

Ginny Morris, the chair of Hubbard Broadcasting/KS95, had been in touch with Broadcast Music Inc. (BMI), a music rights management company that represents more than six hundred thousand songwriters, composers, and music publishers (including Ed Sheeran, Adele, Maroon 5, and Taylor Swift, to name a few). The folks at BMI were so moved and inspired by Zach's story and song they wanted not only to sign him as one of their artists, but also to invite us to come visit their office in NYC to actually sign the papers with a photographer present and give him the whole works. It was treatment most often reserved for bigger, more successful artists. Zach was thrilled, so we were going to New York.

Through the gracious generosity of several entities and people, including Hubbard Broadcasting, CCRF, and Dan Seeman, we were able to take the family (except Alli, who had to stay behind for work) to the Big Apple. The trip was made even more fun when Dan's family; my sister, Lee; my brother-in-law, Jon; and our attorney, Adam, joined us.

We stayed at a hotel in Times Square and had a fantastic time taking in the sites. We went to the theater, visited the World Trade Center memorial, and took a jaunt up to Central Park. NBC Studios was another stop on the list; Zach picked up a Dwight bobblehead doll, his favorite character from *The Office*.

By far, though, the most memorable part of the trip was visiting BMI. We had an appointment at their office at 7 World Trade Center at eleven thirty in the morning on Friday, January 25. We expected to have a quick meeting to sign some papers and then have a little time for photos afterward. We had no idea what they had in store for us.

We knew wonderful things were about to happen when we stepped off the elevator to the sound of "Clouds" being piped into the lobby. There were at least two big electronic poster boards along the wall opposite from the elevator doors with a picture of Zach that had been taken from the "Clouds" video with a big sign that said "Welcome to BMI, Zach." We were greeted by Silvia Davi, BMI Vice President and Head of Strategic Communications and Marketing; Brook Morrow, Executive Director, Creative Development and Writer/Publisher Relations; and Mike O'Neill, Senior Vice President, Repertoire and

Licensing. It was clear the red carpet had been rolled out for us. This was no handshake, sign the papers, it was nice to meet you, and you're out the door affair. These were top executives taking time out of their busy schedules to make Zach feel like a king.

Mike, a tall, polished man in a sharp-looking suit, led us on a private tour of the offices. "Do you want to see something amazing?" he asked with the enthusiasm of someone who wanted to share a secret treasure.

We all, of course, did, and he led us to a gorgeous office at the end of a long hallway. As we stepped in the door, he turned to his right and waved his arm at the display before him. The whole wall was a huge window that had the most amazing and surreal view of downtown Manhattan. We all stood in awe as we took in the sight. It felt almost like we were looking at a beautiful painting; the color, depth, and contrast of light seemed to go on forever. It gave us a sense of how small we were compared to this big city. But it also gave the unique effect of making us feel like we were a part of it. It was stunning.

I stood next to Zach, and we gazed at the scape in silence.

"This is amazing," he said in awe, without averting his eyes. "This is so perfect."

I felt the same way as I looked over at this humble boy who had fought so many battles and who now stood at the top of the world.

"It truly is," I said.

Next we were brought to a conference room where a royal feast awaited us. Platters of sandwiches, roasted vegetables, cheeses, fruits, and desserts had been laid out for us, and everyone took a seat. We all sat around a huge conference table, a view of the World Trade Center memorial just out the window. All my presupposed, small-town ideas of what New Yorkers would be like were dispelled. We felt like we were having a leisurely lunch with friends rather than with top music industry executives.

When lunch was finished, we were joined by Susan Austin, chairman of BMI. She and Zach signed all the appropriate documents that officially made Zach a BMI artist. After the signing, she presented Zach with a beautiful leather-bound journal for his future songwriting. We finished up with a few photos and a video interview in the lobby in front of a bank of screens that read BMI across them.

We said our good-byes, hugs and handshakes given all around. This group of wonderful people had made the day extraordinary for Zach and our family. But it was the friendships they offered that really warmed my heart. There is something powerfully satisfying about a stereotype that is turned on its head and replaced with a memory of people who came together and made something beautiful happen.

Zach opened the huge, glass door in the ground-floor lobby, stepped out onto the sidewalk, and said, "Well, that was fun."

We all laughed at the glaring understatement. It had been so much more than fun, and it would be a memory I would treasure always.

I NOTICED ZACH WAS SLOWING DOWN. IN NEW YORK HE HAD NEEDED a nap every afternoon. After we returned from the trip, he continued to take naps almost daily when he got home from school. There were many days when he would sleep through dinner and come up later in the evening for a snack, but wouldn't eat a full meal. He just wasn't hungry, he would tell me, when I'd try to get him to eat more.

I also noticed his breathing had become more labored, and he seemed to get winded fairly quickly.

"How's your breathing?" I asked one afternoon as he pulled one of his specialty drinks out of the refrigerator.

"It's fine. Why?" he asked with a frown.

"You seem to be a little out of breath lately. I just want to make sure we don't have another collapsed lung on our hands," I responded. I was more concerned that the tumors had grown so large that they obstructed his breathing, but I didn't want to alarm him by saying so.

"No, I'm fine." He walked out of the kitchen and down to his usual spot on the couch in the family room.

He left his crutches in the living room, something that used to drive me crazy. "Do you have any idea how much it would hurt to break your pelvis?" I would chide him. But now I let him do it without much fuss. He knew what could happen, and he was willing to take the risk. And, to be honest, I liked seeing him without them. It reminded me of the good old days.

February 2013

WHILE WE WERE IN NEW YORK CITY, BACK HOME, SCOTT HEROLD had been hard at work. He'd taken Zach's and Sammy's desire to play more live shows and, along with Dan Seeman and the folks from CCRF, hatched a plan for a huge event at the Varsity Theater in Minneapolis. The event would serve as a fund-raiser for the Zach Sobiech Osteosarcoma Fund as well as a release party for A Firm Handshake's new EP, *Fix Me Up*, a collection of original songs written by Sammy and Zach. Anne and I wanted to make sure that the songs the kids had written were recorded before it was too late, and the team who mobilized to record "Clouds" was passionate about making sure the project happened. Zach and Sammy would have to get back in the studio and record the songs in short order if we were going to have the EP ready in time. The date was set for February 16, three and a half weeks after our return from NYC.

A flurry of frantic activity had taken place over the course of just a few weeks to get the event organized and to line up other local artists who would be willing to lend their talents and make this a night people would remember.

Dan called me one day about a week after we returned from New York. "How do you think Zach would feel about headlining with Vicci Martinez?" he asked.

Vicci was fresh off NBC's *The Voice*, and her top-forty hit "Come Along," produced by CeeLo Green, was building steam. Dan had met her through an earlier event hosted by KS95, and he knew she had a soft heart and would be open to helping out with the event.

"I love her song! And I know Zach would be thrilled to share a stage with her." My surprise at the scope of Dan's vision and the lengths Dan and this team of people would go to for Zach continued to grow. Their dedication to him was astounding; it seemed they were on a mission to make his dreams happen.

Several local bands and artists, including Gabriel Douglas from 4onthefloor (whom Zach had joined on stage at First Avenue), my brother Luke's band, Squares, and local legend Kevin Bowe, along with several other artists, would play at the event as well. There was hardly a soul who was approached that didn't say yes when asked to articipate.

There was just one problem. There was no *Fix Me Up* EP.

So Zach, Sammy, and Reed headed back to Atomic K Records to rk with Karl Demer on laying down tracks for three new songs as well as a rerecording of the song "Fix Me Up." The EP would contain all original work; there would be no covers of other artists' songs as there had been on the *Blueberries* CD.

Karl, despite his studio's financial struggles during a difficult economy, had graciously offered to open his studio and master the tracks for the kids. He'd been changed by his first meeting with Zach and was committed to doing whatever he could to help Zach.

He said, "Something inside me couldn't shake the thought of this boy who wanted to leave songs as a reminder that he will never be far even after he was gone from this world. As if someone just hauled off and slapped me across the face, I realized that all of my worries and fears I had been dwelling on regarding my financial situation suddenly became insignificant in the grand scheme of things. I began to take inventory of all the things in my life that I was grateful for and a sense of peace came over me . . . I felt compelled to do anything I could to make this time in his life a little better. It was a time of spiritual awakening."

Our second visit to Atomic K Records was much more relaxed than the first. At least for Zach and me. We knew what to expect, and we knew that Karl would take great care to make sure things were perfect. For Karl, it was a different story. With the unexpected success of "Clouds," the bar had been set high. He wasn't just creating a memento for the family to keep and treasure after Zach was gone. He was mastering music for a known artist whose music was receiving global attention. And he was working with amateur musicians this time around, no studio band. It was just the kids: Zach on acoustic guitar, Reed on percussion, and Sammy and Zach on vocals. On top of all that, we needed the CD ready to go in two weeks!

The same team that donated their time and talent to make the

Blueberries CD happen came back together to do the same for *Fix Me Up*. They had seen what happened with "Clouds" and had been inspired to do whatever they could to keep the momentum going and help A Firm Handshake tell more of their story. We all knew we were part of something bigger than any one of us could understand.

"Fix Me Up" was the most difficult because of all the tempo changes that needed to be mapped out prior to recording the guitar. But once that was out of the way, things fell into place. Most tracks only required one recording. Karl filled in strings and keyboard when he thought it needed it and brought in a friend and fellow musician to add some bass, then spent a long night and most of the next day mixing the tracks to get the master ready for production. Like "Clouds," the project came together without any hitches. It felt guided.

It was a long and exhausting day of recording, but somehow Karl managed to guide the kids through laying down tracks for the four new songs in just eight hours.

Twenty-Eight

. . . .

"SO, HOW MANY PEOPLE ARE IN THE CREW?" I ASKED JUSTIN ON THE phone the day before his film crew arrived. They would spend the week following our family around, filming our every move. We'd had several camera crews to the house by then, but this would be something entirely different.

"There will be eight of us," he responded.

Eight! All the other crews had been three, tops. I wondered how I would tell Sam and Alli that instead of three strangers in the house, there would be eight. Justin must have picked up on my hesitation and jumped in to explain.

"Since we're going to be spending so much time with your family, we need to have a lot of cameras going at once. We need footage from all different angles so we have plenty of footage to choose from when we are back in LA putting it together."

"Okay. So, does your crew stay here with us? Or how does that work?" I'd seen the other videos, and all of them had scenes of people getting out of bed early in the morning. I was mentally calculating the number of blankets, pillows, and amount of couch space we had in the house. I could blow up the air mattress if . . .

"Oh! No." Justin laughed. "We would *never* do that to you!"

"Oh. Okay, well, this is sounding a little better." I laughed. *Thank God!* I thought. That surely would have put everyone over the edge.

Later that night I had everyone gather in the family room. I sat in my rocking chair, command central. Rob was on the couch to my left, Zach and Grace on the couch to my right, and Sam and Alli on the floor, leaned against the hearth. We'd eaten dinner, and there was some bickering about who should clean up just before I called everyone in to give the update.

"Okay, so here's the deal. There are eight guys coming into town—" I started.

"Seriously!" Alli interjected. "Why do they need eight? I thought you said there would only be three!"

"I was basing that off of the previous crews we've had come," I jumped in defensively. "I'm doing my best to figure everything out as I go."

"So where are they all going to be?" Sam asked. "Are we going to have any privacy? Can I at least use the bathroom by myself?"

"Justin assured me that you guys can participate as much or as little as you want. If you don't want them in your room, just tell them. He's a nice guy and really does care about making this as easy as possible," I explained.

"It's just going to be really weird having all these strangers in our house all week. I'll probably spend a lot of time at the Bowersoxes'," Sam said. Reid Bowersox was Sam's closest friend. I used to joke about how Sam was half Bowersox because he seemed to spend at least half of his growing-up years at their home, eating their food. Now their house would serve as a media fallout shelter.

Alli's jaw was set. She wasn't as easily persuaded and was less than thrilled at losing the quiet of home for a week to a crew from Los Angeles.

"I know you say that Justin is a nice guy, but how do you know, really? What if he has some preconceived idea of what our family is about and only shows what he wants people to see? What if it's some Pollyanna version of our family that isn't real?" She had become jaded as she progressed with her degree in journalism and could see how reality can be manipulated into whatever the journalist wants.

"I don't know, Al. I just know from my conversations with him. I know he's a little over the top, but he seems like a very genuine guy, and based on the videos he's already produced, I trust that he will truthfully portray our family."

Grace and Zach sat silently. They both looked forward to the experience, but wanted to allow their older sister room to air her concerns.

"Alli, I understand where you're coming from," Rob chimed in. "We know the media can take something and turn it into something it's not. But we all decided to take this risk together when we chose a month ago to have them come. So let's just leave it in God's hands and trust that there is a bigger purpose. For some reason, out of millions of people who are dying, Justin decided to follow Zach. Let's just see what happens."

Alli relaxed a little. She and Rob had clashed a lot when she was in high school. But now that she was older, she could see how similar their personalities were, and she could appreciate his advice more freely.

"Fine. But I have a ton of stuff I have to do. The timing of this thing just really sucks. So I'm probably not going to be around much with all the magazine projects I've got going with my internship and at school. Not to mention, I have a wedding I'm trying to plan." She was annoyed, but she would do her best to roll with it.

I WORKED ON MY LAPTOP AT THE KITCHEN TABLE WHILE I WAITED for the crew to arrive. I'd straightened the house up a bit but hadn't bothered with the frantic cleaning I'd done a few months earlier when CNN had been in town. By now we were seasoned and media savvy. And besides, this was supposed to be real life. The desk in the kitchen was never clean, so why would I clean it now?

They pulled in around two o'clock on Monday afternoon. I opened the front door and waved as one by one they exited their rental SUV.

"Laura!" Justin exclaimed as he walked up the sidewalk. He pulled me into a bear hug as he stepped into the house. "It is so nice to finally meet you! I can't wait to meet Zach and the rest of the family. I'm already in love with your amazing family and can't wait to tell your story to the world."

My conversations on the phone with Justin had prepared me for his exuberance and passion for his work. Thanks to Google, I was also prepared for his incredible good looks. He was classic—tall, dark, and handsome.

Each of the crew members introduced themselves as they made their way into the house.

"Thank you so much for letting us come hang out with your family," was the collective greeting delivered with a sort of reverence by each as they stepped through the door and laid their gear down on the floor. The sincere appreciation they expressed gave me the feeling that each had come for his or her own personal reasons and that this project meant more than just a paycheck.

A few minutes after they entered the house and were somewhat settled, Zach pulled into the driveway. He'd had a couple of Skype conversations with Justin, and by the spring in his step as he walked down the sidewalk I could tell he was eager to meet everyone.

"Hey, Zach." Justin met him at the door and extended his hand. "It's so great to finally meet you in person. You have no idea how excited we all are to be here!"

"Justin." Zach pulled him into a hug and slapped his back a few times. "Good to see you. Welcome to Minnesota." Zach had a huge grin on his face. He was in his element as he personally greeted each of the crew members.

"So, can we check out your room?" Fou, one of the camera guys, asked Zach.

"Yeah, sure. Come on down. I haven't cleaned up much. My mom said I should leave it since this is all supposed to be real and everything," I heard Zach say as a couple of the guys followed him down the stairs.

Justin turned to me. "Do you think we could take a quick walk around the block just to talk about some stuff?"

"Sure," I answered. "I'll just grab Daisy. She could use a walk." I put on my coat and clipped the leash to Daisy's collar. I figured he wanted to get an update on how Zach was feeling, emotionally and physically. I'd shared with him the night before that Zach had been feeling down and a little anxious about all the demands on his time and that I was concerned the week would prove to be too much.

"Could I take the tags off her collar?" Justin asked. "The noise will get picked up by the sound equipment."

"Of course," I said as I saw Jordan, the sound guy, pick up one of those huge, fuzzy microphones and Emerson and Kieran grab their cameras. *So, we are jumping right in*, I thought to myself.

As we walked down the street, Jordan held the microphone just above Justin's and my head while Emerson ran backward in the snow and ice, his camera trained on us, and Kieran ran alongside.

"So, how is Zach?" Justin asked.

"It's been a rough couple of days. He's just really started to get physically tired, and I think the pressure of having people expecting so much from him is weighing heavy. He told me the other night that he's looking forward to things settling down a bit. He just seems kind of down lately," I said, trying desperately to ignore the men running with cameras around us.

"We're really hoping to help with that while we're here," Justin said.

How are you going to do that when this is the farthest thing from settling down? I wondered.

"Remember that car we talked about? The Nissan GT-R that Zach loves?" he asked.

Of course I remembered. He mentioned it every time we drove down Highway 94 on our way home from the hospital. A couple of weeks earlier, Justin had asked me if there was anything they could do for Zach that I thought he would go nuts for. "Get him a Nissan GT-R," I told him.

Justin called about a week before they flew into town and told me he'd tried, but there simply wasn't a Nissan GT-R to be found in Minnesota or the surrounding states. He was bummed, and so was I; I knew Zach would have loved it.

"Well," Justin said with a glint in his eye as we continued down the block, snow crunching under our feet, "we brought a little surprise." He pointed up ahead.

There, parked a half block ahead around the corner, was a gorgeous, shiny and new, navy blue Nissan GT-R! My mouth dropped, and I could hardly breathe.

"*You* . . . No . . . Oh . . . my . . . gosh! What did . . . How . . . How did you get it?" I couldn't believe what I was seeing. Zach was going to *love* this!

"The folks at Nissan heard Zach's story, and they had it shipped up from Nashville for him. They even put special snow tires on it and everything. He can drive it all week." He laughed at my excitement and was obviously thrilled he'd pulled off such a huge surprise. Now all the cameras made sense.

"I can't wait for Zach to see it," I said. "He's going to love it. Absolutely. Love. It."

We decided the best way to deliver the car to Zach was to have Rob, who was on his way home from work, drive it into the driveway. The camera crew was stationed in the front room of the house, and I had Zach ready near the window. When I saw Rob pull in, I walked over near Zach.

"So, we have a little, tiny surprise for you," I said.

He gave me an incredulous look and said, "I don't like surprises."

"Oh, I think you're gonna like this one," I said as I pointed out the window.

Grace saw it first and gasped as Zach stood from the couch and looked out the window.

"Holy crap," he exclaimed. "Are you serious?!"

"You get to drive it for a week," I said.

He laughed with excitement at the prospect. Not many days earlier he had told me he would give anything just to sit in one. To have the opportunity to drive one was beyond anything he could have dreamed.

Grace knew he loved that car, and they were in the habit of going out and driving around together, especially when they were both bored and needed to get out of the house, so, "You're driving me places," was the first thing to come out of her mouth. She was just as excited as Zach was.

Rob, Zach, and Grace all got their coats on, ran outside, and jumped in the car. The crew scrambled to get their gear and follow.

It was a good start to a week that would hold more surprises. Not all of them for just Zach.

IT WAS WEDNESDAY MORNING. THE CREW HAD SPENT THE PREVIOUS day following Zach around at school to get video footage and a sense of what his life was like. But this day would be spent doing individual interviews. Rob went to work and the kids went to school, so I would be the first to be interviewed.

By then I'd had enough time with Justin and the crew to know that they genuinely wanted to hear our story. For them, this visit was not just a job, but more of a pilgrimage. Justin told me in one of our first conversations that he had always been fascinated by the wisdom of the dying. He was inspired by their unique joy that came from the clarity they had about what is truly important in life. He wanted to use their wisdom to show the rest of us how to really live.

As the crew transformed our living room into a set, I spent a few minutes alone in my bedroom. I was nervous. I had been interviewed several times by then, but this would be different. This interview would go deeper than any of the others, and it had the potential to change lives. I spent my time sitting quietly on the bed with my head in my hands in prayer.

This is Yours, I prayed. *Whatever is accomplished here, today, is for Your glory. I pray only that You bless it and that You give me the words that need to be said for those who need to hear them.* And with that, I laid my anxiety down at Christ's feet and went down for a life-changing interview.

Downstairs I found Daisy lounging in the interview chair in the middle of the room. She was quite content to sit while the crew arranged lights around the room and even outside on the sidewalk that shined in the window. They had set a camera track up in front of the interview chair, along with two other cameras on stands.

I could feel the anxiety well up inside me again. The chair with all the lights trained on it reminded me of an interrogation room. "Remember, this is Yours," I whispered to God under my breath. "Give me the grace to do it well."

I took my seat; Daisy nestled beside me. And we talked. For the next two hours, these eight men, from five different faith backgrounds (Baha'i, Muslim, agnostic, Judaism, and Catholic), and I spoke about the innermost truths of the human heart.

We spoke of love and peace. We spoke of surrender and gain. And we spoke of life, death, and loss. There was no judgment. No agenda. Just a genuine desire to seek and hear truth. To understand how a person could love so deeply that the only thing to do is to let go. To learn how the purest joy in life can come through the most intense and messy suffering. And to understand that peace through the most violent of storms is the most profound of all miracles.

After the last question was answered and the cameras had been turned off, I felt like I had been on a retreat. These men had come to my home to take something away, but they had also brought something: an opportunity for my family and me to speak of things that we couldn't on our own. Things that had been bottled up just waiting for someone to ask for them to be released. I felt refreshed and at peace.

I looked through my tears and saw eight men looking back at me with their own tear-filled eyes. We all knew that something profound and beautiful had happened and that we had been brought together for a reason. We needed one another.

Twenty-Nine

ZACH CAME HOME FROM SCHOOL NOT LONG AFTER MY INTERVIEW ended. The rest of the family members and a few of Zach's friends would be interviewed after dinner. While the interviews were going on in the living room, the rest of us needed to be extremely quiet and tucked in the family room at the back of the house. By seven o'clock that evening, we were all exhausted. About that time, Alli trudged through the knee-high snow across the backyard and walked in the back door. Sam had called her an hour earlier frantically asking where she was.

"I don't want to do this alone," he said on the phone. He had concerns about the intrusion into our family life and was reluctant to bare his soul to people he had just met. He and Alli are both introverts, and talking about such a personal thing as their dying brother seemed too personal and even exploitive.

Alli told Sam she was on her way and that they would talk about it when she got home. They'd become close through the ordeal, commiserating with each other.

I put a finger to my lips indicating she would need to be quiet as she shut the door and knocked snow off her feet onto the tile floor.

"What's with all the huge lights on the front sidewalk?" she asked, looking a little annoyed. Our yard and house were so lit up it looked like it was midday rather than evening. We were drawing some attention in the neighborhood; cars would slow to a crawl as they drove by.

"I guess that's how they do it," I whispered with a shrug. "How was your day?"

"Busy," she answered brusquely. "There was all sorts of drama with the magazine today, and our deadline is tomorrow. I'm the editor, so it all falls on me if things don't get done. Not to mention I have a huge paper due tomorrow in my American lit class." She looked through the French doors to where the crew was set up in the living room. "Am I going to be able to get to my room soon?" She was exhausted and wanted some peace and some time to Skype with Collin, but her home had been overrun by strangers and turned into a beehive of activity. She was near her breaking point.

"They should be wrapping up in a few minutes, then you can go down to your room. Have you decided if you want to do an interview?" I asked cautiously as she removed her jacket and tossed it on a pile of coats by the flickering fireplace. I didn't want to pressure her, especially at the end of such a hard day. But she was a huge part of Zach's life, and I wanted her to be part of the story we were trying to tell.

"I just don't get why we have to sit down with strangers and pour out our feelings when we don't even do that with each other," she said as she plopped down on the couch next to me. "Why would I want to talk to these people who have no idea what we are really going through, people who have their own agenda? I just feel like instead of turning outward and telling our story to the world, we should be turning inward and focusing on us—on our relationships."

"But, Alli, the rest of us have been here working on this thing together. We have a story to tell as a family. I just don't see this project as something that is distracting our attention from each other; I see it as something that can bring us closer together," I responded.

I knew she was dealing with a lot of stress with school and her internship, but more than that, she was struggling with the conflict of emotions she felt when she thought about her upcoming wedding. Her wedding and Zach's death were two dots on the horizon; one would be a time of joy, the other a time of utter sadness. Somehow, she had to walk the road to both points without breaking. It sometimes turned into a nasty cycle of joyful anticipation followed by the intense guilt of knowing what Zach would have to go through between now and then.

She craved our old lives, how it used to be before cancer and cameras, when a big event like a wedding would have had our undivided attention. She longed for those days when it was just the six of us around the dinner table each night sharing a meal and the day's adventures with one another. She had given up an opportunity to study in Rome for a semester so that she could stay home with her family and dying brother, but now he seemed more interested in hanging out with strangers than his own family. She simply could not see how any of this media stuff would benefit the family.

"Sam isn't so sure he wants to do this either. He called me a little bit ago wondering when I'd be home. So I'm not the only one who isn't thrilled about this," she said. "And it's not like I hate the crew or anything. I've had a chance to talk with them, and they seem pretty cool. I just want to be focusing on other things right now, and

I don't get what our 'message' is, Mom. I mean, really, we haven't been through the worst of it yet. How do we really know what our message will be?"

I empathized with her desire to focus on family life. The week wasn't even half over, and I was exhausted and wanted nothing more than to have a quiet house with just my family. But it seemed obvious to me that God had something big planned. That He was using Zach and our family for some purpose that I wasn't entirely sure of yet. Alli wasn't convinced and saw the intrusion as wasted time. As we sat in the room together at odds with each other, I decided the best thing to do was to step back and let God do His thing.

It's Yours, I prayed. *If You want her, You work it out with her.*

Alli and Sam were a huge part of Zach's life, and I desperately wanted them to be part of the project. But I wasn't driving this thing. It wasn't in my hands.

"Sam is in his room. After they wrap up Grace's interview, why don't you go up there and talk about what you want to do? Neither one of you has to do the interview; it's completely up to you."

Alli was pulling her computer out of her bag to start working on her lit paper when Grace busted through the door.

"I totally nailed that interview," she exclaimed with the excitement of a girl who had just conquered a hidden fear. "I had every single one of those guys crying! They were all in tears!"

She stood before me with a hand on her hip, still in her basketball uniform with her long blond hair pulled back into a ponytail. Her face beamed with pride, her big green eyes shining and a huge grin on her face. I had been nervous about sending her down for the interview. Grace wasn't much of a talker when it came to her emotions. Depending on her mood, she could get a little edgy when people asked personal questions. And these would be the ultimate personal questions. But she'd obviously decided this was her deal, and it was on her terms. She was tough enough to let people in, and I was so proud of her.

Justin joined us in the family room. "Oh my gosh. Grace was awesome!" I could see he'd been crying.

"I heard." I chuckled as I looked to where Grace stood with a smile still shining on her face. "Who do you want next?"

"I think we'll do Sammy and Mitch next, then we'll do Sam and Alli, if they're up for it."

"I'll talk to Sam about it," Alli said as she got up and walked into the kitchen.

I went up to Sam's room and knocked on the door.

"Sam, you and Alli are up in about an hour if you want to do the interview," I called through the closed door. He opened the door and stepped into the hallway.

"Is Alli home?" he asked.

"Yeah, she's grabbing a bite to eat."

He came down to the kitchen where Alli was seated at the counter. The crew was scurrying between the living room and family room on the lower level as they moved the set and lights.

"Are you going to do it?" Sam asked Alli.

"I guess so. I'm not sure what I'm going to say, but since we're doing this thing, I suppose I should be part of it."

"Yeah, I've thought about it too. I guess I'll do it. To me, it's not so much about the crew and what they want. I'm doing it for Zach, and I think that's what we should focus on," Sam responded. He had a hard time watching his brother battle cancer, and his way of dealing with it was to avoid thinking about it. This interview would be a huge sacrifice for him. He was stepping forward to lay himself open and raw.

Justin walked into the room. "So, what are you guys thinking? Do you want to do the interview?"

"Sam?" Alli turned to him.

"Yeah. We'll do it."

"If it would be easier for you two, we can interview you together."

Sam and Alli looked at each other and nodded in agreement. They would do it together.

"I'm going to be totally honest, no matter what," Alli said to me as she headed down the stairs to her bedroom. "It's our story."

"The more honest you are, the better. People need to hear it," I replied. She was right. People needed to hear it like it was.

It was close to nine o'clock when Sammy and Mitch wrapped up their interviews. Alli and Sam took their places on the couch. Both were fighting their own internal battles, neither one wanting to be there. I stood at the top of the stairs and watched as they got settled and listened as the crew offered cordial banter to put them at ease. As the door closed, I offered up a prayer.

Lord, this is Yours. Do with it what You like, but please bring our family together. We need to be together.

About an hour later, Alli and Sam came back upstairs.

"How did it go?" I asked cautiously.

"It went well," Sam said. He was upbeat. "It actually went better than I thought it would." He pursed his lips thoughtfully and nodded his head. "Yeah. It was good." He bounded up the steps to his bedroom and shut the door.

I turned to Alli. "Well? Was it horrible?"

"No, it wasn't horrible," she said. "They asked some leading questions, and a couple that I thought were inappropriate, but it wasn't horrible." She picked up her backpack from the family room floor. "I thought I was going to have to do most of the talking, but Sam really surprised me. He poured his heart out. It's the most I've seen him cry since this whole thing started." I could see she'd been crying too. Her tone had softened, and she seemed more thoughtful. "I'm glad we got to do the interview together; it kind of opened some stuff up for us." She turned to go downstairs to her bedroom. "I've got to work on some stuff, and I want to Skype Collin before I go to bed."

I was relieved and grateful that Sam's and Alli's anxieties over the project had lessened.

Justin pulled me into Zach's bedroom. He had his cell phone in his hand and was pulling something up.

"I have to show you what we've been working on," he said.

Then he handed me the phone and tapped Play. It was a video of various celebrities lip-syncing to "Clouds." There were musicians I knew Zach loved, and actors and actresses from shows that Zach loved watching. It was incredible to think that all these people took the time to do this for Zach, but equally incredible that Zach's song had reached them.

"We would really love to have Zach's close friends and family members in the video as well," Justin said. "I just think that would mean the world to him."

"Really? You want each of us to video ourselves singing 'Clouds'?" I imagined how that might go with the kids and Rob. I would have to do some convincing, and it wasn't something I was thrilled about doing either. It had been a really long day, and now we would have to sneak around the house and video ourselves singing.

"Okay," I relented. "I'll get everyone together, and we'll do it."

I went down to Alli's room and tapped on the door. "Hey, Al? I have to ask you for one more thing tonight."

She opened the door. "What?" Collin's face was on the screen of her computer that lay on her bed.

"Hey, Collin." I waved as I stepped into the room. He waved back.

"Justin wants us to video ourselves singing 'Clouds.' It's a surprise for Zach."

"Yeah. I can do that. Where should we go so Zach doesn't see us?"

I was relieved by her willingness to participate. Things were so much easier when Alli was on board; she had a way of rallying the kids together when she wanted to get things done. She said good-bye to Collin and shut the computer screen down, then we got everyone together in our master bedroom. I explained the video that Justin was putting together as a surprise for Zach and told the rest of the family what he wanted us to do. I was surprised at how little cajoling it took to convince them all to participate.

"I suppose Dad and I can be the first to do it," I whined.

"I'll take the video." Alli took my iPod off the dresser and knelt at the foot of the bed. Rob and I took our places.

"Somebody should get Daisy. She should be in the video," Grace said.

"I haven't seen her in a while. She's probably downstairs in the interview chair." Sam chuckled. Daisy had managed to make her way into a lot of footage.

"Yeah, she's probably down there right now spilling all the deep, dark family secrets," Alli said, laughing.

"Okay, let's do this." Alli positioned herself at the end of the bed. I had my computer with the song ready to play. "On three. One, two, three . . ."

Rob and I started to sing the song. It was horrible. Rob forgot the words, and I kept laughing. After several false starts, we finally sang through the entire song. Everyone piled on the bed and watched what we had recorded.

Rob and I looked terrible! All five of us broke into peals of laughter at the sight.

"Hey, guys, we need to keep it down," Rob said. "We don't want Zach to find us." Zach was hanging out with Sammy and Mitch and the crew in the family room downstairs.

"Rob! You look like you're drunk! Next time try sitting up a little," I scolded. "And I look like a ninny . . . blech. Redo!" I handed the iPod back to Alli.

After several more takes, we finally got something we thought would work. By then we were all a little punchy and weren't taking things too seriously. Alli and Sam were up next. It was a minor miracle we got through their session at all. Sam kept breaking out into goofy hand gestures while Alli fought to keep a straight face. Grace nailed hers on the first run. Get in, get out was more her style. She wasn't interested in shenanigans.

As I uploaded the footage and sent it to the editor in Los Angeles, I realized what an answer to prayer this little project had been. We had been so polarized lately and hadn't come together like that and just laughed in such a long time. It was a relief to know that we still knew how.

The next day before the house filled up with people, I took Zach aside. I knew he had sensed some of the tension, though we'd tried to shield him from it.

"If Alli seems edgy it's because she is under tons of stress and having a hard time with all the chaos and cameras," I explained. "She's better after last night's interview, but it's still tough. She misses you."

"Yeah, I noticed," Zach responded. "I get it. It's not like we've had a whole lot of time to relax and get away from everything."

Zach had been going constantly. That morning Amy had surprised him with a trip to the Viking's stadium where she had a picnic ready for him on the fifty-yard line to replace the one they missed when his lung collapsed the previous summer. When they got home, a camera crew from a local station was waiting for them in the kitchen; they wanted to do a story about the "Hollywood" crew that was doing a documentary on Zach. So he understood the chaos, and he understood feeling disconnected from the family.

Later in the evening the crew came back, and the house began to fill up with people. Sammy, Mitch, and Amy had come to hang out for a while, and they were all in the kitchen when Alli walked in the door after a long day at class. She hung up her coat and set her backpack on the chair by the front door, then kicked off her boots and went to the kitchen to get something to eat. Her class had run late and she missed dinner.

Zach had just reached up and pulled a mug from the cupboard when Alli stepped up to the counter. While the cameras were rolling, Zach pulled Alli into a hug.

Alli described the moment in her blog series, *Married in the Mourning, Sailing with the Knight*:

But here, this hug. This is what made me let it all go: the anger, the self-pitying, and my misconceptions about the filmmakers. If you watch the three seconds of this clip, you'll see me rolling my eyes. I was annoyed, I felt like Zach was trying to create some sort of fakey scene to show how "loving" our family was. But here's the kicker: this hug was the most genuine hug he had ever given me. I could tell he knew I was having a hard time with the documentary, the cameras, the cancer. He knew, quite simply, that I just needed a great, big, brotherly hug.

At this moment, here in this picture, I had a pretty intense revelation: that this wasn't about me, this wasn't even about our family, it was about my brother's message, and darn it he deserved to tell it to the world. I wasn't even sure exactly what the message was at the time, none of us were sure. But I discovered that despite death, there is love. That even if your life is totally derailed, there are moments, like this hug, that bring you back. You just have to look for them. And when you find those moments, they change you and your perceptions.

Cancer causes a lot of things. For me, it amplified my personal flaws and made me deal with them head-on. Whenever I see this clip, I get a little embarrassed because I think, "If only they knew what I was thinking before this . . ." In all honesty, I am still dealing with a little anger, a bit of selfishness, and a tad of resentment because of Zach's death, but I've figured out a lot. And if I had to reduce what Zach did for me in one moment, summed up in one photo, this would be it. He helped me let go.

Things changed after that. Alli was freed to see the good that could come from Zach's message of hope being shared with the world. It didn't mean that she always agreed with the methods, but it allowed her to honor what Zach was trying to do.

Our week with the crew from *My Last Days* was a lot of things. It was emotional, agonizing, and exhausting. It was fun, exhilarating, and enlightening. But most of all, it was a week of healing. It was a time of scraping away the misunderstanding and hurt and starting out new, like an infected wound that had been cleaned and now could heal properly. We were able to look into an uncertain future with less fear because we were stronger together, and would face it together.

As we said our long good-bye to the crew, sad to see them go, it was clear that they would walk away changed as well. Each of them expressed their deepest gratitude to our family for what we had given them. They had seen a family that was real, with real people who struggled with some hard stuff. But who also, through it all, chose to have hope in the midst of suffering. Who didn't give up on life because life was hard, but sought to understand and looked for meaning in all the little crevices. And a family who learned to trust that God's hand was guiding it all.

They also saw a boy who had every reason to despair, yet chose instead to hope and love. A boy who could have chosen to indulge but chose to honor instead. And a boy who understood that a simple smile given to a stranger could change the world. A boy who taught them they didn't have to find out they were dying to start living.

Thirty

. . . .

February 10, 2013

IT WAS SUNDAY NIGHT. ZACH FOUND ME IN THE FAMILY ROOM KNIT-
ting a pair of socks with my iPod earbuds in my ears. I was listening to
Zach and Sammy's new *Fix Me Up* EP that Karl had mastered and sent
over a few days earlier. Sammy and Reed had come over earlier in the
day to practice for the big release party/Zach Sobiech Osteosarcoma
Fund benefit that was scheduled the following Saturday.

It was two days after Justin and the crew left. We already missed
them; they had truly become friends. But we were happy to have the
peace and quiet of home life back. I'd spent the previous day putting
the house in order. We'd had a house full of family and friends the
last night the crew was in town. Partly so everyone could meet them
and partly to surprise Zach with the big celebrity tribute video that
featured several musicians and actors: Jason Mraz, Bryan Cranston,
Passenger, the Lumineers, Jenna Elfman, Rainn Wilson, and several
others. It had been an incredible night full of laughter and camaraderie.

"Mom." He sat down on the couch next to me. "I think I'm done with school."

He was dressed in his favorite skinny jeans that were too short, wool socks, and a plaid shirt. Daisy hopped up on the couch and crawled into his lap. He stroked her head, and she closed her eyes and nuzzled in.

"Any particular reason? Is everything okay?"

"I just don't see the point anymore. It's become more of a hassle than a constructive way to use my time. I'm just ready to be done."

"Getting tired?"

"Yeah. I'm just ready to settle down. The media stuff is great and everything, but I think I need to step back and focus on the family and my friends. I'm tired of being pulled in so many different directions."

He had obviously given it a lot of thought and was certain of the decision.

"What about the Varsity event? You don't have to play that night if it seems like too much. There isn't a soul on the face of the earth who wouldn't understand."

He cocked an eyebrow and looked at me with a mischievous grin.

"Well, Mom. Let's not get crazy," he chided. "There's no way I'd miss that."

February 16, 2013

THE VARSITY THEATER, MINNEAPOLIS, MINNESOTA

It was two o'clock and freezing cold. Zach and Sammy stood on the sidewalk under the iconic Varsity Theater marquee, which read:

Up, Up, Up
A concert for Zach
with Vicci Martinez

"Now that's cool," Zach said as he adjusted his tie. He looked sharp in a black shirt and gray vest. The colors accentuated how pale he was, but it wasn't hard to miss the excitement in his eyes. "Any last words before we go inside?"

"Just three," Sammy said.

Zach nodded.

"Don't screw up," they said in unison.

They stepped inside and looked around. The Varsity was a big, empty room with huge, dusty chandeliers that hung from the ceiling. A second-floor balcony surrounded the main floor, a blue-lit stage at the front of the space. The place was abuzz with activity as sound techs and members of the other participating bands hustled around to get ready for sound checks. Rock the Cause employees manned a merchandise table filled with A Firm Handshake CDs and T-shirts.

As I watched the goings-on, Vicci Martinez came up beside me. I introduced myself to her and thanked her for coming. "No, this is cool," she said. "And probably the most important show of my career."

Zach surveyed the room. "Exactly how many people are coming to this thing?" He looked a little surprised by the size, maybe even a little nervous. Sammy did too.

"Well, the room holds over twelve hundred and the show sold out in seventy-two hours," Scott said. He'd seen us enter the room and made his way over to us. He had a clipboard in his hand and a spreadsheet of all the bands and their sound check times.

"Sold out?" Zach asked.

"You're a hot ticket," Scott said. "KS95 has been advertising the event for weeks. Everyone wants to help you celebrate the release of your EP and raise money for the fund. Your sound check starts in five minutes. You kids ready?"

Zach grinned. "Let's do this."

Over the next few hours, all the bands took their turns with sound checks. Some of the bands were long established in the Twin Cities market. Others were up-and-coming high school bands, like the Swedish Revival. Everyone was excited.

By six o'clock, a line had formed out on the sidewalk and around the block. Hundreds of people stood huddled against the cold— hearty Minnesotans having chosen to leave their jackets in their cars. They jumped up and down and pounded on the doors until Scott Herold gave the okay for them to be opened. The people flooded into the warm room. I stood on the steps that led to the balcony where we had a semiprivate section for our family and those who had been involved with the production of the EP and "Clouds." Given the size of our family and friends and the number of people who had been part of the production, the balcony was already packed with people chattering with excited anticipation.

I watched as throngs of people handed over their tickets and entered the room. There were familiar faces; at least seventy of Zach's and Sammy's friends and classmates came through the doors. Friends I hadn't seen in ages, some since high school, waved as they came in from the cold. Nurses and doctors who had treated Zach had also braved the cold to support him. I was most touched to see Lance's mom, Laurie, come in. It had only been four months since Lance's death, and I was encouraged to see her looking well. I left my perch to worm my way through the crowd and give her a hug.

There were many unfamiliar faces as well. I felt like a celebrity as I worked my way through the crowded space.

"Is that Zach's mom?" I would hear people yelling into each other's ears as the din in the room grew louder. A few of them stopped me to tell me how much they loved Zach's music and what a profound effect he'd had on them. "You must be so proud of him," they would say. Of course, I agreed. I couldn't have been more proud.

There were people from all walks of life and every age group. There were plenty of teenagers and middle-aged women. But I was surprised by how many young children were there with their parents or even grandparents.

I remember one little girl around six years old. As I walked by where she was seated, her eyes got wide; she obviously recognized me, so I walked over to meet her. When she heard on the radio that Zach would be performing, she had begged her grandma to take her.

On the opposite side there were two women who looked to be in their sixties who sat with an elderly woman. My sister Amy had been talking to them and heard their story. She hustled across the room to where I stood.

"You have to come meet these ladies," she yelled above the noise. "They have quite a story."

As I approached, one of the women stood to greet me.

"This is my ninety-two-year-old mother," she said as she gestured to the elderly woman. "When she heard that Zach would be playing tonight, she insisted on coming. She absolutely would not be talked out of it! She hardly ever gets out of the house and never stays up past nine o'clock, but she insisted on being here tonight."

I bent down to introduce myself, but it was evident she couldn't hear a word I was saying and wouldn't take her eyes off the stage.

She was here for Zach and Zach alone. My heart melted at the sight of her.

The love and support of all these people was amazing. But those who had made it all happen were the ones I was most grateful for. This team of people had come together and used their talents to make something magical happen. This night would be the summit of Zach's musical career.

The room pulsed with as much energy and love as pulsed from the bass and drum. Bands played and the people danced, even making a conga line that snaked through the room. Finally, it was time for the main event.

Rob went up to the corner of the stage and took the mic. He thanked everyone for coming and thanked everyone who had organized the night. He encouraged people to help us in our fight to wipe osteosarcoma from the planet. He amazed me with his eloquence as he stood up there pouring out his heart in front of twelve hundred people. In short, he made me incredibly proud.

Dan Seeman followed and announced the debut of the "Fix Me Up" music video, which played on a big screen, bringing the audience to tears as Sammy and Zach sang back and forth to each other:

> *Don't you lose hope the sky's not falling.*
> *Please just listen cuz I'll be calling.*
> *Stay with me just one more moment.*
> *I know you're in pain just please don't show it.*

It was a very heavy reminder of why we were all there, gathered together as both musicians and audience: to watch Zach and his band play their songs, knowing that unlike so many other young musicians, this was not only the beginning of their musical journey together, but also the middle, and the end.

As the last note lingered in the air, then fell silent, Staci, one of the DJs from KS95, took the microphone and said, "And now . . . welcome to the stage . . . Zach Sobiech . . . and his band, A Firm Handshake!"

The crowd roared. Zach walked on first, raising his hands toward the crowd. Sammy followed, wearing a black daisy T-shirt, red velvet shorts, and black tights. Reed wore a black ruffled tuxedo shirt with suspenders. They looked like a seasoned band. They took the stage with confidence, natural and relaxed, like they belonged there. It was then that I finally realized—they did belong there.

They played a full set, Sammy at the center microphone carrying most of the vocals, with Zach to her right on guitar and Reed on her left, moving between the cajón and drum kit. They played "Blueberries," "Sandcastles," "Coffee Cup," and "Fix Me Up." Zach's voice was noticeably raspier than it had been one month earlier when they recorded their EP. I didn't know if that was a symptom of the disease's effect on his lungs, or the result of talking to friends and fans for two hours before hitting the stage. I tried not to think about it too much.

Sammy announced that their last song would be "Star Hopping," which, she joked, "would be happier and shorter than 'Fix Me Up.'" It was the perfect way to close, reminding us all that it was okay to "stand there waiting, wishing, wanting to take off and go star hopping." Zach joined in with "start the countdown: three, two, one, let's go."

With that, the three friends waved good-bye under the pink lights, and Vicci Martinez took the stage with a rousing set. Afterward, she invited the kids back to the stage to join her for the singing of the

Lumineers' song "Flowers in Your Hair," with Zach on lead vocals and Vicci and Sammy pulling in the harmonies.

Finally, all the bands that had played throughout the night came onstage to join Zach in singing "Clouds." Kevin Bowe added lead guitar, as did my brother Luke. The whole audience sang along, and the song stretched through several choruses before confetti fell from the ceiling. It was the perfect ending to a perfect and magical night. I watched from the balcony as Zach held his arms up in triumphant gratitude and mouthed the words *thank you* to the adoring audience, some of whom had fallen asleep in their mothers' arms, others who had tears streaming down their faces.

There wasn't a prouder mom in the whole state, maybe the whole country. Make that the world.

The concert was reviewed the next week in the Minneapolis weekly *City Pages*:

> Songwriting has long been a tool to express the aches and worries of difficult living—and the examples of artists who met early and tragic ends, like Elliott Smith or Jeff Buckley, are numerous. The difference for Sobiech, however, is he has a disease beyond his control, but his mind is sharp, and the situation completely in his comprehension. So, with the straight-ahead lyrics of *Fix Me Up* ("I know you're in pain, just please don't show it") and *Coffee Cup* ("I would like to know myself before I have to die"), he can pair the deepest issues of the human condition with the light-hearted arrangements of youth. Trying to pack a lifetime's worth of expression into a short time is a tall order, but he's doing it.[*]

---

[*] Reed Fischer, "Zach Sobiech at Varsity Theater," February 16, 2013, http://blogs. citypages.com/gimmenoise/2013/02/zach_sobiech_varsity_theater_2013.php?page=2.

Thirty-One

. . . .

February 2013

ONE WEEK AFTER THE VARSITY CONCERT, ZACH CAME INTO THE porch where I was lying on the couch, watching mindless television and relaxing. Daisy slept in her usual spot, perched on the back of the love seat. The light from the fireplace flickered on the ceiling, its warmth permeating the room. It was late Sunday night, and I was unwinding from the busy weekend. Zach did this often when he had something on his mind, coming to me in the quiet of the evening, so I sat up to hear what he had to say.

"I have a weird thing going on here, on my left side." He pointed to the place where his crutch would rest, just under his arm and in his rib cage.

"What kind of weird? Is there pain?" My voice was steady, but my heart rate began to rise.

"I don't know," he said. "It's just weird." Over the years, Zach tried many times to find the words to describe how it felt to have a beast grow inside of him. It was frustrating for him because he knew it never translated well.

"Do you think it's a tumor?" I asked. I'd been expecting this, but I still didn't want to hear it. It was so easy to think we had more time when he seemed so well and was able to go to basketball games, record music with Sammy, and be normal.

"Yeah," he answered in a matter-of-fact tone. He'd been fighting this war for a long time. He knew.

Nine months earlier I'd been given a health-care directive form to fill out with Zach. At the time, I had glanced over it and promptly stuffed it in the coffee table drawer. I hadn't been ready to discuss the real stuff back then, the details of how the end would be. But I had given myself permission to think about them, and I did almost every night right before I went to bed. I would put my iPod on the "Sad Songs" playlist and cry as I let my mind wander through the scenes of Zach's death and funeral, almost like watching a play being acted out. It had become a part of my nighttime routine. But I couldn't talk about it, especially not with Zach.

It felt too much like we were giving up.

But time had passed, and a lot had changed as the months went by. New therapies had been tried and failed. We had done all we could do. The future had gotten real in a big, big hurry, and now the details needed to be talked about and written down.

Zach and I sat in silence for a moment. He knew what was coming and waited patiently for me to gather the strength.

"I think we need to start talking about how you want things to be at the end. And I think we need to start talking about your funeral," I said with as much practical resolution as I could muster while I pulled the health-care directive form out of the coffee table drawer.

He nodded his head slightly as he rocked slowly back and forth in the rocking chair, no trace of emotion betraying what went on in his head.

~ I looked at him hard and tried desperately to imprint his image into my brain: the smooth face with a few spots of missed stubble, the round green eyes, the dark blond thinning hair from years of chemo, the gray jeans that were too short and too saggy, the well-loved brown plaid shirt, the wool socks that he got for Christmas.

He draped himself in the black and maroon comforter he'd brought up with him from his bedroom. He'd had that blanket since the seventh grade and had taken it to the hospital with him for every stay. It would go in the wash after each visit to rid it of the hospital smell.

I locked onto his eyes. Those big, beautiful eyes that took my breath away the first time he opened them. The desperation of deep, heartbreaking sadness crept from my chest to my clenched jaw. I fought the tears that forced their way out. They wouldn't be stopped this time.

"I don't want to do this," I croaked in that awful crying voice nobody likes to hear. "I don't want to say good-bye."

I leaned forward and rested my forehead on my fingertips. I couldn't burden him with my tears. He continued to rock slowly, the steady click of the chair keeping time with the clock on the wall. He didn't divert his eyes, but he didn't speak either. He knew it would only make things worse.

He doesn't want to cry, I thought. *He needs to be strong*. It was one of the struggles of parenting a dying child. How to keep the balance between showing enough emotion, but not so much that my grief became a burden. He had enough of his own.

I recovered my composure and grabbed a tissue from the Kleenex box on the end table. I picked up the form and took a deep breath.

Zach moved from the rocking chair to the floor, rested his head on the couch seat, and stared at the ceiling. Daisy hopped down from her perch, her dog tags clinking as she trotted across the floor and crawled into Zach's lap.

I skimmed through the questions on the paper, skipped over the legalese, and jumped to the pertinent questions.

"How and where do you want to die?" I read off the sheet.

"Skydiving and Florida." He lifted his head and turned to me with a smug look on his face, one bald eyebrow cocked. He was bored and it was late.

"Funny. Seriously. I need to know. Do you want to be at home or are you okay with dying at the hospital? We need to think about this stuff." I felt like I was in two separate worlds: Practical-Mom World and My-Son-Is-Dying-and-I-Don't-Want-To-Do-This World. That happens to mothers of dying children a lot.

"I'm fine with being in the hospital. It's practically a second home," he finally answered as he rubbed a hand over his face. "I want to be alert for as long as possible," he continued. "I don't want to be doped up on a bunch of pain meds. I want to be awake enough to say a proper good-bye."

I set the sheet of paper down on my lap and closed my eyes for a moment. Oh, this boy. This boy who battled the pain of a vicious disease for over three years and who should be tired and ready for whatever comfort medicine could offer had chosen the hard way. He would battle to the end, just to stay close to us.

I didn't question his decision. He knew. He'd seen the scan. He'd felt the tumor. He'd made a truce: cancer could take his life, but he would claim every minute he had left.

We continued.

"CPR?"

"No."

"Intubation or ventilation?"

"No."

"Feeding tube?"

"No."

"Organ and tissue donation?"

"Yes."

"Have you thought about your funeral?" I asked.

He yawned and looked up at the clock. He wanted to get to bed, but I wanted to press on. I wanted to get it done before it was too late. Saving it for another day was no longer an option. Another day was here.

"I want bagpipes," he said.

"Bagpipes? Really?" He was neither Scottish nor old, both prerequisites for having bagpipes at a funeral in my book.

"They have a sound that reaches the soul," he explained. "I don't want Psalm 23. It's overdone. And I want the gospel reading to be the one about the talents. I like that gospel. It makes sense to me."

He went on to tell me that he wanted to wear a shirt and tie with his suit vest, but no jacket. A jacket would be too "uptight" looking. Everything else he would leave to me.

We wrapped up the conversation and moved to normal talk about normal life stuff. I don't remember what it was, maybe something about his day or about a television show he'd watched, or some new fact that he'd learned on the Science Channel. I remember thinking how strange it was to live these parallel lives of living and dying, and I marveled at the grace we'd been given to do it.

Zach set Daisy on the floor, and we both laughed as she trotted to her crate, rooted around, and tucked herself in bed so only her nose peaked out from the blanket. His laugh stirred up a cough. My ears perked up to listen for any rattles or wheezes as if the sound could tell me how much time he had left.

"Relax, Mom. It's just a tickle in my throat. I'm not quite there yet." He looked down at me, a smirk on his lips.

We said good night, and I reached up and placed my hands on his cheeks.

"I love you." I kissed his forehead as I stood on my tiptoes. That phrase we had said without much thought for so many years was now packed with meaning. It meant, *I am proud of you, I will miss you, and I will never, ever forget you. I love you.*

Zach hobbled down the stairs to his bedroom, his blanket dragging behind him. I made my way up to my own bedroom and quietly crawled into bed next to Rob, who was already in a deep sleep. I laid my head on the cool pillow and stared at the wall as I replayed in my head the conversation I'd just had. I thought about the gospel of the talents. It was so Zach. Of course he would want to leave people with the message that God had given them something precious and not to squander it like a fool. He'd had a taste of what could happen if you tapped into the gifts God had given, and he wanted everyone to experience the same.

And the bagpipes! Ah, Zach. My dear boy always did love quirky pomp. If it were allowed, I was certain he would have loved to be sent down the St. Croix River on a great floating pyre. In his shirt, tie, and vest—no suit coat, because that would be over the top.

I smiled to myself as hot tears welled up and spilled out onto the pillow, soaking it. Oh, I would miss him.

Exhausted, I reached up, turned the lamp off, and flipped the tear-soaked pillow over. It would be a beautiful funeral. We just had to get through the dying part.

IT TOOK ME A COUPLE OF WEEKS TO FORCE MYSELF TO TRANSCRIBE the notes I had taken to fill out the health-care directive. To write it all out in permanent ink on a legally binding document was just . . . well . . . hard. I didn't want to do it, but it had to be done. There were people who needed to know how we wanted things to happen. In particular, our nurse practitioner, Melissa. She had periodically over the course of the last several months asked if we'd had a chance to look over the form. Melissa had been with us from the beginning, from that first hospital stay when Zach was so miserable. She had allowed herself to go beyond the normal confines of the "professional relationship" and become our friend. She knew how to talk to Zach, and Zach trusted her. She laughed with us, and she wasn't afraid to cry.

When I finally gave the form to her, Melissa was relieved to have the document in hand. It would serve as a guide for Zach's care. She had always wanted him to be involved in the decision making, and it was especially true now, as he was nearing the end.

Zach got progressively worse after our conversation. He coughed more, he lost weight, and he started to feel more intense pain in his hip. It kept him up at night, and he wasn't able to go out much anymore. I called Melissa a few weeks later to inquire about pain medications; he needed something more powerful than what he was currently using. She asked if I would like to begin palliative care, which specialized in pain management. The team would be able to set up a regimen that would be preplanned and accessible. As Zach's cancer grew and his body demanded more medication to achieve the same amount of control, we would have standing orders to bump up the dose without having to wait.

In other words, she was asking if I wanted hospice care. It was another declaration of the end. I told her that we would discuss it, all the while feeling like another piece of Zach was being ripped away.

Melissa and I talked in more detail about what Zach's wishes were, especially about the pain medications and how they would affect his alertness. He'd made it clear over and over that he didn't want to take a medicine that would make him too sleepy or foggy. He wanted to be able to enjoy his friends when they came over, as they still did on a near-daily basis. He didn't have time to sleep all day.

We also talked about what happens at the end and what I should expect after he died, whether that was at home or at the hospital. She told me that she would call the county coroner's office to tell them Zach's was an expected death so we wouldn't need a medical examiner to come to the house when he died. My heart ached, and I felt it break under the pressure. Those blasted sobs made their way out again, from my tightened chest, up through my jaw. I bit down on my bottom lip—a tactic I'd only read about until cancer entered our lives. It used to annoy me to read about a person doing it. Really? Like biting your lip would help. Turns out it does. The tears needed to wait. This was practical stuff that had to be done.

"So," Melissa said, "I see that you have checked the box for tissue and organ donation." She spoke slowly with a touch of airiness in her voice that indicated she knew she was treading into fragile territory. Melissa was a mother too. Her first son was born just months before Zach's diagnosis. Her son and Zach's cancer grew up together.

"Yes," I said as I held the phone to my ear. I sat on the oversized chair in the living room, the afternoon sunshine filling the room.

I had been enjoying the afternoon curled up with a book and a hot cup of tea. It had been a gloomy couple of weeks, cloudy and cold. We were desperate for the warmth and colors of spring, but it hadn't made its way north to us yet.

Melissa continued, "I'm not sure Zach's organs will be viable for donation, given his disease and the chemotherapies he's had. And I'm assuming you don't want to donate his body to be used for science . . . by med students," she asked in a tentative voice.

"No," I responded resolutely. The sun no longer provided the warmth it had just moments earlier.

"The only other thing that they would likely take would be his eyes," she said.

The image that filled my mind was a moment almost eighteen years earlier. I held Zach in my arms for the first time, and he opened his eyes. It took what seemed like forever for that little baby to lift his lids—his eyes, they were so huge! I gasped, then chuckled as I watched him try to focus. A little frown formed on his face. It was such a big and bright world, and he didn't seem quite ready to be part of it.

The next image that flooded my mind was of me, standing over a casket and looking down at Zach knowing those beautiful eyes were gone.

I couldn't do it. I couldn't bear the thought. Those eyes were too precious to me. They were mine.

Melissa had already moved on to another topic, but I interrupted her, saying, "No. Not the eyes. I can't give up his eyes." Tears ran freely down my face. No amount of lip biting was going to stop them. Melissa could hear the tears in my voice so she gently ended the conversation. My tea had gone cold and so had the room, the sun hidden behind a cloud. I walked into the kitchen and began to clear the clutter from the table to make room for a meal that would be delivered by one of the hundreds of people who had taken care of us these past three years. As I poured the now-cold tea in the sink, I looked out the window at the snow that just wouldn't go away.

Laughter rose from the basement where Zach and Amy spent each afternoon. I wiped away the tears and smiled at the sound.

Thirty-Two

. . . .

WHILE THE CANCER SLOWED ZACH'S BODY DOWN, THE INTERNET attention picked up speed. By the end of February 2013, the story about how he wrote "Clouds" had been running on various Internet and television news programs for months. With each bit of coverage, downloads surged and then dwindled. "Clouds" had been averaging around sixty downloads a day, then jumped to around a thousand. And then CNN Student News ran the story and was viewed by thousands of middle school children across the country, which resulted in tens of thousands of downloads.

For many, the response was deeply emotional. They imagined themselves in Zach's shoes and what it must be like to know you are dying at such a young age. He was a kid close in age to them with many of the same dreams and struggles, but he was going to die and lose it all. Through the eyes of Zach's story, they were able to see things more clearly and gain perspective on their own lives. What seemed like a problem before hearing Zach's story wasn't such a big deal anymore. Their perspectives on life changed, and many of them were profoundly affected. It seemed as though the message they heard on the news that day was delivered just for them.

Every hour, hundreds of people visited the "Clouds" video on YouTube and posted comments:

"Zach, you are my hero."

"You showed me how to live a better life and I'm going to do it."

"You are amazing and we love you."

"I've never cried for a video before but this one made me bawl like a baby."

"You showed me what is really important in life and I will never forget that."

"Thank you."

Thousands of comments like these were written over the next several weeks. A movement had started, and it just kept growing. One mom wrote to me about how her ten-year-old son came home from school and told her a story he'd seen on the news. It was about a teenager who got cancer and now was writing songs to say good-bye to his loved ones, and he wanted to download one of the songs he wrote called "Clouds." She said she listened to him go on and on about this teenager and his song all evening. She thought he would eventually lose interest in downloading the song, but he didn't and he was relentless in his begging. Finally, she gave in.

"I am so glad I did," she wrote in her comment on the "Clouds" video. "The song and Zach's story have not only inspired my son to be thankful for what he has, but it has inspired me to be grateful for every day that I have with him."

"Clouds" was reaching the hearts of children and adults all over the world. Hundreds of YouTube tribute covers of the song were being posted every week—countless teens from across the country, professional musicians in their twenties and thirties, and even toddlers were all singing "Clouds."

Of course there were "trolls" too. Trolls are lazy people who want attention, so they cowardly choose the easiest route and post nasty anonymous comments online in order to provoke anger and disgust from those who read them. It seems the troll's chief target is anything that promotes positive thought and change. And so it was with "Clouds."

Initially I was disturbed by the comments. Zach had enough to deal with. He didn't need to see comments like: "He's just another kid with cancer and not a big deal" or "His song is only popular because he's going to die."

How could people be so cruel? I wanted to fight back and make my own snide comments to cut them down and shame them. But that was exactly what the trolls wanted, to provoke people into an angry reaction and pull them into a public argument. One comment in particular got under my skin. It said something like: "Ha ha, he's dying! Why waste time caring about someone like him. He's already dead." After the initial surge of disgust and anger, I began to realize how sad some people are. If hearing a song like "Clouds" and knowing Zach's story provoked hate, jealousy, or bitterness in a person's heart, then how messed up must that person's life be? Despair is an ugly thing, and it does ugly things to a person's soul. So rather than sling anger back at them and feed their despair, I began to offer up little prayers for them instead: *Lord, You know what's going on in this person's life. Please give him the grace he needs at this moment to heal.* It seemed like a more productive way to deal with them and brought me peace.

All the attention that Zach received on the Internet didn't alter his life much. By now there had been almost three million hits on the

"Clouds" video, and hundreds of covers of the song had been posted as well. But Zach could easily block all that out of his life when it got to be too much by simply shutting down the computer or phone. He would occasionally, though, check the comments on the various videos, and of course, he enjoyed the uplifting ones. He was pleased to see how many people the song had touched. But the cruel comments were difficult to take. Not so much those that were critical of the song itself; most of the musicians who commented complimented him on the composition and lyrics—they knew it was a good song even if they didn't particularly care for the song itself. It was the fascination people had with his dying that got under his skin. It really irritated him when people would ask if he had died yet, or worse, assumed he already had. He felt like people were eager for it to happen, almost like they wanted it to happen.

But he didn't let it get him down for long and eventually quit looking at the comments altogether. His time with family, friends, and especially Amy was much more important to him. Whatever was going on in cyberspace didn't have much to do with what was going on in real life.

Thirty-Three

. . . .

BY MID-MARCH, THE TUMORS IN ZACH'S LUNGS WERE HUGE. THE biggest one was seven and a half centimeters in diameter and was between his lung and rib cage, just under his left arm. He could feel it rubbing on his rib cage when he breathed, and it hurt. Radiation was the best option to shrink it, as well as to provide some pain relief, so we made daily trips to the hospital for three weeks straight. Radiation made Zach tired, but it also shrank the tumor enough to stop it from rubbing every time he took a breath.

His daily appointments were scheduled for eleven o'clock in the morning so he could sleep in. I usually drove him in, but occasionally Zach would drive himself. I got the impression he preferred for me to take him so he didn't have to be in the waiting room by himself. The children's hospital didn't have the proper equipment to treat his lung tumors, so he had to switch to the adult hospital, which meant sitting in a waiting room full of adults.

"It's like sitting in a funeral home," he would say. "They all look so mopey and worn-out, like they have no life left in them." And he had a hard time listening to the complaints of people who were so much older than himself and who'd had the privilege of a long life. One morning there was a particularly obnoxious woman who felt it necessary to air her every complaint to the waiting room full of people. I caught Zach's eye when he looked up from a worn-out copy of *ESPN Magazine*. He rolled his eyes, shook his head, and smiled.

"Do you think she's ever thought that maybe some of those doctors are the reason she's still alive and able to complain?" he joked as we walked toward the exit.

"Maybe we should write complaint letters to those doctors for keeping her around," I replied. It was crass and insensitive, but sometimes it helped to joke about stuff. And it certainly helped to have someone to joke about it with.

Most days, when Zach got home from radiation, he would grab a small snack and whatever drink he was into that day, head for his favorite couch downstairs in the family room, and sleep for a couple of hours before Amy came over after school. It was strange for her, not having Zach at school anymore, and she missed him. She would stay with him for a few hours, then go to dance and come back, sitting with him until late at night, often not getting home until midnight or one o'clock. Then she would do it all again the next day.

Zach managed to muster up the energy for some important things. He did his best to make it to Grace's basketball games. He loved watching her run down the court like he had done a few years earlier. Grace liked having her big brother in the stands, but made it clear she didn't want him judging her or harassing her about how she could have done things better. Zach complied.

One of the major radio stations in the Twin Cities, Cities 97, extended an offer through Scott Herold for A Firm Handshake to play at one of their Studio C sessions. It was a small studio where the latest, most popular bands would play for a private audience, then donate the recording of the session for charitable purposes. It was an exciting opportunity for A Firm Handshake, and they jumped at the opportunity.

A few days after their studio performance, Zach and I were headed back to radiation.

"Oh, forgot to tell you, Ma. We're going to Studio C again. They invited us to come back to see Walk Off the Earth." He was thrilled. It was one of his favorite bands, and he would have the opportunity to see them up close and even meet them. "It starts at noon, so if they're not on time at the clinic, I'm out of there."

"Seriously? Zach, what's really more important?" I teased.

"Do you even have to ask? Geez, Ma. Duh," he came back. He knew the real treatment for what ailed him. So did I.

The next week he managed to take an hour to drop in at his first-grade cousin Amelia's school to surprise her for her birthday and read her class a story. He had been reluctant to go because he was tired and really just wanted to nap. But as we walked down the halls of the school and saw the excited faces of the children when they saw who had entered their school, I could see the energy it produced in him. It was sweet to see the reactions of the children.

"Is that Zach Sobiech?" we heard whispered as we made our way to Amelia's classroom. Little ones as young as kindergarten came to a dead stop, jaws dropped, as they walked to their next class and caught a glimpse of Zach.

One of the teachers popped out of her room and called after us. "Zach Sobiech?!" She invited us to drop by her classroom after we had finished reading to Amelia's class.

The look on Amelia's face when we stepped into the room after the teacher had announced that the class had a "surprise reader" was precious. She turned beet red as she walked across the room and gave Zach a big hug. She loved him dearly, even from the time she was a baby. We stopped by her brother Owen's class as well, and then saw Ian, her oldest brother, in the lunchroom. The little ones knew Zach wouldn't be around much longer, and this visit meant the world to them.

JEFF DUNN, OUR PHOTOGRAPHER, WAS A GODSEND. HE HAD BEEN our photographer for two years now. He was interested in adding video production to his business, so he offered to make two of A Firm Handshake's songs, "Sandcastles" and "Star Hopping," into music videos.

Jeff had a vision of Zach and Sammy floating in a pool with a guitar for the "Sandcastles" video. It was difficult and physically taxing as it required Sammy and Zach to be in a pool for hours dressed in jeans and shirts. Zach was exhausted by the time we got home, and he slept for hours. But when he got up from his nap, he was ready for more adventure.

It had been a long winter and a hard one. By now it was mid-March, when Minnesota starts to warm up and the end of winter is near. But winter didn't want to let go. The temperatures had been bone-chilling cold and the snow just wouldn't stop. We were all suffering from intense cabin fever, crawling the walls and praying that some sign of spring would come soon.

One afternoon, Zach came upstairs after his nap. Amy would be over any minute and dinner was ready to put on the table, but he had something he wanted to ask me, so we sat down in the family room.

"Mom, if I'm still around on my birthday, can I go on a cruise with my friends?" he asked.

My heart broke. His birthday was May 3, six weeks away—an eternity. I was certain he already knew the answer: there was no way I could let him go. He already struggled so much and barely had enough energy to do a couple of outings a week, let alone a trip. But I couldn't tell him that as he sat there looking so hopeful.

"I'll think about it," I replied. There had to be some way we could get him out of this cold, depressing weather and feel the warmth of the sun again. I wondered if he just needed to feel summer one last time.

Later that evening, Dan Seeman called me. We had been conspiring with Zach to figure out a unique way for him to ask Amy to the senior prom that was six weeks away, the day after his birthday. All the other boys had asked their dates back in January. But Zach had put off asking Amy because he didn't know if he would be well enough to go or, for that matter, still alive, and he didn't want her to plan for it and be heartbroken, with a dress in her closet she would never wear. The radiation treatments had slowed the tumors some, and though he got sicker with each passing day, it seemed like he might actually be able to go.

"So, I'm wondering if you should ask Amy to prom," I had probed. There had been a lot of prom talk among their friends when they visited the weekend before, and I knew he had to be thinking about it.

"Yeah. I was wondering about that too. What do you think?" There is nothing more pleasing to a mom than to have a son ask for advice. Prom advice was the crème de la crème!

"I think you should go for it. Amy should have the chance to do all the fun stuff that comes before prom, all the planning and shopping that a girl does. If you end up too sick to go, then so be it; but at least she had the chance to dream."

"Yeah, that's kind of what I was thinking. At this point, I think it would be worse to miss out because I didn't even ask than to miss it because I was too sick. How do you think I should ask her?"

How a guy asked a girl to prom was everything. Some of Zach's friends had gone to great lengths to ask their girls to prom. Mitch went so far as to stage a carjacking. Just when his girlfriend thought it was real, the fake offender held up a sign that read "Will you go to prom with me?" After she slapped him in the face, she said yes.

Sammy's date set up a scene straight out of a musical. When she entered the choir room one morning, she was pushed into a desk chair with wheels and pushed down the hallway of the high school. As she passed, a flash mob of friends poured out of classrooms and joined in as nearly one hundred kids sang "You're the One That I Want" from the *Grease* soundtrack. At the end of the hallway her future prom date stood waiting with a sign that asked if she would be his date for prom.

Needless to say, Zach had his work cut out for him.

"Well, you know some pretty cool people who have some pretty cool connections. Maybe you should tap into them," I suggested. It would have to be something simple but unique. "How about asking Dan if you could somehow get on the radio and ask Amy? You certainly have friends in radio these days."

Zach raised his eyebrows and thought for a moment. "That would be cool. Actually, that's a great idea."

Now I was on the phone with Dan working out the details.

"How is Zach doing?" he asked. "I haven't seen him since the Varsity. I know he had some tough scan results not long after. How is the radiation going?"

"He's doing okay. He's tired most of the time; the radiation really wipes him out. But he's pretty happy. He's getting a little spring fever, and he really wants to go someplace warm. The winter is just dragging him down."

"He should come to Fort Myers with me! I leave on Sunday and come back on Tuesday. It would be the perfect opportunity for him to get away for a bit. You and Rob could come with him." Dan always came through with some amazing thing he could offer Zach. It was hard sometimes to believe that this man who had made such an impact on Zach's life had only known him for four months.

"That would be perfect!" I don't know why, but I was still surprised by God's timing in bringing even the smallest things together. There always seemed to be someone that God was moving into the right place at the right time.

"Can Amy come?" Zach asked as soon as I told him. She'd been in New York attending a journalism class for a week at Columbia, and he missed her. I realized that week how much I missed her when she was gone too. Zach relied on her to keep him steady and positive; without her presence, he was feeling a little like a boat without an anchor in a raging sea. Without Amy around, Zach seemed lost.

Rob accompanied Zach and Amy to Fort Myers, and I stayed home with Alli, Sam, and Grace. Amy was home from New York less than twenty-four hours before she was back at the airport on her way out of town again. The trip was a whirlwind of activity packed into just a few days' time. They went to a restaurant that served alligator (Amy stuck with chicken); they went to a Twins spring training game, and Dan set up a meeting with several of the players. Zach's favorite time was the afternoon that he and Amy spent on the beach building sandcastles. When they got home on Tuesday night, Zach looked refreshed and content. He'd gotten to experience a little bit of summer in the midst of a hard, cold winter that refused to loosen its grip. And he got to experience it with his best girl by his side.

THE DAY AFTER ZACH GOT HOME FROM FLORIDA, WE DID SOME retakes for the "Sandcastles" video and shot the whole "Star Hopping" video too. It was a day filled with great energy, but it really wiped out Zach. He needed to go home between shoots to take a three-hour nap before filming the final scene, which required him to climb a ladder onto a rooftop and dance and sing in the cold March air. It was a nerve-racking moment for me, but so much fun for the kids. Later Sammy commented that singing with Zach on that rooftop would be one of the most cherished moments of her life.

We were at a point in Zach's life where it felt like the last few miles of a marathon. He had run so hard and for so long that his energy was running low, but the finish line was in sight, so he pressed on to accomplish as much as he possibly could. There was a part of me that wanted to put a stop to everything. I knew he didn't want to waste his time away, sitting and waiting for death to come, but I was seeing the toll it was taking on him and wondered if he was doing all of this for himself or if it was really just for us.

The next day Zach didn't leave his bed until the late afternoon when he was scheduled to visit a couple of church youth groups. One was a local church, St. Lucas, where his grandpa Jim belonged; and the other was our home church, Church of St. Michael, or St. Mike's for short. He and Sammy went to both churches to talk to the kids about their experiences as a band and about their faith. The kids at St. Lucas were a bit starstruck.

"Zach was eating it up," Sammy told me when they got back to our house. "It was pretty funny how the little girls were swooning for him and asking for his autograph. I just stepped back and let him do his thing." She went on to tell me how he spoke to each and every child that approached him and left that child feeling special, like he or she had been the only one in that room with him.

"How? What would he say to them?" I asked.

"Oh, it was nothing big or profound. Just in little ways. Like this one little boy came up to him and just blurted out, 'I have a brother!' He so badly wanted to connect with Zach. It was so cute. Then Zach bent down and said, 'Really? That's awesome! I have one too!'"

The kids at St. Mike's were a different kind of crowd. Zach and Sammy were there to talk with the ninth-grade Confirmation class about their faith and how it had gotten them through some tough times. Most of the kids had known Zach and Sammy for a number of years (Matt, Sammy's younger brother being one of them), so they weren't so much starstruck as they were interested. They knew Zach's story, that he had been diagnosed with cancer when he was their age. And they knew that cancer would end his life.

Zach got up in front of the group of about fifty kids to talk about his faith. He chose the same gospel to inspire them as he had chosen for his funeral: Matthew 25:14–30, the gospel about the talents that had been given by the master of the house to the servants before he'd left on a long trip. Each was to use his talents in a wise way that would be productive. Two of the servants had done well and increased what they had been given. One, however, had been afraid of the master and rather than use his talent and take a chance at increasing it, instead buried it.

That gospel reading resonated with Zach. He had seen so clearly how it had played out in his own life. He had taken something that

God had given him—a love of music and a story to write about—and turned it into something beautiful. It wasn't an easy thing, but it wasn't a terribly difficult thing either. He simply took that first step without fear. God did the rest.

I wasn't there that night when Zach got up in front of those kids. But I am told they listened. Perhaps it was because he had written a song they could relate to or perhaps it was his charisma. But I like to think that Zach was a vessel who allowed God to fill him up and spill over to those around him, and that his love of God and gratitude for what God had given him was what spoke to their hearts.

He was a boy who understood that although the door to eternity was close at hand, he already lived in the kingdom of God. Through all that he suffered, he still retained a childlike wonder for the world around him. He sought joy wherever he was, whether it was onstage in front of twelve hundred people or in a hospital room all alone. He saw the good in people because he chose to look for it. To Zach, it was all very simple: use what you have to make another person happy, and joy will be returned to you.

Thirty-Four

. . . .

THE PAIN IN ZACH'S HIP HAD INCREASED SIGNIFICANTLY. WE HAD A hard time keeping on top of the pain, and he hated the medications he was taking for it because they made him sleepy.

"Maybe it's time to think about a palliative care team," Melissa, our nurse practitioner, recommended again. I thought I had been ready when we talked about it a couple of months earlier, but in the end I hadn't been able to resign myself to it yet. "They are really good at managing pain and keeping ahead of it."

"You're right. I think it's time," I answered, resigned. It wasn't that the idea caught me off guard; I'd been thinking about it since we'd spoken of it. I just didn't want to be there yet, that place in time I'd saved for another day. I know some people get angry when the doctors recommend end-of-life care. They feel somehow like it's giving up. But I was grateful that there were people ready to help us with the transition. Zach was dying, and he was dying now. Placing him on hospice didn't feel like giving up; it felt more like being prepared.

"Let's go ahead and set up an appointment," I said. "We need help with this."

Alli came in the room after I got off the phone with Melissa.

"What's going on?" she asked. She'd picked up on parts of the conversation.

"I set up an appointment with hospice. They will be sending a nurse out tomorrow to talk to us and Zach about how he wants the end to be."

She broke down and cried.

"I just can't believe this is all going to happen right now. The wedding and Zach dying . . . it's all going to happen on top of each other and there's nothing we can do about it." She looked at me through tears. "How are we going to do this, Mom? How are we going to get through this?" She curled up on the couch and let the tears go. "I wish Collin were here. At least I could find comfort in him. It's just so hard doing this on my own, planning a wedding and watching my brother die. I feel guilty every time I find myself excited about the wedding."

I waited before I spoke and let her cry it out. Months of agony poured out of her. The wedding was less than two months away, and every thought of it, every bit of excited anticipation, was matched with equal amounts of guilt. We had decided not long after the engagement that we would keep the wedding date despite what cancer had thrown our way. Years of life being tossed and turned by cancer had taught us to hold steady and trust that God would take care of us. But like Peter walking to Christ on the turbulent sea, sometimes it was hard not to look down at the waves crashing at our feet. The countdown to the wedding paralleled the countdown to Zach's death. As time went by, it seemed the two events had fallen in step together.

"Mom, what if Zach dies right before the wedding? Or what if he dies on my wedding day? I feel so guilty even thinking about it. I get so down when I think about having a wedding right after a funeral. I always dreamed of a wedding where I look out to see a church full of people who are so happy to be there. Zach and I have talked about the wedding a lot. I know he wants to be there and he keeps promising that he'll make it, but I think we both know that's not going to happen." She pulled the pillow from under her head and hugged it. "How can any of us be happy at a wedding without Zach? All I can picture is a church full of people who are heart-broken and somber."

I sat silent for a few moments to collect my thoughts. I'd been through the same scenarios in my head, all the what-ifs that could happen. What if we had a funeral just days before the wedding? What if Zach was on his deathbed while the wedding was happening? Where would Rob and I choose to be? I'd played all the scenarios out over and over in my head.

One Sunday afternoon a few weeks earlier, while Zach slept on the couch downstairs and the rest of the kids were out of the house, I lay down next to Rob on our bed. He'd just woken from a nap.

"I'm wondering what we'll do if Zach is in his last hours on the wedding day." We lay on our stomachs, our faces turned to each other. "What do we choose? Being there for Alli and Collin to witness them getting married? Or being there for Zach when he dies?" The choice seemed impossible to make, but I needed a plan, and I needed Rob's wisdom.

"I've been thinking about the same thing." He sighed with a sort of relief. We had learned over the past couple of years how much we really needed each other to shepherd our child safely to death while still taking care of the other children. And we had learned that there was so much we didn't have control over. We knew that we could only do our best to work together, praying that God would give us the grace we would need to make the right choices.

"It's hard to believe that we have to do this, decide whether we attend our daughter's wedding or our son's death. How can we miss either one? Should we split up? One stay with Zach and one go to the wedding?" I asked.

He thought for a moment and then said, "I think we need to go to the wedding."

"Why? What's your thought process?"

"Alli and Collin will remember that day for the rest of their lives, and I think it's important that they be able to look back on it and know that we were there for them," he said. "If we did our job right, Zach will be ready when his time comes to die. At that point there won't be anything else that we can do for him. While I would hate not to be here, I know he would understand our decision. He gets it."

Rob's clarity in difficult circumstances was one of the things I loved about him.

"I think you're right. I think we should ask Amy and her family to stay with him if it should come to that," I said. Zach had become close with Amy's family. He loved Amy's brothers, Tony and Joey, and her parents, Mary and Vic. I knew he would be comforted by their presence. "If he dies while we're at the wedding, do you want to be called?"

"No," Rob answered. "Let's wait until we get home. It won't change anything for us to know sooner."

Once Alli was done crying and dried her eyes, I finally answered her. "Dad and I have a plan, Alli. We will have Amy's family stay with Zach while we are at the wedding."

She sat up and held the pillow in her lap. "Really? Are you sure that's a good idea? He's going to need you here, Mom. I wouldn't blame you at all if you were at home with him."

"I'm sure. Your wedding day is important, and we need to be there. Of course, we hope we don't need to worry about it, but we do have a plan that I think will work for everyone."

"But what if he dies before? I can't see how we can have a joyful wedding without Zach there. It just makes me so sad to think of us at our wedding and all of us just so sad."

"Alli, this is what we do. Our family has always taken hard, awful things and turned them into the most amazing memories. Remember the day Uncle Dave died last summer? We had the big camping party planned with all your aunts and uncles and cousins that night at Grandma and Grandpa's house?"

"Yeah," she said. "That was a good night. I'll remember it always."

"That's right! We could have canceled it and all stayed home to mourn Dave in private. But we didn't. We got together and mourned together. It was sad and there were tears, but there was also a lot of laughter. Because that's how we do it. It's actually what we do best! During the worst times, the hardest, most agonizing times ever, our family gets together to have a party."

She grabbed a tissue from the box on the coffee table and wiped the tears from her eyes.

"Yeah! We are good at this crappy hard stuff, aren't we?" she said, laughing.

"That's right. There is none better," I agreed. "Al, whenever I think about your wedding, I don't imagine some sad and somber event where people are standing around with cake and talking in hushed tones to each other. I picture everyone with a beer, the DJ is playing the Proclaimers' '500 Miles' song, and all your aunts are in a conga line dancing across the room."

She grabbed another tissue from the box. The tears had started up again.

"Thanks, Mom. I needed to hear that so badly. I felt so selfish wanting to have a fun wedding. I just assumed you thought it would be horrible and that you weren't looking forward to it at all, like it was just this huge burden on everyone."

"Oh, honey! Not at all! I've always thought of your wedding like the light at the end of a long, dark tunnel," I assured her. "It's going to be a beautiful wedding, and you are going to be a beautiful bride."

I pulled her into a hug and held her close. This poor girl had been through so much. All the emotional turmoil of watching her brother dying while being separated by thousands of miles from a fiancé in the navy and having to plan a wedding and finish her degree—it was a lot for one person to have on her plate.

"I just wish that Collin could have some time with Zach. He's only met Zach a few times, and I hate that the next time he will see him will likely be when Zach is gone."

"Then let's bring him home. Why wait? Even if Collin has to forfeit leave for Zach's funeral later, I think it's more important for him to be with Zach now. And you need him here now," I said. "A man got in touch with Mindy from CCRF and offered frequent-flier miles if we need them. I think bringing Collin home would be a worthy enough cause."

Collin came home a few days later.

Thirty-Five

. . . .

Mid-April 2013

ZACH'S DECLINE HAD SLOWED SOME. THE RADIATION HAD HELPED alleviate the discomfort from the lung tumors, and the hospice team had him on a pain regimen that had worked well. The pain was managed without making him feel so loopy. He had a system down: sleep until ten o'clock in the morning, shower, watch *The Price is Right*, eat a snack, then nap until Amy came over at one o'clock. Amy would stay until he fell asleep, then she would head home. A few days a week she would have dance practice. There was a competition coming up and team Topaz would be competing. She also had something new she'd been working on, a solo.

One night in early April, Zach went with Amy's mom, Mary, to watch her perform the solo she'd been working on for months. It was a dance dedicated to Zach and their love, and it was her way of saying good-bye, her "Clouds."

I hadn't been able to go with them that night; I'd fallen ill with a serious bout of vertigo that had me bedridden for over a week. As I lay there wondering about God's timing—why now, when Zach was so sick and had so little time, did God choose to allow this illness?—I realized I wasn't panicked by it or even angry about it, just curious. I was truly learning to trust in all things.

Zach didn't say much about the dance, but Amy's mom, Mary, told me about it and Zach's response. He had been deeply moved by it, openly crying as he watched from the bleachers.

Amy shared with me what she wrote about the day in her journal:

April 3rd

On Wednesday, April 3rd, it was Zach's and my 10-month anniversary. I was performing my solo for the first time. Throughout the day it was all I could think about. I was nervous about performing it, but I was also nervous that Zach might not be able to go.

After school I texted him and asked if he was going to be able to make it. He said that his mom was sick and he would need a ride. Luckily my mom was able to give him one. When they arrived, I was so relieved. I knew Zach would be able to see the dance at least once. He and my mom greeted me with flowers. I gave them each a hug before I went backstage. They wished me luck and took their seats.

Backstage, I brought my iPod and listened to my song over and over again. When I had only two dances left before mine, I went into a back hall, sat down by myself, and listened to the song Zach wrote for me, "Our Souls." I began to cry thinking about my dance for him and how it could be the only time he would ever see it. Knowing he was out there watching me, I felt ready to perform. As I waited backstage, my teacher Katia gave me a hug and we started to cry. She said, "Do it for Zach."

Already crying, they announced my name and I walked on stage.

Dancing for Zach and knowing he was watching felt so good. I performed like I never had before and let all my emotions take over. After I was done, I walked offstage still in tears. I got myself together and went to find my mom and Zach in the lobby and I could tell they had been crying. I was overwhelmed as Zach limped over to me, tears running down his face. My mom stood back, allowing us space, tears running down her face as well.

Zach pulled me in and hugged me tight. As we stood there against the wall crying in each other's embrace, he said in my ear, "I'm not letting go anytime soon."

"What did you think of my dance?" I asked as our tears subsided.

Tears welled up in his eyes again. "It felt so surreal," he said. "When you ran across stage holding your arm out, I knew it was like you were trying to pull me along, like you wanted me to keep going—to stay with you. I felt connected to you and I understood everything you were trying to tell me."

It was an amazing feeling to know it meant so much to him because it is so important to me. It was a night filled with so much sadness, but at the same time I was so glad Zach got to see my dance for him. I will cherish that day for the rest of my life.

"YOU SHOULD PROBABLY LEAVE IN ABOUT TEN MINUTES," I SAID AS Zach walked up to the kitchen to grab an energy drink from the refrigerator. "If you're supposed to be on the air at three o'clock, you never know how traffic is going to be. Are you okay to drive? I can drive if you need me to."

"No, Mom. I'm fine. Besides, that would be totally lame having my mom with me when I ask my girlfriend to prom," he said, rolling his eyes.

It was the happiest I'd seen him in days. His meds had been working but the pain had gotten worse, and now he needed to bump up the dose almost every other day. And he was just down. Fighting pain has a way of doing that.

He hobbled over to the coat closet, grabbed his crutches and keys, and headed out the garage door. I watched as he expertly maneuvered around a fallen rake and a bag of old clothes that lay in his path. *Why didn't I move those out of his way?* I scolded myself.

"Good luck! Hope she says yes, or that could be very embarrassing," I called out cheerfully. I did my best to fuel the good mood he was in.

"Yea. Thanks, Ma." He opened the door to the car, tossed his crutches over the backseat, and lowered himself into the seat. He winced in pain as he pulled his legs in. "Hey, Ma, could you grab the handicap tag off the desk? I don't see mine in here," he called out before he shut the car door.

I ran over to the desk and scrounged around for it. I finally found it tucked between the "Wedding Songs and Readings" and "Funeral Planning" booklets we'd gotten from church. I ran it out to him, kicking the rake and clothing bag off to the side as I passed them.

"Here ya go." He took it and set it on the seat beside him. I kissed my fingers and transferred the kiss to his forehead with a tap. "I love you."

"Love you too," he said as he closed the door.

He was headed to KS95 to be on the Moon and Staci afternoon radio show where he would ask Amy to the prom. Amy, of course, had no idea what was really going on. She thought Zach was going in to record a promo for an event that was happening at a local shopping center in a few weeks that would raise money for Zach's fund.

306

Grace had a basketball game that afternoon, so as I drove into Stillwater I listened to the show. It was perfect! They had Zach participate in a game they do every afternoon called "Smarter Than Staci." A series of the same questions is asked of both the contestant and then Staci. Whoever gets the most right, wins. Instead of the usual listener call-in, they had Zach play against Staci. At the end of the game, he turned to Amy and asked her if she would go to prom. At first she was confused and stumbled with her words. Then she answered with a resounding "Yes!"

I cheered in the car, ecstatic that Zach had pulled it off. Not just the surprise itself, but that he was able to execute the plan. It had taken a ton of effort, but he loved Amy and he wanted to make it special for her.

Prom was the day after Zach's birthday, two and a half weeks away. Practically a lifetime.

JOURNAL ENTRY ·

April 23, 2013

We head into high school for Zach's "graduation." His diploma has been delivered early, and the staff and I thought it would be nice to give it to him in a memorable way. His teachers and friends are gathering in the office for a little ceremony.

Zach isn't feeling well. He's tired but says he will go. We pull up to the school, and I see that Zach is crying. He says he's feeling really sick and begins to panic. His breathing is rapid. I'm afraid he might pass out. Rob asks him if he wants to go home, but the point is moot. It's obvious he won't make it into the school.

Zach says he feels like he needs to vomit. There are cars, busses, and kids everywhere. School has just let out. I have no choice but to pull ahead, right in front of a bus, and let him out of the car. We get out and walk to a tree. He stands by it, coughs a bit, and then vomits.

Kids watch from the bus. They turn away when they see I am looking at them.

We get back into the car and drive home.

That's it.

No more planned events.

JOURNAL ENTRY

April 25, 2013

I'm cleaning out the refrigerator. I grab a Cool Whip container, open it, and see leftovers from a dinner that Zach made for us earlier in the week. It hits me that this is likely the last thing he will ever make.

For the tiniest moment, I wonder if I should keep it. Like all those art projects brought home from school when he was younger that eventually need to be thrown away, a pang of guilt squeezes my heart as I toss the leftover spaghetti in the garbage.

Letting go.

Always letting go.

JOURNAL ENTRY

April 26, 2013

He sleeps a lot. Most of the day. Today he gets up at one o'clock, walks from his bedroom to the bathroom, then to the couch. His couch.

He is panicked. He can't catch his breath. It's scary. Very, very scary.

Hospice comes just moments later for a scheduled appointment.

The social worker comes down and helps calm him with meditation through visualization. It works. His breathing becomes more normal. He's calm again.

Rob and I leave him with Alli and Amy so we can talk to the nurse and social worker in the kitchen. Alli is in tears at the horror she has just witnessed. Amy walked into the room right in the middle of it all. That girl is a rock. I love her for loving my son.

The nurse tells me that if he panics again, I should give him the Ativan to help calm him. We decide it might be a good thing to give him right now. I take it down to him.

He smiles at me.

"No," he says, "I'm not taking that. It will make me sleepy."

Old Zach is back for the moment.

He feels well enough after an hour to come upstairs and sit out on the patio for our first spring-like day. The sun is shining and warm on his skin, birds are chirping, and the buds on the trees are beginning to open.

JOURNAL ENTRY ·

April 27, 2013

I get up early. It's sunny. A Saturday morning.

I love mornings when I'm the first one up. Something about the serenity and quiet of the morning. It's a peaceful start to the day.

I go down to give Zach his meds and I find him and Amy both asleep in his bed. She stayed the night, and they are in each other's arms, asleep. Like a married couple.

I wonder at the appropriateness of it. Then I think about what they will never have, and I silently shut the door and walk back upstairs.

I stand at the kitchen sink and look out the window onto the patio.

There are two empty chairs pulled close together, facing the yard.
I cry for the future they will never have.

May 3, 2013

IT WAS ZACH'S EIGHTEENTH BIRTHDAY. I'D LEARNED FROM Christmas that most any gift would only serve to remind Zach that he wouldn't be around to enjoy it for long, so I figured the best gift would be something he could enjoy for a day or two. For years, Zach and Sammy had unsuccessfully searched the Twin Cities for Play Dough ice cream, their favorite flavor. They had only been able to find it at the campground in Northern Wisconsin where our families camped every Labor Day weekend. I knew Zach would love to taste that ice cream once more, so I recruited the one guy I knew who would be able to track some down: Dan Seeman. Sure enough, Dan did not disappoint, and on Zach's birthday, along with his wife and daughter, he delivered a three-gallon tub. We feasted on the bright-blue frozen treat with balls of red and yellow cookie dough for days. I don't know what made me happier, seeing Zach thrilled by the gift or the fact that he was actually eating.

May 4, 2013

IT WAS ALL PLANNED. DINNER RESERVATIONS WERE MADE AT A little restaurant they'd found online. It was quaint with a menu that offered something each of them would like, Zach being more adventuresome, Amy, a little less. Amy had found a beautiful royal-purple dress, and Mary had ordered the corsages and set up a limo and driver to pick them up at our house. Amy had even picked out a couple of ties for Zach and brought them to the house so he could choose.

A collection to help with the cost of prom had been taken up at Oakland Junior High School where Mary worked as a seventh-grade English teacher. She'd brought the card and money over about a week before prom to show Zach; he'd barely been able to muster a smile, he was in so much pain that day. A couple of weeks earlier he only needed one medication patch to stay on top of the pain; now he was up to eight.

Zach was determined he would make it to the prom for Amy.

I was terrified.

I wasn't sure he would be able to walk from the car to their table at the restaurant and was afraid he would pass out, leaving Amy to figure out what to do. Or what if he couldn't breathe in the car on the way to prom? What would she do then? But Mary had thought of all that for me. She'd called the restaurant manager and explained the situation. They had heard of Zach and knew his story, and assured Mary they would take good care of the couple. Mary had also talked to the limo driver to let him know what the kids were up against. He assured her that he would help Zach in any way he needed and wouldn't leave Amy to fend for herself should Zach need care.

Zach prepared by going to bed early the night before, loaded with pain medication. He had new patches laid out on his table and a timer set to go off when he needed to switch them out. He planned to sleep until mid-afternoon, then he would give himself plenty of time, an hour and a half, to shower and get dressed in his gray suit and purple tie.

While I paced and prayed, people from our parish filled the little adoration chapel at our church. For months they had someone posted in the chapel every hour of every day, praying for Zach and our family. In response to a plea for prayer I had posted on CaringBridge, on this day they doubled their efforts to carry Zach through the day by filling the chapel. And that evening, Mass was dedicated to Zach and Amy; the church was full of people praying fervently that the kids would have a fun evening.

Zach hadn't left the house in days. The last time had been for Sammy's brother Matt's Confirmation two weeks earlier. A private ceremony had been arranged for Matt so that Zach would be able to attend. We didn't think Zach would be well enough to go to the regular ceremony.

Now, two weeks later, I was glad we'd moved the Confirmation ceremony up, but prom had me worried. I couldn't see how Zach would pull this off. A wheelchair had been delivered the day before and that would help. But, still, he was having a hard time just sitting up these days. And he was so thin. I worried that if he ate anything rich it would make him sick to his stomach.

Well, maybe he'll be okay . . . Please, God, let him be okay, I thought and prayed as I watched the clock. Soon I heard Zach stir downstairs.

"Hey," I said as I peeked through the door. Rob was sitting on the couch. He spent most of his time at home keeping vigil while Zach slept. "How are you doing?" I asked Zach.

"Tired. But the pain is okay. I actually feel pretty good," he said, taking a breath every third word. The nurse had heard fluid in both lungs just the day before.

"Did you want to wait a bit before you hop in the shower? Can I get you something to eat or drink?" I asked.

"Could you get me a juice out of the fridge?" He pointed to the little dorm refrigerator behind the couch. He had his private stash of all his favorite drinks tucked inside. "I'll hop in the shower in a little bit."

"Okay. Let me know if you need anything else. Dad can stay down here with you."

I went down the short hallway and into his bedroom. As I removed his suit from the closet and laid his shirt and tie out on the bed, I thought about the parable Jesus told of the wedding guest who had not properly dressed for a marriage feast and was thrown out by the king into the darkness. I sat down on the bed and smoothed the wrinkles from the shirt and thought about the years I had spent preparing Zach to enter that feast, the banquet hall of heaven. When he was young, I would lay out his clothes for him. But now he was a man and had to make his own choices. Had I trained him right? Was it enough? He was so close to the entrance of the heavenly banquet hall—any day he would reach out his hand to push open the door. Would his shirt be pressed? Would his tie match? Would his pants be long enough? Had I done my job? Was he ready?

I knew Zach would recognize Christ when he saw Him; he had spent his life looking for Christ in those around him. But there was a spirit of fear that had begun to torment Zach. As his physical body declined, his soul became restless and at times, in the darkness of night, he would be overcome with fear.

Late one night a few weeks earlier, I went down to check on him before I went to bed. The lights were off, so I thought he was sleeping. But when I opened the door to the family room, I found him awake and sitting on the couch wrapped in his comforter. I sat down next to him, and by the light of the stairwell, I could see tears rolling down his cheeks.

"Hey," I said as I stroked his hair, "what's going on? What's wrong?" It always sounded so stupid, but there was really no other question to ask. He buried his face in his blanket and sobbed for a moment. I got up on my knees and rested my cheek on his head. "What is it, hon? Things are better when you talk about them. You can lay it out for me. I can take whatever you have to say," I coaxed.

"I'm just scared," he uttered huskily. "I'm just scared of what's coming. I don't want to die." He broke down into more sobs, and I pulled him into a tight embrace.

"Oh, babe." I kissed his head and stroked his face. "Of course you're afraid. No one wants to die, and especially not a seventeen-year-old with so much life that should be ahead of him." Tears ran down my own face. "You are in a place that I have not been, and I know I have no words to make it better." I pulled back and looked into his eyes. "But I do know that God is very, very close. He will not abandon you. Sometimes, when things are darkest, it is because God's hand is overshadowing you."

He wiped his eyes on his blanket. The sobs had stopped, but the tears continued to flow down his cheeks. I reached up and wiped one cheek with the palm of my hand.

"I'll sit up with you. You don't have to fight this thing alone."

"I know. I called Amy a little bit ago, and she's on her way over. She can stay for a little while."

I heard the front door open. Daisy barked from her crate.

"Okay, hon. I'll go tell her you're down here." I stood and kissed his forehead. "I love you."

He reached up and squeezed my arm. "I love you too, Mom."

Amy was taking her shoes off at the front door. "Hi," she whispered when she saw me at the top of the steps.

"Hi. Thank you for coming over this late and through the

snow. It seems this winter will never end." I hugged her. "He's really scared."

She nodded her head. "Yeah. I know. He called and asked if I could come over. He sounded pretty shook up."

"He was. But I think he's a little better now. He just really needs to talk it out. I'm so glad you're here. He really needs you."

After she disappeared downstairs, I closed myself in the bathroom and leaned against the counter. How dare Satan torment my son! What a coward, going after a dying teenager! Every protective, motherly instinct reared up inside me and, filled with a holy anger, I was ready to do battle. I dropped to my knees onto the cold tile and prayed with every fiber in my being.

"Dear God! Send Your holy archangel, St. Michael, to defend Zachary in battle. Do not leave him unprotected from the wickedness and snares of the devil. Protect him from the spirit of fear that torments him." That was the formal prayer that came to mind. It was mingled with an informal, mother-bear prayer that went something like this: "Dear God. Kick Satan's butt and keep him away from my son! Please."

I got up, went down to my purse, and texted a group of family and friends I knew would pray their hearts out for Zach and asked them to storm heaven with prayers for peace. Fear would not have a foothold in this house! Not on my watch. I sat up reading until I heard Amy leave, then went down to check on Zach again. He slept peacefully. He'd managed to work through the fear.

Now, on the night of prom, he was focused on making sure Amy was taken care of. This day was about her, and he was determined to do everything in his power to make it special.

Zach had showered and was dressing in his bedroom while Rob

and I waited in the family room. I heard the handle of his bedroom door and stood from the couch as he walked into the room. "Wow! You clean up nice." I rubbed my hand across his smooth, clean-shaved cheek, then straightened the knot of his tie. "Amy won't even recognize you without your sweats and a T-shirt on."

"Thanks, Mom. I do look pretty sharp." The glint I hadn't seen for weeks was back in his eyes. Even though he was gaunt and pale, his smile was bright. He was happy and excited.

Amy pulled up with her family. She looked beautiful in her long purple gown with sequins that circled her neck and traveled down her back. She'd spent the day with her mother at the salon getting her hair, makeup, and nails done. Now it was time for pictures. It had looked like it would rain all day, the sky solid clouds, until Amy pulled into the driveway. The clouds broke up, and within minutes the sun shone bright and it began to warm up. We went into the family room to take some photos, then out onto the patio in the sunshine. When we got back into the house, Zach was hot (his body's temperature regulation had gone haywire as his health declined), so I threw the family-room windows open even though the screens had not yet been put in.

The limo driver packed up the wheelchair, and the kids got into the back of the car and waved as they drove off. I looked at Mary and said under my breath so the guys wouldn't hear, "Should we hop in my car and follow them?"

"I was thinking the same thing." She smiled. "But Amy knows what she should do if something happens. We've talked through every scenario possible, and she's prepared." She rested her hand on my back. "They're going to have a great time."

I hoped so.

We decided to go with Amy's folks out to dinner ourselves. It was better than sitting around wondering how the kids were doing and waiting for a desperate call from Amy. In the middle of dinner, my cell phone rang. It was Alli.

"Mom! You won't believe what happened," was all I could hear. The restaurant was too loud so I rushed out onto the sidewalk, my heart racing. "What's wrong?" I asked, panic rising in my chest.

"Daisy caught a bird in the family room. She murdered it," Alli said with disgust.

"What? That's it? Daisy caught a bird," I said, relieved but confused.

"Just wait until you get home."

We walked in the door to find feathers all over the floor. Hardly a square inch was left bare.

"We cleaned up the gross stuff, but we left this as evidence of her dirty deed." Alli and Grace stood in the doorway as we entered the room. Daisy sat, bewildered and confused, in her crate. She'd only been protecting her home, after all. A bird had apparently flown in the windows I'd opened earlier in the evening when Zach had gotten hot. I'd forgotten to close them before we left for dinner.

I waited for the kids to come home. I'd expected they would only stay at prom for a few minutes, but it was going on three hours. My worry had faded away as the night went on. Zach had been known to push himself harder than he should, but he had gotten better at recognizing his limits. I knew that if they were still at prom it was because they were having a good time and Zach was doing okay.

Zach and Amy walked in the door about midnight. They were both beaming and bursting with energy.

"Hey, Mom, Amy and I are going to have some of that ice cream the Seemans brought yesterday." I stood, shocked, as they headed downstairs. I hadn't seen either one of them this happy and refreshed in a long time. I followed them downstairs and grilled them for details.

"Well! How did it go?"

"It was perfect," Amy said as she sat next to Zach on the couch in their usual spots. "The dinner was amazing. All our food was ready to go when we got there because my mom had called ahead with our order. The staff was so nice to us. They knew 'Clouds' and were excited to meet Zach."

"Yeah. They even comped our meal," Zach said.

"How was the dance?" I asked.

"It was fun," Amy answered. "Everyone was so happy to see Zach. It was pretty funny when we walked into the room; one by one we could see faces turn toward us as the word spread that we were there. Zach had people coming up to him all night," she said as she turned to look at his face.

"It was nice to see everyone again." He hadn't seen most of his classmates for almost two months, since he'd stopped attending school.

"I'm so glad you two had such a great time," I said as I rose from the couch. "Who wants some ice cream?" They both raised their hands.

I set the bowls down in front of them, kissed them both good night, told them to be good, and went off to bed. It had been a weird day. But it was also a day of small miracles. The little kind that we sometimes miss if we aren't looking for them.

I've learned to be watchful.

Thirty-Six

May 9, 2013

ROB AND I DECIDED WE NEEDED TO GO TO THE CEMETERY AND PICK out a plot for the burial. We were both crabby before we went. Rob wanted to wait for a time when the church secretary could walk around with us, and I didn't.

"We have the map," I reasoned. "Let's just go and get the general lay of the land and at least figure out what section we want to be in."

It was a nice day, the cemetery was only a few minutes away, and Zach was resting comfortably with Amy at his side, so Rob finally agreed to go. We got out of the car, and I opened the sheets of paper, three of them taped together, showing all the available real estate with three or more plots circled in red.

"There are eight available over there," I said, double-checking the map.

"Nope," Rob said with barely a glance.

"Okay . . ." I looked back down at the map. "There are two up along that road, next to that big black monument."

He regarded the space for a moment. "Nope."

I took a deep breath. I could feel the irritation building up in me. This is how it worked with us sometimes. I would throw out ideas, and he would shoot them down without any real reason. Selecting baby names had gone that way, and choosing a house—the same thing. It drove me a little crazy.

"Okeydokey. Let's walk down this way," I said, doing my best to keep the edge out of my voice as I walked to a grove of trees. "It looks like . . . one, two, three"—I counted out the plots from the road to the tree that was noted on the map—"these four here or . . . one, two, three, four . . . these four here are available."

He walked around for a little while, looked up at the sky, then turned around a few times. "I like it here, but I don't like those."

"Why?" I couldn't take it any longer. "Why do you like that one, but not those? They're the same exact trees, just opposite from one another. I don't get it."

"I like the way the shade lands on this side," he said, a little surprised by the irritation in my voice.

"Why does it matter?"

"I want to like the place I'm going to be buried," he said matter-of-factly.

"I hadn't thought about that," I admitted, softening a little. "I was thinking more about where I want to be standing at Zach's grave."

We finally worked it out and found the perfect spot. It was far enough from the road, but close enough to see as we drove by. And it had nice shade in the summer. It was a pretty spot.

ZACH WANTED TO SEE *IRON MAN 3* SO HE, SAM, ALLI, AND AMY WENT to the afternoon show. By the time he got home he was wiped out and spent the rest of the day in bed. The only time he got up for two days was to shower. Then he went right back to the couch where he spent the rest of the day.

JOURNAL ENTRY ·

May 11, 2013

The old Zach, with all his boundless energy and high spirits, is gone, buried under disease. I miss him. He still fights for it, to get it back. He tries to sit up when people visit. He tries to participate in the conversations. He tries to laugh. But his strength is gone. His world is small and getting smaller each day. There is no room for nonsense. He is being refined. And we are being conditioned to let go.

ZACH SPENT MOTHER'S DAY SLEEPING ON THE COUCH BUT MANAGED to sign the card Alli bought for me. "Love you so much, Zach," he wrote. Alli told me he pondered for a long time before he wrote it.

Sammy, Mitch, Reed, and some of his other friends came to sit with him and keep Amy company. He didn't sit up anymore and only occasionally threw out a comment or two. He mostly just listened.

His grandparents came to sit with him. He tried to stay awake and converse. He managed for a while, then fell asleep.

Rob stayed downstairs with him during the day, sitting quietly or watching television.

I would go down periodically to help him change his medication patches. My time with him was at night, after everyone else had gone to bed.

Alli, Sam, and Grace tried to sit with him. It felt weird. Like they were waiting for him to die.

Daisy lay at the top of the stairs and wouldn't go down anymore. Zach was different. He was leaving. And she knew it.

Amy held her post daily and for hours at the end of the couch wrapped in a blanket, guarding her from the freezing air of a fan that blew on her and Zach constantly. It would ease the feeling of suffocating, the hospice nurse told us.

My sister Maria brought her baby, Henry. Zach reached out to touch his face. We took video so Henry could see when he was older.

Father Miller came to anoint him. Eyes shut, Zach lifted his open hands eager to receive the scented oil.

The adoration chapel at church filled with people. They prayed. We watched and we waited.

JOURNAL ENTRY

May 18, 2013

I'm sitting here with Zach. Watching him as he lingers between sleep and wake.

His hands are in perpetual motion. At times he seems to be playing his guitar, at other times he turns knobs on an invisible amp. Now he is waving at someone. There is a smile on his face. Now a frown.

He has a foot in this world and one in eternity.

AMY, SAMMY, MITCH, AND REED CAME. I CALLED THEM. IT WOULDN'T be long, I said.

They flipped through the booklets the hospice social worker gave us. They read about what to expect as they watched their friend die.

Sammy got up and went into Zach's room. She was cold and needed to borrow one of his sweatshirts. She pulled the University of Minnesota sweatshirt over her head. She sat down on the bed and began to cry.

The sweatshirt, the rumpled bed, the cluttered bedside table, the recording equipment, the leather-bound notebook, the clothes strewn about, the backpack still full of books, the posters on the wall, the football trophies, the six pairs of shoes, the guitars hanging on the wall, the disco ball. She said there was more of Zach in his room than there was of him in his own body. She could feel him leaving, and she missed him already.

JOURNAL ENTRY ·

May 19, 2013

I feel like a woman in labor, pacing the house with my mind focused on the big, painful event about to ensue.

Rob and I are alone with Zach. He has been lying on the couch for several days now. His hands have been working for several minutes waving to unseen people, playing a guitar that is not in his hands. He floats between worlds. Rob tells me that earlier in the morning, when I was at Mass with the girls, it looked like Zach was shooting hoops and throwing a football. We look over and Zach has his arm extended and hand held out like he is expecting someone to grab it. I stand up and sit on the coffee table in front of him. "He is smiling," I whisper to Rob. And I put my hand in his open palm. His hand is warm as it closes around mine and squeezes it tight. He smiles for a bit longer, then his expression shifts to utter sadness in a split second. I squeeze his hand and hold it to my face. So warm. Still so strong. His fingertips are rough and calloused from years of sliding on guitar strings.

His breathing is rapid. Forty breaths a minute. His pulse is too. A hundred twenty a minute. He'll be leaving soon.

"Zach," I bend down and whisper. "I love you. I will miss you so very much when you are gone." The tears come, uninhibited, and fall on his blanket. "But you don't have to stay here, you don't have to hang on for us. We'll be okay. It's okay to go."

His eyes remain closed, but he hears and he nods his head. I kiss his hand and set it on his chest. I walk to Rob, and he holds me for a long while. Then I leave so he can say his own good-bye.

Rob comes upstairs, his eyes puffy, and he sits listlessly on the couch. Then Alli goes down. Zach tells her he doesn't think he can go on, that he doesn't think he will make it to the wedding. She sobs. She hates seeing him so sad and wants desperately to make him smile. She tells him she doesn't want him to die, but if he has to, to remember that his suffering was just like collecting gold coins in the video game *Mario*. Dying was like leveling up. He smiles. Alli holds his hand for a while, then Sam goes down and tells Zach that he will never, ever forget him, and he promises to visit his brother's grave every May 3, on Zach's birthday.

Grace is out at a basketball game with a friend. She isn't supposed to be home for a few hours, but I call her and tell her to come home early.

"He's not good," I tell her. "You should probably come home."

I'm downstairs with him when I hear the front door open and close.

Grace wastes no time and runs downstairs. I watch as she throws herself down by Zach's side and grabs his hand.

"I'm here," is all she says.

He lies there for a moment, then turns to her and opens his eyes. And he looks at his baby sister, whom he has looked after and protected for fourteen years. His baby sister, whom he loves. And he sits up and hands her the remote to the television.

"You can watch whatever you want, Grace. It doesn't really matter to me. We'll watch together." He moves down the couch to make room for her.

And they watch together. He continues to protect.

May 20, 2013

I WAS SLEEPING ON THE COUCH ACROSS THE ROOM FROM ZACH. I had been there the past two nights. Amy stayed the night and was on the floor next to me. It was five o'clock in the morning when we heard Zach unexpectedly bolt down the hall to the bathroom, shut the door, and lock it. I threw the covers off and ran to the bathroom door to stand vigil in case he needed help. He had been fiercely independent throughout his battle, but now he was weak.

I heard something clatter, then silence. My heart was racing as I fumbled around trying to find the key for the door where I'd stowed it months ago, on the wainscoting ledge.

"Mom! I need help," he cried.

I popped the door open with the key. He was sitting on the stool we had placed in front of the sink.

"What's wrong?" I asked as I rushed in.

"I can't breathe." He stood, then collapsed into my arms.

"Amy," I yelled. "Get Rob!"

I lowered Zach onto the floor, then ran to the kitchen to get the Ativan. I had tried for days to get him to take the Ativan to help with the panicky feeling that came with his shortness of breath. He refused. It made him too groggy, he said, and he didn't want to lose the little time he had left to sleep. But now he was panicking and needed the drug desperately. I got to the refrigerator, yanked the door open, and plucked the little brown bottle from the top shelf of the door. *Where is the measuring dropper? . . . I had just seen it yesterday . . . Where is it!* I started throwing things off the counter. Panic was creeping in, and my mind was freezing up.

"Stop it," I scolded myself out loud. "You don't have the time to lose it."

I remembered I'd set the dropper on the table the night before, out in the open where it was easily seen. I grabbed the phone, picked up the dropper, and ran back downstairs and gave Zach the medicine. Then I called 911. We needed to get him into his bed, and I knew he wouldn't want Rob and me to do it. He hated the thought of burdening us and he would try to help, but he didn't have the strength. There was comfort knowing my friends from the fire department would be walking through the door in just minutes. I needed them.

While I was on the phone with the dispatcher, Rob had gotten Sam and Grace out of bed. Alli had heard the ruckus and come from her room. She knelt on the floor next to Zach as we waited for the crew to arrive.

"Remember the sea turtle, Zach? The one you saw in Mexico? Remember how peaceful it was, how beautiful?" She held his hand

and tried to soothe him. Zach nodded, staring straight ahead but not seeing as he gasped for air.

Amy knelt on the floor opposite Alli and stroked Zach's hair. Grace sat next to Alli, silently crying, and Sam stood behind her. There was hardly any space to move. Rob moved a shelf out of the way so that the fire department could get in with the stretcher.

I had my pager and heard the crew check in on-scene. I went to the door to let them in.

"He's on the floor in the bathroom," I instructed. "We need to get him into his bed across the hall. It's going to be tough using a longboard, though. It won't make it around the corner."

The kids and Rob cleared out of the bathroom as I knelt by Zach's side.

"Honey, the fire department is here. They are going to move you to your bed." I stroked his hair. "Don't help. Just try to relax. They know what they're doing." He nodded in response, fighting for every breath. I stepped out of the room as the crew swarmed in. Within a minute or two, they had Zach in his bed.

"Do you need anything else, Laura?" Jim, the assistant chief, asked.

"No," I answered. "I just needed you here. We just needed help."

He nodded in understanding. Then the crew packed up everything and left us.

THE ATIVAN BEGAN TO WORK. ZACH WAS CALM. HIS BREATHING slowed.

We were all there: Rob, Alli, Sam, Grace, Amy, and I. All of us sat around him as he lay on his bed. We prayed. We told him how much we loved him. I hummed a hymn while I stroked his hair.

Amy kissed him. We told him it was okay to go. We would see him again.

And then he died.

My beautiful, precious boy died.

ONE BY ONE, WE LEFT THE ROOM.

Rob and I stood in the hall, outside his bedroom door, and held each other. There was an odd sense of accomplishment mixed with the horror of what we'd just been through. But now he was gone.

"We did it," I said to Rob as I rested my head on his shoulder. "We held him until he stepped into eternity."

"His suffering is over," Rob whispered, "and he's gone."

Alli stepped out of the room and joined our embrace.

"You are the best parents he could have asked for," she sobbed. "You were both so strong through it all."

Amy was curled up on the couch with Zach's favorite blanket. I sat down next to her and patted the seat for Grace to cuddle up next to me.

"Do you mind if I call my mom?" Amy asked.

"Oh, sweetheart. Not at all," I replied. "You need her."

Sam quietly emerged from Zach's room and sat down on the couch next to Alli.

"Six thirty-five," he said. "He died at six thirty-five."

I was surprised at how late it was and yet couldn't believe how much had happened in a short amount of time. Time had seemed to stop as we sat through that last hour and a half with Zach. I was grateful that Sam had thoughtfully taken note.

After a few moments of silence, I got up from the couch and walked upstairs with the phone in my hand. Zach's friends would be leaving for school soon. They would need to know that Zach was gone.

WE HAD A PLAN, A "CALLING TREE," TO REACH THOSE WHO SHOULD hear the news first, before the media was alerted. Anne, Sammy's mom, woke Sammy and told her the news, then called Zach's closest high school friends before they left for school, as well as the school counselors and the local paper. My friend Stephanie, who had bathed with us in the water at Lourdes, called St. Croix Catholic School and a few of our close friends. I called Justin Baldoni and Mindy Dykes at CCRF, who alerted Dan Seeman, Karl Demer, Scott Herold, and Adam Gislason.

Within a couple of hours, our house began to fill with family and friends and food . . . lots of food.

We kept Zach's body with us, in his bedroom, for several hours so we could each have a chance to be with him, alone.

It was nice, that time with him. I held his still-warm hand to my cheek and kissed it. That precious warmth. I didn't want to waste it, so I just held his hand until it was cool. And I cried tears of relief and agony.

He was free.

But he was gone.

The funeral home sent a van to take him away. As they carried him toward the front door, I stopped them and kissed Zach one last time. The house full of people was silent as we watched the van pull away.

How many times had I watched as Zach drove away down that very same road? And how many prayers had I offered up for his safe return?

I wouldn't have to worry anymore.

He was safe. Forever.

TWO DAYS LATER, WE HELD ZACH'S WAKE IN THE GATHERING SPACE at the Church of St. Michael. The funeral home was too small for the anticipated number of people.

Rob and I stood for five straight hours. The line of mourners serpentined through the room, ran up the hallway to the atrium, and out the door. For five hours the line never broke. And there were stories. Lots of stories.

"He said hi to me in the hall," one girl told me with a look of astonished gratitude on her face. "He said hi to me and he didn't even know me." It was such a small thing, a tiny, friendly gesture, but something this girl had apparently not experienced enough of. Zach made a difference in her life by simply acknowledging that she was there. He saw her.

Another man in a business suit stopped by to offer his condolences. "I'm from North Carolina, but I was in town on business, just an hour away. My wife and I have been following Zach's story. He's changed our lives."

"Zach stood up for me," another girl spoke through tears. "He stood up for me when I felt really stupid and everyone was teasing me."

"Zach saw me crying in the hall one time between classes," said another. "He didn't know me, but he took the time to ask if I was okay."

"I came from Minneapolis. I didn't know Zach other than his story and his music. But he changed my whole outlook on what's important," said a man in his early twenties.

"I never got to meet him, but I miss him," a middle-aged man said.

A teacher from a grade school in Minneapolis brought a handful of her students. They had seen the video in school and wanted to offer their condolences.

They kept coming.

Hundreds of people—both friends and strangers—poured into the church and waited in line for hours just so they could have the chance to tell us how Zach had touched their lives and changed them. They were no longer faceless people typing comments on a YouTube video. They were real people with real lives who had experienced something powerful that had made a profound impact on their lives, and Zach had given that to them.

At the end of the evening, Scott Herold approached Rob and me. "I don't want to bother you by talking business right now," he said, "but I thought you might want to hear what 'Clouds' is doing." He pulled out his cell phone to show me the screen. "It's been climbing the charts all day, and it just hit number one. It seems Zach has started some kind of a movement."

Rob put his arm around me, and I laid my head on his chest. Our brave boy who battled for so many years and who had no hope for a future, through his death, was spreading hope to the world.

May 23, 2013

MAY TWENTY-THIRD WAS A PERFECT DAY. THE KIND OF SPRING DAY that gets us through the long, cold winters in Minnesota. The sky was completely clear—cloudless, many noted. The air was crisp, but the sun was warm on our skin. It was the day that we would say goodbye to Zach.

The Church of St. Michael was packed to overflowing with people who had faithfully carried our family through the past three and a half years of Zach's battle. They had filled the adoration chapel at all hours of the night and day to pray that God's grace would carry us through no matter what came our way. They had prayed, in many cases despite their own suffering, for a boy whom many of them had never met. They filled the pews and aisles and even spilled out onto the sidewalk that was lined with pale blue and white balloons that gently twirled in the breeze, the words *Up, Up, Up* written on them.

Four priests concelebrated along with Father Miller at the funeral. Zach had touched each one of them in some way. Father Miller and Father Lynch had been particularly impacted by this teenage boy whom they had visited countless times over the years to bring the comfort of the sacraments and prayer.

The choir lifted our souls to heaven on the wings of angels, and Father Miller soothed our grief with a beautiful homily that encouraged us to take Zach's message of hope, and that of the gospel, with us into our hearts.

At the end, our dear, sweet Sammy stood before twelve hundred people and delivered a eulogy befitting her lifelong friend. Her final thoughts were these:

> There are two very important things in particular Zach has said to me that I will keep with me for the rest of my life. The first is to think of him whenever I eat a taco, because he really loved tacos. The second is that life is really just beautiful moments, one right after the other. He has taught me to see beauty and joy in everything. And although today is very sad, it is also very beautiful.

Because what is more beautiful than a congregation full of lovely people celebrating the life of a beautiful, young man?

As she finished and left the pulpit, the choir sang "Clouds" and hundreds of mourners, who all knew the words by heart, joined in as the casket was prepared to depart. There was a barely audible ripple of laughter from Zach's closest friends as the casket was rolled out of the church to the sound of bagpipes. It was so . . . Zach.

For months I had prayed that Zach's funeral would be a time when heaven and earth would meet. I prayed that the Holy Spirit would fill the space and permeate each soul with profound hope, and that Zach's simple message of love would be heard.

My prayer was answered. As the mourners poured out of the church and back into the crazy world, something amazing was happening. Millions of people, all over the globe, clicked on a video and heard for the first time about a boy who wrote a song to say good-bye. They did not know that boy, they had never met him personally, but somehow his spirit had touched them in deep and unfathomable ways. They had been changed by this boy who had every reason to despair but who chose instead to fly a little higher.

Epilogue

ZACH'S MUSIC CONTINUED TO TRAVEL ACROSS THE WORLD AND into people's hearts. The week of June 8, 2013, "Clouds" debuted on *Billboard* magazine's Hot 100 list at No. 26 and No. 1 on Rock Digital Songs, making it the first song in music history to ever reach such status with only the backing of a nonprofit and exposure from digital media. No major record labels were involved, and there was virtually no radio play outside the St. Paul/Minneapolis market.

A Firm Handshake's *Fix Me Up* EP made it to No. 20 on the Billboard 200 for the same week and reentered Folk Albums at No. 1. The songs Zach and Sammy wrote and performed together continue to climb the charts in countries around the world.

On September 28, 2013, the "Clouds" video won an Upper Midwest Regional Emmy award for musical composition/arrangement. Karl Demer, Mike Rominski, Rob, and I accepted the award on Zach's behalf. At the end of December, 2013, CNN named Zach as one of their "Five 'Extraordinary People' You Have to Meet."

The *My Last Days: Meet Zach Sobiech* video that SoulPancake produced has also reached unprecedented numbers. The twenty-two-minute video was intended to reach thousands. To date, it has been translated into twenty-one different languages and received over ten million hits from people across the globe.

At the writing of this book, Zach has been gone for four months. We still receive messages daily, in various forms, whether letters in the mail or comments on the various videos, expressing how much Zach and his music meant to people. We treasure them. They make Zach feel close.

But then, he's closer than ever, isn't he? He shows us sometimes.

As our family pulled out of the church parking lot and followed the hearse to the cemetery on the day of his funeral, out of the blue we heard a familiar sound. The radio in the car had been turned down so low that we didn't know it was on until we suddenly heard the first notes of "Clouds" played out on the glockenspiel. I turned it up as we drove to the burial site at the cemetery.

A couple of weeks after the funeral, Father Miller was saying the closing prayer at Mass. As he turned to walk past the altar and into the sacristy (the little room off to the side of the altar where the priest's vestments are stored), a green balloon gently floated at about the height of a man from the church atrium through a door and into the front of the church. Father Miller didn't see the balloon as it floated around the communion rail, up the steps past the altar, and followed him into the sacristy. My friend Molly and her children, who associated "Clouds" with balloons, were stunned as they watched. Father had walked through the sacristy and directly to another door that led to the atrium where he stood and greeted people as they left the church. He never saw the balloon that had followed him. Molly opened the door to the sacristy and found an altar server standing with the balloon in his hands. "Is this yours?" he asked with a confused look on his face.

"No, but I think I know who it belongs to." She took the balloon and brought it to Father Miller. "Have you been thinking about Zach lately?" she asked.

"Yes, as a matter of fact, I've been thinking about him a lot these past couple of days," he answered. He had been struggling with severe pain in his feet for several weeks, and it was starting to get him down. Over the months of visiting Zach, watching him suffer and administering the sacrament of Anointing of the Sick, he had developed a unique spiritual connection to Zach.

"I think this is for you." Molly handed him the green balloon.

Father Miller was shocked, but not totally surprised, as he took the balloon from her. "You know, I think you're right." The color of the balloon matched his vestments. Green, the color of hope.

A few days later, Father Miller traveled to his parents' farm in rural Minnesota. It was a sanctuary for him, a quiet place where he could rest and pray. As he was walking the farm with his father, they came to the milk house.

"The strangest thing happened a few days ago," his father said. "Out of nowhere, a clump of green balloons came out of the sky and settled on the ground right here." He pointed.

It would happen to Amy too. He would show up in little ways. She pulled into a park for a graduation party not realizing that it was the same park where she and Zach had planned their first picnic. It was weeks after his death, and she didn't think she could handle the memories, so she decided to go home. Just as she began to back out of the parking spot, "Clouds" came on the radio. It was as if Zach was letting her know he was still there with her. She decided to stay.

A week before she went off to college, Amy was down in Zach's room, hanging out like she sometimes did when she wanted to feel close to him. A glint of something caught her eye in the middle of all the knobs on the microphone soundboard Zach had in his room. She walked across the room to find it was a pin she had given him more than a year earlier, the pin we all desperately tried to find before his funeral because Amy wanted to place it in the casket with him. *Dancer's Boyfriend*, the pin said. She'd gotten it at a dance competition as a joke, but he wore it proudly on his jacket all winter just to tease her. He liked to tease.

"You'll find it when you need it," I'd told her the day before the funeral after we'd searched the room two and three times over. "It's here somewhere, and he's probably just waiting for the right time to give it to you." And there it was. Right there where it couldn't have been missed.

She left for college the following week, and when she moved into her dorm and began putting her things away, she opened the top drawer of the empty desk and there were two guitar picks waiting for her. She asked her roommates if one of them had placed them there. They hadn't.

Some of Zach's closest friends went on a day trip to Duluth, Minnesota, in his honor before they all headed off to college. Zach had always wanted to go with his friends, but never made it to the beautiful north shore of Lake Superior.

The kids spent the day on the rocky shore reminiscing about Zach and vowed never to forget him, each of them memorializing him with a tiny *Z* tattoo etched into the inside of their middle fingers. To commemorate the trip, they all gathered on the rocks in front of the lake and had their picture taken. The day was clear with a few tiny clouds dotting the vast blue sky. Later, after the picture was uploaded onto Facebook, they realized there was a lonely cloud in the shape of a *Z* just above Amy's head.

He got his trip to Duluth after all.

On December 6, 2013, a year after KS95 played "Clouds" for the first time on the radio and interviewed Zach and me for the "KS95 for Kids" Radiothon at the Mall of America, Rob, Grace and I returned to the mall for another radio event. This time, KS95 invited those in the community who wanted to remember Zach and honor his legacy to come to the mall and join in singing "Clouds" together. They hoped to get one thousand people to respond. They got five thousand.

The place was buzzing with excitement as the rotunda filled with choirs and groups from across Minnesota, all clad in light blue T-shirts with white clouds and the words "Up, Up, Up" written across the front. The talk at the mall and all across the Twin Cities was about how unusual it was to see a rainbow on that clear and sunny December day positioned directly over the mall, just a few puffy clouds floating lazily in the sky. It was then I recalled another rainbow that appeared years earlier on a dark and cloudy November day as we traveled home from the hospital—a sign of hope to keep us going.

I HOLD ON TO LITTLE THINGS. THE CLOTHES IN HIS DIRTY-CLOTHES basket are still there. I hold them to my face sometimes and breathe in their scent. For weeks, I left his toiletries where he had carefully placed them on the bathroom sink. Sometimes I cradle his toothbrush and remember his smile and what it felt like to kiss his cheek. His room remains as it was the day he died, and it will for some time.

Rob visits Zach's grave daily. He has a hose in the back of his car that he hooks up to the faucet and waters the grass at the site. Zach's grave is the only patch of green in the parched cemetery. Football is wrapping up. He misses watching the Vikings games with Zach.

Sam grieves quietly. He finds the best way to honor his brother is simply to live. He studies diligently and hopes to one day join a research team that unlocks the secrets of osteosarcoma. Sam has vowed to visit Zach's grave every May 3, on Zach's birthday.

Grace, too, grieves quietly. She misses Zach's presence as she moves into high school. She teared up after getting her schedule for her first semester at the high school.

"I would have taken this to Zach, and he would have told me about all the teachers," she said. He would have been there for her, offering his support and guidance.

Alli had started a blog called *Married in the Mourning, Sailing with the Knight*. She grieves through writing, laying it all out—raw and real.

Eight days after Zach's funeral, we all reentered St. Michael's for Alli and Collin's wedding. We felt Zach with us there most especially. It was a tumultuous day, weather-wise. There were clouds churning all around the Twin Cities, violent storms popping up all around us. Yet as dark clouds rolled in from every direction, the sky above us remained clear. It was a night that defined us. Despite our mourning, we all came together, family and friends. We filled the dance floor and danced until our feet hurt, and then we danced some more.

And we remembered.

We remembered that beautiful boy who showed us that hope could raise us to a better place where the view was a little nicer. A place where we could look and never see the end. A place in the clouds.

Acknowledgments

. . . .

ZACH'S STORY IS ABOUT GOD BRINGING THRONGS OF INCREDIBLE people together to make beautiful things happen. The task of adequately thanking all those who have held my hand, scooped me off the floor, dusted me off, and sometimes even thrown me over their shoulder to carry me as I voyaged through writing our story is daunting. I would like to acknowledge all of them, but these pages aren't big enough, so I am forced to acknowledge just a handful.

Zach, thank you for showing us how to be a channel of grace through suffering. You make your dad and me so proud. We love you and miss you.

Rob, you held me through tears, laughter, and everything between. Thank you for trusting me with the telling of our story. I love you.

Alli, Sam, and Grace you are each amazing in your own unique and wonderful way. My life would be so much less beautiful without you. I am so grateful to have you in my life and to be your mom.

Mom and Dad, thank you for sacrificing for faith and family and teaching us what true hope is. Adam, Lee, Andrea, Amy, Maria, and Luke, I could not have chosen better siblings. I love you all.

Thank you to Zach's friends for pulling in closer when many would have fallen away.

Thank you, Sammy Brown, for bringing the melody of love through friendship to Zach's life.

Thank you, Amy Adamle, for your example of courage and self-less love. You are the strongest woman I know.

Thank you to my dearest friends, Anne Greenwood Brown and Stephanie Landsem. This book would never have happened without your constant encouragement, guidance, and practical sensibilities. Anne, you taught me to jump without overthinking and Stephanie, you taught me to have a parachute at the ready. I love you both so very much.

Thank you to the communities of Church of St. Michael and St. Croix Catholic School for all the countless ways you supported Zach and our family over the years. We were fed by both your constant prayers and meals. I would especially like to the Father Michael Miller and Father Brian Lynch for their prayerful support and for bringing us the grace of the sacraments.

Thank you, Danielle Magnuson, for the late nights of editing.

Jacquie Flynn, my agent, thank you for your unwavering confidence that I could actually do this when I wasn't so sure of myself.

Thank you to the folks at Thomas Nelson for taking a chance on me, especially Brian Hampton, Chad Cannon, Emily Lineberger, and Kim Boyer. And thank you to my editor, Katherine Rowley for cleaning it all up and making it look pretty.

Dan Seeman (Hubbard Broadcasting), Karl Demer (Atomic K Records), Scott Herold (Rock the Cause) Jeff Dunn (J. Dunn

Photography), Adam Gislason (Snyder Gislason Fraiser LLC), Mike Rominski (Whoolly Rhino Productions), and Justin Baldoni (Wayfarer Entertainment/SoulPancake) without your vision, countless hours of hard work, and dedication to bringing Zach's music and message to the world this story would have been very different.

Thank you to Children's Cancer Research Fund, especially John Hallberg, Kris Huson, and Mindy Dykes, and the University of Minnesota Amplatz Children's Hospital. You have given life to Zach's legacy of hope that children in the future will not have to suffer and die from osteosarcoma.

Zach Sobiech
Osteosarcoma Fund
of Children's Cancer Research Fund*

Zach Sobiech wanted to make a difference for children with cancer through his music and message of hope. Before he succumbed to cancer, Zach and his family established the Zach Sobiech Osteosarcoma Fund at Children's Cancer Research Fund, where proceeds from Zach's music and donations made in his honor are directed.

The Zach Sobiech Osteosarcoma Fund supports leading-edge research to find out why children get this rare cancer, and to discover life-saving treatments. **To learn more or to make a donation, please visit ChildrensCancer.org/Zach.**

Children's Cancer Research Fund | 7301 Ohms Lane, Suite 460, Minneapolis, MN 55439

Fix Me Up—Deluxe Edition
by A Firm Handshake

Available worldwide on Compact Disc, DVD, or Digital Download

Includes *Fix Me Up* EP original master recording of "Clouds," as well as
the Largest Clouds Choir version, acoustic version, and new music
from A Firm Handshake, featuring Sammy Brown, Zach Sobiech,
and all your favorite A Firm Handshake videos.